# POLLBOOKS
## HOW VICTORIANS VOTED

# POLLBOOKS

## HOW VICTORIANS VOTED

J. R. VINCENT

*Fellow of Peterhouse, Cambridge*

CAMBRIDGE

AT THE UNIVERSITY PRESS

1967

Published by the Syndics of the Cambridge University Press
Bentley House, 200 Euston Road, London, N.W.1
American Branch: 32 East 57th Street, New York, N.Y. 10022

Library of Congress Catalogue Card Number: 67-10160

Printed in Great Britain
at the University Printing House, Cambridge
(Brooke Crutchley, University Printer)

# CONTENTS

B  Constituencies analysed by occupations (*cont.*)

B  Constituencies analysed by occupations (*cont.*)

# PREFACE

This book is rather protean. The largest part of it is a compilation of data about voting in England in the nineteenth century, giving much material of which no use has been made here, but which might form a starting-point and source for others more acquainted with particular problems and localities. The introductory essay is concerned with the meaning of this heap of evidence, mainly at a rather general level. The traditional problem on which it chiefly throws light is the place of class in electoral politics—a problem better and more neutrally defined as one of the relation between the type of social situation a person is in, and his political outlook. It is on this question that discussion is concentrated.

The two concluding essays pursue the point from a different angle. The first analyses the social situation in Cambridgeshire in the middle of the nineteenth century, by using probate records, and suggests that the structure of capital ownership corresponded to certain distinctive features of contemporary political sensibility. The concluding essay ventures some thoughts on the change from Liberal to Labour, considered in terms of the function of politics in relation to the personal needs of the ordinary voter. The common thread uniting these fragments is a preoccupation with tracing political consciousness back to its roots in a personal situation, by yoking the surmises of sociological theory to empirical data gained from door-to-door interviews with the dead.

J.R.V.

# ACKNOWLEDGEMENTS

The kindness of others has greatly assisted in the making of this book. Mr George Cunningham and the History of Parliament Trust have generously allowed me to draw on the fruits of their own researches into pollbooks. The compiler has also been able to draw on inquiries made by Mr N. P. Brecknell, Mr James Chadwick, and Miss Margaret Leslie, concerning Norwich, Dublin and Carlisle respectively. Miss J. Chambers gave stalwart assistance with some of the most burdensome work. Mr Brian Harrison drew my attention to some very interesting statistics which are referred to below. I am greatly indebted to Miss C. A. Stoakley for the skill and care given to the typing of a difficult manuscript. All faults of conception and execution, however, stem peculiarly from the author.

I am very grateful to the Master and Fellows of Peterhouse who gave me the opportunity to do this work, and to the Trustees of the Twenty-Seven Foundation for a grant towards the cost of publication.

# I

## INTRODUCTION

Pollbooks are lists of voters at a given election, accompanied by indications of which candidate or candidates they voted for. This is the only feature common to all of them. (Lists of voters which do not state their votes exist fairly commonly in the form of electoral registers, and are of no use at all.) Most pollbooks were printed, but a few survive in manuscript. Most pollbooks were in pamphlet form, but some were weighty and expensive books, those for the West Riding for instance costing up to a pound. Most pollbooks give the address of the voter; but even this is not always to be found. Their internal arrangement varied considerably. Some grouped the voters by villages, wards, or even by streets. Others listed their names alphabetically, or according to the order of voting. Some distinguish between freemen electors and ten-pound householders, and between resident voters and out-voters: others make no such distinction. So far as can be seen, the jobbing printers who usually published pollbooks acted under no responsibility to anyone, and the consequences of their having had a free hand—sometimes good, sometimes bad—are evident in the complete lack of standard presentation in pollbooks. In a few cases pollbooks were published by political bodies, but in general everything depended on the free will of some small printer looking around for a small profit.

Hence there is little rhyme or reason in the distribution of places for which pollbooks were published, and the oddities which are most marked are those a historian would least desire. In times of political excitement, the printer had most incentive to publish a pollbook, and so the elections of the 1830s are very well represented. But when one turns to see what the new voters were doing in 1868, the pollbooks are taciturn, presumably because the great increase in the electorate would have made pollbooks too expensive to sell easily. The same considerations no doubt lay behind the absence of pollbooks for very large constituencies. No pollbook is known for Manchester after 1839, for Birmingham after 1841, or for any London seat after 1841. Everything depended, not on the social interest of the data, but on the chances of the printer recovering his costs.

Nevertheless, a very thorough search made by the History of Parliament Trust in 1953 revealed about 1,750 titles for England and Wales published over the whole period 1694–1872. The chances of a pollbook not surviving or, if surviving, of not having been found, are certainly high, but the figure of 1,750, including as it does all the titles in the handful of large collections, is a practical maximum. As an unsupported guess, one might say that a third to a half of all contested elections between 1830 and 1872 were reported in a printed pollbook.

Now all pollbooks might conceivably be made use of in relating party preferences to certain variables like occupations (taken from directories), wealth (taken from ratebooks), kinship (taken from the census), religious denominations (taken from congregational lists, if such exist), and the amount of savings possessed (taken from probate records).* Such investigations are conceivable and perhaps desirable, but for one person to try to find in such ways sufficient data to make generalizations at a national level, would be impossibly laborious.

It is fortunate therefore that a certain number of pollbooks give the occupations of those who voted. This kind of pollbook forms only a small fraction of the total, and therefore a still smaller fraction of all elections are described in this way. There are for instance no pollbooks giving voters' occupations for either Manchester or Birmingham. Nevertheless, where occupational pollbooks do exist, they enable one to relate party preference to that variable one would choose most to know about—occupation and social position—in a mechanical and exact, though still sufficiently laborious, way.

Nearly all the pollbooks between 1830 and the end of open voting in 1872 which give occupations of voters, are for borough constituencies, not for county seats. No county pollbook after 1852, to my knowledge, makes any pretence of stating occupations, and no county pollbook after 1835 does the job in a full and proper way. This is quite a lacuna, but it is not so important as the number of county seats would suggest. For on the one hand, the agricultural seats did not include as constituents the rich variety of human types found in the borough electorate: on the other hand, voting in the counties was much more related to the pattern of landownership and of traditional territorial influences than it was

* For a use of probate records on a local scale, showing at least the difficulty of deploying them, see ch. 11 below.

to occupation.* Analysis of the county vote by occupations would not be wrong exactly, but it would tell a very small part of the story. So the impossibility of such an analysis may be accepted with a good grace.

Most of the pollbooks which allowed analysis of voting by occupations have in fact been so analysed, and the results are set out in chapter III below. The few pollbooks which might have been analysed, and yet were not, were quite unimportant. Some elections in 1837, for instance, were omitted, when the same constituency had been analysed for 1835 or 1841. A few boroughs which were hopelessly corrupt or 'closed' were omitted. Some entirely one-sided elections where a freak candidate forced a poll, but with derisory results, were not worth considering. Some pollbooks in local libraries were too inaccessible to be worth a special journey. But the range of elections analysed below comes as near the maximum as it is worth while to go.

It may be objected that the range is too wide, that much of the material gathered below has no special interest, exhibits no striking features, and advances no great argument. This is undoubtedly true, and no one has felt this as much as the compiler. But in dealing with a new type of evidence, the defect of method which would be involved in reporting only 'interesting' results would much outweigh the gain in amenity. The world is quick enough to forget the existence and the importance of the merely amorphous, without doing its work for it.

It is not clear why some pollbooks give occupations and others do not. It may be a question of the balance between printers' costs and printers' pride in their work. Neither is it clear how the occupations got into the pollbooks at all—whether, for instance, some polling clerk wrote them down, and if so, how far he did so on his own ascriptions, and how far he accepted the self-assessment of the voter; or whether the printer himself added the occupations from common knowledge (possible only in a small town) or from street directories. The text for working purposes, then, is the text of the pollbook as it stands. One cannot, so to say, discern by internal evidence a 'historical election' standing behind what is reported to us, and make allowances accordingly. For the purposes of this book, pollbooks are texts which emerge *ex nihilo*, bearing

* For this point see D. C. Moore, 'The Other Face of Reform', in *Victorian Studies*, V (1961), and the analysis below of village block voting in the Lincoln-shire election of 1823.

within them, as will be seen, certain kinds of pragmatic verification, and so long as they are analysed as texts, rather than as historical realities, no question of methodological error arises.

Unfortunately no occupational pollbooks are known to exist for Bradford, Manchester, Birmingham, Salford, Liverpool after 1841, Norwich after 1830, Bristol after 1852, Portsmouth, or any of the London constituencies at any date between 1830 and 1872. The bias is strongly towards the medium-sized constituency of 10,000 to 50,000 people, normally a market, county, or cathedral town rather than a manufacturing centre, which was in any case the central element in the English electoral system. The pollbooks throw little light on the politics of great cities, of the Industrial Revolution, on the tendencies which rose to importance chiefly after 1872, and this is a pity so far as knowledge of political behaviour goes. But their bias in this respect is really rather salutary, as it corresponded to the actual bias and weighting of the electoral régime. It brings one nearer to the actual social structure and economic life of the country, to Dickens' England, than an attention to the precocities of Lancashire would.

## 2

The question now arises what kinds of inquiry are and are not advanced by the occupational analysis of party preferences. There is also a third group of topics, to which the tables below are relevant, but no particular effort has been made in this work to develop the data incidentally included there. Among this third group are such questions as which occupations tended to vote for persons, which for parties; which respected legitimate traditional influences most; which occupations changed proportionately to the electorate between 1832 and 1865; and what the effect of the Reform Bills of 1832 and 1867 was on the social balance of a constituency. For example, a comparison of the Cambridge pollbook of 1866 with that of 1868 brings out exactly the effect of Reform on the constituency. On these and other topics, the tables given below will probably be found to have something to say: and their extensive publication may be worth while in this respect, as a work of reference, reaching no conclusions itself, for others to quarry from.

Even in some questions of electoral politics, pollbooks are a broken reed, and the method of occupational analysis the wrong method. For precisely as it is well suited to the analysis of the main structure and substance of political behaviour, so is it ill suited to the analysis of contingencies, events, and small fluctuations. Of course it is very useful in giving quantity and social locality to the eruption of Reform in 1830–2, but it is an insensitive instrument for recording political changes in the very evenly balanced 'normal' elections between 1835 and 1872, let alone for interpreting them. Pollbooks are not much use for writing a history of the course of events at national level. Detailed analysis of many constituencies of much the same type, in order to derive the fate of a nation, an election, or a constituency from some final inconsequence or loose end, is hardly a step forward from leaving the causes of the ups and downs of Victorian elections as undefined and anecdotal as at present. Perhaps when a more systematic approach than argument by the accumulation of instances has been adopted in the study of general elections, the tables below may come to illustrate, what they cannot now demonstrate. 'The need is not so much for more studies of...constituencies, as for a classification of the range of constituencies, followed by studies of sample constituencies of widely differing characteristics.'* The analyses of individual constituencies given below do not pretend to have the usefulness that a quantitative typology of constituencies would have for the writing of the history of events.

Since knowledge of Victorian political behaviour has hitherto been nearly entirely qualitative, not to say anecdotal, it is hardly necessary to apologize for the omissions inherent in a quantitative study. Numbers do not record fervour, and they do not directly record effort, a rather different quality. (It must be remembered that corruption is the obverse of somebody else's zeal, organizing skill, and financial sacrifice.) The excitement which men were feeling over a particular burning issue appears in the tables only in the form of some general occupational tendency to prefer one party to another. And so on: the losses and gains of such matters are well rehearsed. Apology is needed more for statistical omissions than for statistical excesses. The voting of clerical personnel and contemporary literature all suggest the immense importance of religious denomination for political and indeed for every kind of behaviour. It would therefore be very useful to relate party preference among the laity to religious denomination. But unfortunately there is no royal road here as there is with occupations. In certain fortunate cases the relation might be worked out on a small scale,

* H. J. Hanham, *Political Studies* (1955–6), p. 151.

though the results would be hard to obtain and probably, owing to the duplication of common names, rather inaccurate.

The question of the relation between voting and wealth, as shown either in the ratebook or in probate records, was not nearly so insuperable on the technical side, but it was much more super-fluous. For occupation, taken by and large, gives an implicit and politically sufficient assessment of wealth, without taking the matter further by inquiries into the means of actual individuals. The divergence between rich and poor shoemakers, for instance, may have been quite considerable, both as regards fortune and as regards politics: but it was as nothing compared with the differ-ence between shoemakers in general, and gentlemen in general.

Though their fortunes might vary considerably upward or downward, all shoemakers shared in a body of social opinion about what kind of people shoemakers were, which in turn derived from an objective economic homogeneity* natural to skilled small producers competing in a free market. Shoemakers were poor enough to feel poor, or to be felt to be poor by others, and they were rich enough to feel independent, or to want to be so. Never-theless, studies of probate records may have much to add, if they can show, what one suspects, that the capital and savings of skilled non-factory workers and small shopkeepers were high, relatively both to their own earnings, and to the savings/income ratio† of skilled factory workers or unskilled workers then and now. This would be a convenient conclusion, for it would bring together many hints that the 'people' in the towns were, in economic type and in political psychology, not proletarians selling their labour on the market, but something closer to the peasant type than English rural conditions had allowed in most parts of the country for some time. Urbanization, Dr Kitson Clark has succinctly said, preceded mechanization, and in this one fact there is a world of political consequences. It would do much to explain the reverence for property—so long as it was small property—in Radical oratory and

---

* See ch. II below.

† Working-class savings now are probably low in relation to annual income: see the recent studies by the Acton Society, *Acton Survey of Manual Workers' Savings Habits and Attitudes to Share Ownership* (1965) which found that over one-third of workers interviewed had under £50 saved; and by Dorothy Wedderburn, *Redundancy and the Railwaymen* (1965), which found that 54 per cent of the workers interviewed said they had no savings at all, and another 10 per cent said they had less than £50, whereas only 25 per cent claimed to have over £100.

practice. It would make less puzzling the resemblance between French and English radicalism in the later nineteenth century, if both arose from a similar economic type of small producer and proprietor, mainly urban in England, mainly rural in France. The ethic of thrift, too, came from a lower social level than that of businessmen, from a kind of poor person who was as, or more, concerned about his capital than about his income, unlike the proletarian to whom capital is an accidental and rather functionless surplus from income. As a working hypothesis which at least fits a number of phenomena which would otherwise be puzzling, it may therefore be suggested that while the Industrial Revolution produced proletarians in some factory districts (and these were often the wives and children of men* engaged as independent producers in non-factory work), over the country in general the economic growth with which it was associated worked for quite a long time in favour of a wider distribution of small property and a diminution of the relative power of large property (for which in the towns an institutional framework, such as the industrial joint stock company, and an economic *raison d'être* were alike lacking). Hence the emergence of Liberalism, which had always been endemic in the social strata now given that strength which was all they had ever needed.

We are left with three present and solid objects to pursue for which the method of occupational analysis is quite suitable. The first is the provision of miscellaneous information about voting behaviour of strictly limited significance—about the existence of anomalies, archaisms, pressure groups, economic and local interests, and institutionally, ecclesiastically, or educationally shaped voting. The second object is to test traditional explanations or descriptions of political behaviour in the light of the facts given by occupational analysis. Thirdly and more positively, it is then reasonable to try to construct a general description, which will also be partly an explanation, of voting behaviour inductively, by grouping many minute particulars into a few typical probabilities or ratios of voting preference. Having arrived at a general account of the

---

\* English cotton operatives in 1871:

|  | under 20 | over 20 |
|---|---|---|
| Male | 69,996 | 118,276 |
| Female | 118,602 | 161,268 |

(G. Phillips Bevan, *The Industrial Classes and Industrial Statistics* (1876), p. 7.)

phenomena, it is then possible to check against it some of the
various possible ideas of class, to see whether these ideas have
either factual value or explanatory insight.


3

The difficulties of interpreting pollbooks come under two heads.
On the one hand it has to be asked whether one is arranging accurate data in an intelligent way. On the other hand, it has to be
asked whether the votes given, though accurately recorded and
collected, are empty of the kind of meaning they would need to
have to be sociologically useful—either because, though freely
given, the votes had no general significance for the person who
gave them, or because votes often represented the wishes of anyone
but the voter.

I am his Highness' dog at Kew.<br>
Pray tell me Sir, whose dog are you?

The accuracy of the data cannot be checked against the anterior
reality of which it is a recension. But strong checks for internal
consistency and inherent probability can be applied, from which
pollbooks emerge with flying colours. First there is a reasonable
congruence between the numbers and preferences of the various
occupations in successive elections in the same town. Secondly, the
results of occupational analysis do not conflict with the general
direction of traditional knowledge, they only strengthen or dilute
it. Church and chapel, rich and poor, as recorded in the pollbooks,
never vote in ways that outrage one's sense of reality. Thirdly,
where there are two candidates on each side, their voting can be
shown to differ only where electoral reason says it ought to: e.g.
the Leicester publicans voted Liberal in general, but abstained
point blank from supporting a Liberal Temperance candidate.
Fourthly, there was no motive for falsification except laziness, and
still less for the falsification of group voting, which would not be
apparent to the reader of the pollbook. Fifthly, certain consistent
national patterns do emerge from pollbook after pollbook. Such
pragmatic justifications cannot prove the accuracy of any particular
pollbook on any particular detail—this just cannot be done—but
they do suggest that broad generalizations may safely be made
from large collections of these figures, each one of which taken
alone would be entirely open to question.

The figures in the pollbooks are probably usually accurate in detail and taken as a whole they are self-validating. The question is how to use them meaningfully. This depends on the choice of occupational categories, on the homogeneity of the categories chosen, and on the statistical significance of voting variations in fairly small groups of people. The actual definitions of the occupations used are given in the note in chapter II below. So long as only some and not all occupations were tabulated, inaccuracy of a kind was bound to arise, since no occupations were exactly typical of some general group of occupations. The operative question, however, is whether a selective analysis of occupations led to special rather than marginal inaccuracies, and this can be largely answered by looking at the few constituencies (e.g. Ashton, Bedford, Rochdale) where every occupation was analysed, and noting the degree of correspondence between the 'typical' occupation selected (e.g. grocers, shoemakers) and the stratum to which it belonged (Craftsmen, Retailers).

No assumptions are made in this study about the homogeneity of the occupations analysed. It would make for smoothness of argument if people of the same occupation corresponded to a certain stratum of society and were in much the same circumstances. This was no doubt often so. Small producers and small shopkeepers competing under conditions of free entry tend to a general equality of condition, and the few big shops in the High Street, which would be politically influential, were submerged in elections by the 'average' grocer in the ubiquitous corner shop. On the other hand, some occupations like the clergy and officers were distinctly vertical, hierarchical groups, and a curate at the bottom might earn much less than a farm labourer with an employed family. The idea that occupation as analysed below corresponded generally to fairly homogeneous horizontal strata may be a cornerstone of one's imaginative understanding of the situation, but it cannot be derived from exact knowledge.

Many of the figures given in the tables below are small: mostly below 30, many below 10. Can such low numbers really show any meaningful tendency? They certainly can where they are meant to, but often they are not meant to. Where a very few railwaymen, farmers, or weavers are listed, this is not because their voting is thought to provide evidence for the political behaviour of such people in general, but is intended simply as a convenient reminder that these people were not important in this election. The number of bankers in each town was very small, and their party preferences as measured below simply record whether one banking family was larger than another. However, by addition of evidence from many towns, one can draw general conclusions about the politics of bankers. They were in fact quite Liberal—at least as much so as the labourers—which was to say nothing extravagant, but something very different from the position of bankers after 1880.

With clergy and dissenting ministers, who were necessarily sparsely distributed, very small numbers in each locality accumulate nationally to give a very strong indication of party preference. With normal secular groups, however, a high degree of significance is reached only when there is a fairly sharp preference within groups of at least 30 people. In Rochdale for instance the butchers voted Tory in 1857 by 25 to 16. The chances against this result being purely accidental would be about 500 to 1, according to the binomial theorem. The real difficulties in the tables below lie in determining what meaning, if any, the votes given had, not in their potentialities as statistical material.

Corruption and influence may affect the occupational analysis of political preference in five ways. Occupational analysis, at the very least, can show the incidence and social locality of corruption, if indeed a separate class of corrupt votes existed. A second possibility is that even in general corrupt conditions, an underlying genuinely political preference may shine through against all that gold and influence could do. The Norwich and Beverley elections are perhaps cases of this. Thirdly, corruption may on balance have coincided with a genuine preference by voters, and simply have intensified or revealed what was always latent. Fourthly, much of the less flagrant pressure on voters had nothing to do with open voting or the special conditions of Victorian England, but simply represented the irreducible tendency for genuine political preferences to be shaped by the situation in which people find themselves, and especially by the more important people within their daily horizon. This would be as important now as then.

Fifthly, it is possible that external influences completely obliterated the will and intention of great sections of voters, and that no conclusions, except as to proneness to corruption, can be reached from their votes. In the extreme case of servants, it must readily be admitted that the voting of servants should be understood as a double vote for their employers.* (Servants in fact rarely voted

* E.g. the voting of servants at Preston in 1830.

before 1868.) Yet in all other cases, it is doubtful whether influence alone controlled any important group of urban voters. The Toryism of Cambridge college servants, for instance, however agreeable to their employers, can plausibly be seen as coincident with a real political preference.

Only on the most extreme hypothesis, therefore, does corruption and influence nullify the value of occupational analysis. So far as electoral results went, in the period of political balance corruption probably decided the day very often. But it did not touch the core of political behaviour. In fact limits, social and geographical, can be set to the extent of corruption. Manchester and many larger towns never produced a clear case, and this although there was a great incentive for the losing side to get up a petition. Lawyers and publicans were bought, under face-saving conventions, and labourers and the waterfront population expected their due. But money had to flow pretty freely—as at Preston—before small shopkeepers would take the risk of voting against the non-monetary pressures of kin, denomination, and customers. Open voting and small town opinion created its own safeguards against people being lured away from the ruts into which they were born, into doing things they did not really agree with. The evidence of election petitions cuts both ways:

I think you find Norwich to be this: that you would find on the one hand, amongst the general class of voters, a very large class of partisans most anxious to do all they can to assist the candidates and their cause at the slightest expense, taking a most enormous lot of trouble, and never thinking of asking for a farthing of remuneration; whilst another class will take all they can get...one half would labour without the slightest remuneration for the most intense hard work.*

Another important point in suggesting a limited view of the importance of corruption, not in determining election results, but in determining political behaviour generally, is that though the relative will and power of each party to buy votes varied enormously from election to election and from candidate to candidate, the patterns of occupational preference remain relatively stable from year to year and from one place to another. Croesus fought many elections, but he never made shoemakers into good Tories, or butchers into good Liberals. Again, some electoral patterns are very hard to ascribe to influence. In many cases the rich or the

* *Parl. Papers* 1852–3, H.C. 243, q. 517 (Norwich Election).

employers in a town were fairly evenly divided, yet those beneath
them showed sharp preference one way or the other. *A fortiori*,
cases (like the Rochester bargees in 1868), where men vote strongly
against the influential people closest in contact with them, are
most likely to arise from genuine feeling.

Corruption means that any case of occupational preference in a
particular election has to be treated with caution unless one is un-
usually well informed as to the local circumstances. But when one
finds a pattern recurring in different elections in different places,
then corruption can almost be forgotten about. There is a partial
exception to this, however. This is because the Tories, especially
after 1860, had the advantage in money, both centrally and in most
localities, and therefore the Tory vote among labourers, shopkeepers, publicans, and craftsmen has to be construed with one eye
on corruption. But this Tory vote existed—possibly only from
habit—even at the most apparently pure elections, and there are
many other, less adventitious, explanations for popular Toryism.

What of the vote which, though freely given, means nothing to
the man who gives it? Mindlessness is perhaps a constant in
political behaviour. But in 1850, probably more than now, the
world was full of sharp reminders for the thriving earthworm that
politics existed. There was a popular political culture as there was
a popular musical culture, and the urban voter lived in packed and
noisy streets where things happened. Very high polls,* very strict
voting for a party ticket in the two-member seats, and broken
windows bear witness to the strongly and consciously political
intent of the electorate.

Nevertheless, often the vote given must have borne no relation
to the man or his life, or have been entirely unconnected with any
general political feeling. So be it. One can only hope that this kind
of vote, which is an empty box, is evenly enough distributed among
each group and party to make no difference.

---

* The county council elections in Cheshire can be cited to illustrate the difference between the modern and the nineteenth-century sense of mass involve-
ment. The average poll in contested seats in the first two elections was over
70 per cent. In two cases a poll of 89 per cent was recorded, and polls under
50 per cent were almost unknown in county council elections before 1914. At
the 1946 election, on the other hand, the average poll in contested seats was
only 31·8 per cent. Sources: John M. Lee, *Social Leaders and Public Persons:
A Study of County Government in Cheshire since 1888* (1963), pp. 53, 165.
Cf. the high turnout of 94 per cent at the Lancaster election of 1865, below.

4

Pollbooks provide much information which is either pure detail or else can only be generalized at a very low level. For instance, the sweeps of Cambridge, Maidstone (1870), and Ipswich, perhaps personally affronted by reforming legislation, all voted Tory in the 1860s, and there is an end to the matter. Other kinds of detail, however, can be grouped and brought to focus on hypotheses. There is only room here to discuss the light thrown by the tables of voting on the relation between occupation and party preference, but it should not be overlooked that much else may be illustrated from them. For instance, the tables can show the effect of enfranchisement in 1832* and 1868 on the size and nature of the constituencies (see especially the tables for Cambridge, 1866 and 1868). It can show, in the great crisis of 1830–2, which parts of society were the moving, which the yielding, and which the resisting part. The *non possumus* of the clergy, for example, in the great debate comes out very clearly in the tables for Northamptonshire, Hertfordshire, and Cambridge University. This in turn bears on the interpretative crux on the first Reform movement—whether Reform was egoistic or altruistic, conceded or taken, wisely yielded by the influential, or harshly grasped by the uninfluential. (The second Reform crisis does not show up in the pollbooks, as the general elections of 1865 and 1868 were not fought on this question.) But much else lies latent in the tables following, which I do not now seek to elicit: the social location of the floating vote, in constituencies where a long run of elections have been analysed; the convention by which both Tories and Radicals, in many small boroughs, as at Tamworth and Chichester, voted both for their own candidate, and for the nominee of a (probably Whig) aristocratic patron; the pressure of appearances which brought many professional men, especially in Liverpool, to split their votes between the more popular candidates on each side; and the degree of correspondence in votes polled between candidates of the same party, an important indicator of ill-disguised social cleavages, and enlightening as to whether people voted for the party label or for the man. These matters, which concern more the patterns of voting peculiar to an occupation, rather than its party preference,

---

* For a comparative view of the preferences of old and new voters after the first Reform Act, see the tables for the Huntingdon election of 1832, and the Ipswich election of 1835.

are not intended to be specially exhibited in the tables, though these must necessarily include much information about them.

About certain occupations, there is little information. Coal miners appear in force only in Bristol in 1841 and in Shropshire in 1832, in both cases as Liberals. The only agricultural labourers recorded are those dismally Tory villagers who voted in the Leicester borough elections. The silk industry is represented only by the Lancaster election of 1865, where the silk interest voted Liberal by 17 to 4, despite the adverse effects of free trade on the silk industry. The many farmers whose votes are analysed, including an unexpected number in Oldham and Leeds, give no idea really as to the state of agricultural politics and the influence of landlords. We are left with three types of constituency about which there is sufficient information to build up a typical picture: viz. (1) the northern industrial town like Ashton, Warrington, Bolton, or Rochdale; (2) the provincial metropolis like Bristol, Norwich, Liverpool, Glasgow, or Leeds; (3) the cathedral, market, or county town of medium size and traditional economic character like Ipswich, Maidstone, or Cambridge. (The East Midlands towns of Leicester, Northampton and Nottingham combined features of all three types.) The problems and hypotheses which follow relate to widespread voting habits, which stand quite apart from the general grounds of political orientation on the one hand, but are yet so obviously structural as to require a sociological explanation. These are (1) the effect on the boroughs of rural intrusions from the Conservative countryside; (2) the relation between the party preference of a retailer or artisan and the typical social status of his customers; (3) the existence of an anomalous Toryism among the seafaring and longshore population of great ports; (4) the existence of an anomalous Toryism among labourers in boroughs; (5) the conflict between the drink trade and some Liberals; (6) the conflict between Church and Chapel; (7) the effect of higher education on party preference; and (8) the use of minor public employees and officials for party purposes. The type of conflict involved here takes place essentially within a situation of small scale; it is not conflict about the structure of the national political and economic order, though in some cases, for instance Church and Chapel, an apparently 'horizontal' conflict between competing interests was really the *alter ego* of dispute about the whole national society.

One line of division between the parties in the boroughs lay in the tendency of the Liberals to represent the essence and core of the town—business, shopkeeping, and craftsmanship—the general self-esteem of the townspeople, and their social ethic and common culture while the Tories, the minority party, were a coalition of 'outs', of those who could not quite be fitted in, operating under the hegemony of the outside forces of the countryside, as a fifth column within the gates of bourgeois Liberalism. The lawyers, doctors, coachbuilders, clergy, schoolmasters, architects, saddlers, wine merchants, butchers, jewellers, bookbinders, artists, and hatters, who looked for reward in higher quarters than from mere townspeople, appear in the pollbooks as epiphenomena of a mainly Tory landed ruling class, as a sort of upper servants. No disrespect is intended to their sincerity. It was simply a question of how far the pattern of their lives wove them into, or set them apart from, the mass of the borough population. Law, in particular, was an urban industry dependent on rural raw material, and the voting of lawyers in such county towns as Wakefield and Norwich marks this well, they being far to the right of the upper class in general there. (In Norwich, the solicitors nearly monopolized the local Tory leadership.) The pollbooks offer much evidence of the intrusive pressure of rural influences in market, cathedral, and county and to a lesser extent in some provincial capitals like Bristol or Norwich.

There are considerable and sociologically significant differences in voting of different kinds of craftsmen and shopkeepers, mostly along the lines one would expect. In Bolton, Preston in 1841, and Rochdale, for instance, cloggers, who sold only to the poorest, were entirely radical, while shoemakers, themselves little better off than cloggers, but selling to all kinds of persons, were more mixed in opinion. Beersellers, who chiefly served the dregs of society, were normally significantly more radical than publicans, who hoped for more catholic congregations. The difficulty here lies not in the evidence being unsympathetic to basing the voting of shopkeepers on the social position of those they sought to supply, but in the existence of alternative explanations. For, even setting aside the difference between emporium and corner shop within the single trade, there is great variation in economic position of the average of each trade. It is impossible to distinguish how much the Toryism of wine merchants (like Ruskin's father) depended on their own substantial stake in society, and how much rubbed off from a Tory clientele. The point remains, that in most boroughs the shopkeepers are radical, by a good deal less than two to one, and that they and the craftsmen provide the backbone of the Liberal vote; but that politically they are internally divided along a line running from completely Jacobin sympathies, to complete identification with the 'county', this gradation being governed less by what they think they think, than by their kind of customers and their own position. The two latter criteria tended to go together (chemists are a case in point). The exception lies in the case of the butchers and grocers, the single stark revelation these inquiries have produced. Over generations, Tory butchers have been locked in combat with Radical grocers: the statistics are beyond doubt: but of this, no explanation, no word of description even, has come down to us. It is easy to form conjectures as to the reason for such a schism in the High Street, once one knows of it; but more salutary to reflect, how little one's stock ideas could have enabled one to predict this homely fact *ex ante*.

In the ports of Liverpool and Bristol, while the carpenters, cobblers, and shopkeepers were as radical as elsewhere, the shipwrights, mariners, pilots, sailmakers, and so on, constituted practically a bloc vote on the Tory side. Traces of the same thing may be found at Ipswich, Hull (possibly), and in some Kentish ports. Everywhere the pilots seem to be under some Tory spell.* To all appearances, there was a militant Tory working-class community down by the docks, and an equally militant radical working class—capable, be it remembered, of the very effective Bristol riots of 1831—among the artisans and shopkeepers of the landward districts. This was no case of a 'popular' Tory party acting as the means of conflict with a Liberal business oligarchy (party names differing but the conflict being the same) but something falling outside the category of class explanation entirely. To some extent, conflict arose from interests, such as the West Indies trade and the Navigation Laws, which were put in jeopardy by the Liberals. But the duration and depth of this deviation suggest something more chthonic—a separate sense of identity, hereditary solidarity, and a closed world of experience—acting to turn a temporary perception about material advantage, into a lasting political habit.

There is also much evidence of a less deep-seated, but more widespread, tendency for labourers in towns to vote Tory rather than Liberal, and to vote less Liberal than the craftsmen and shopkeepers, on the occasions when they did vote Liberal. In the towns for which this category was analysed, there were 41 elections in

* Except at Sandwich in 1868.

which the leading Tory candidate received more votes than the leading Liberal, against 20 cases where he received less. Disraeli's idea of an untapped Tory stratum lying beneath middle class radicalism had a certain amount of justification over the period 1832–68, though it should be noticed that in 1868, where there were many labouring voters, as at Cambridge, they were radical. Before 1868, the Toryism of the labourers is largely accounted for by their fewness and their corruptibility, but sometimes there is rather more to it than that. For instance, why should the Maidstone papermakers have voted Liberal by 2 to 1 from 1857 to 1865, while the Maidstone labourers were Tory? First, the condition of life of labourers did not permit the kind of radical political consciousness which required literacy and some leisure; secondly, labourers were in frequent contact with the less amiable face of the lower middle class and the labour aristocracy. At some points, e.g. over limitation of, and premiums on apprenticeship, the radical élite met the labourers in something like class war; at all points, they met as foreign bodies with distinct fates and without fraternity.* The Tory vote among the labourers, originating in contingencies, chance attachments and pressures, had by 1868 hardened into a deep-rooted habit, rationalized by better explanations than the genetic one.

The pollbooks do not show the social location of the Temperance vote, though this undoubtedly existed as such in the great provincial cities in the 1860s. They do, however, show the operation of the drink trade as a pressure group from the late 1850s onward, not indeed uniformly, but only where the Liberal candidate was thought to be 'dry'. Examples are the Rochdale election of 1857, and the Leicester elections of 1859 and 1861, where the publicans boycotted the Temperance Liberal, J. D. Harris, while still voting for the other Liberal candidates. It is possible, too, that the Beer Bill of 1830 had some effect in throwing the trade behind Reform; the liberalism of the trade in Liverpool in 1832 is surprisingly marked. The trade can also be found rallying round Liberal members who were its lobbyists in Parliament, like Berkeley at Bristol. What matters most for national history, is the vigorous *ils ne passeront pas* with which the trade met the

---

* There was 'a certain understood dignity and exclusiveness of caste pertaining to the artisan class which every individual of it is compelled to respect and support. A mechanic when out of work can scarcely take work as a labourer, even if it is offered him' (Thomas Wright, 'A Journeyman Engineer', *Some Habits and Customs of the Working Classes*, 1867, p. 258).

Temperance movement. This was a perfect example of a pressure group—a sharply defined group of people organized to defend their economic interest by rational electoral pressure, uninvolved in general political issues and without ideological overtones. What is remarkable is that the drink trade is perhaps the only interest, apart from the Catholic Church, which really operated in this way. There is no sign at all in the pollbooks that beneath the 'conventional issues of politics' one can find an earthy 'reality' consisting of the mutual pressures of rationally egoistic small-scale groups. The explanatory value of the idea 'pressure group' in electoral politics is negative, as indicating how political opinions were *not* normally formed. In the case of the publicans, their conviviality, their established trade societies, their training in reality, all fitted them to react to the unfairness of the Temperance threat in a cool, utilitarian, effective way. Their behaviour was not distinguished only in Victorian politics: for it is unusual anywhere for a lower middle-class group, faced with an appalling threat to its livelihood, to react by turning to intelligent manipulation of the traditional party system, rather than revolting against the system altogether.

Many things, at first classifiable as pressure groups, are really special cases deriving from a more general conflict. Thus at Bristol, the local struggle of the West India interest (the clergy supporting slavery) coincided with the general contest between the forces of order and the scruffier elements of society. Likewise one can trace in the conflict of Church and Chapel how education and tradition can harden a broad, but hardly imperative, division of interests, into a quite rigid difference of political culture. No other occupation was so partisan, so militant, so unfloating, as the Dissenting ministers. They were a sort of Communist hard core to the Popular Front. (Incidentally, the traditional impression that Wesleyan ministers were Tory is not borne out by the limited evidence so far found.) Moreover, clerical militancy was as great in Manchester (1839) as in rural areas like Suffolk or in the old county towns. Conversely, the voting of Anglican clergy, sextons, organists, and gravediggers was more unevenly split between the parties, by a long way, than was the voting of the most reactionary or the most revolutionary secular occupation.

Higher education had, in lesser degree, the effect of ecclesiastical employment in sharpening party preference. To some extent the issues merge, since so much of higher education was an Anglican preserve. However, the upper crust was broadly divided within itself on an educational basis which did not obviously correspond to economic or social inequalities. The Liberal professions were most likely to be Tory: the gentlemen, *soi disant*, were usually fairly evenly split; and the business world was inclined to be Liberal, though not by very much. This corresponds fairly well with the differing degrees of education endured by each type.

The serious reader will find no theoretical meat in the frequent instances given of the politics of bumbledom. Policemen, lamplighters, turnkeys, beedsmen, pilots, firemen—the preferences of these belong only to the curiosities of literature and the malpractices of Conservative electioneering, so far as individual cases are concerned. Not that what happened could cause anything but grave suspicion: the postmen of Shrewsbury in 1868, the pilots everywhere and always, the turnkeys in county towns like Cambridge, Lewes, Leicester, and especially Maidstone, at election after election, behaved so as to suggest that public authority, somewhere along the line, was turned to private use. But taking these contingencies as a whole into account, a point of some importance surely emerges: that, even on a cursory inspection, a wide range of occupations can be found, in which institutional influences caused a marked deviation from the pattern of voting normal to that condition of life in general. This deviation was normally in the direction of the Tories, but in all cases it produced a much more marked affiliation to one or other party than would otherwise have been the case. The institutional structure of borough or county injects a tincture of exact and socially determined opinion into the general welter of merely mental opinion, so to say, with the result that, through the growth and connection of families and changes of employment and home, any strong and exact body of opinion formed in one part of the polity must dissolve and diffuse and multiply till it colours a fraction at least of all parts of society. This is the permanent countervailing process, on the animal and ecological side, which ensured that in no section of society did the preference for one party over another rise to a very high ratio.

In conclusion, let us point to three details which may be cherished, as bearing on the proverbial side of human character. At Rochester* in 1868, all the bargemasters voted Liberal, and all the bargees Tory. At Cambridge, the college servants voted Tory

---

* At Rochester, in the same election, the eight postmen voted Liberal, while the postmaster voted Tory.

in season and out of season. It is still more agreeable to find that
the Roman Catholic clergy, in the age of Newman and Pio Nono,
swallowed their principles and voted almost solidly Liberal.*
Here, as with the publicans, calculation quite overlaid feeling,
showing the successful function of parties in creating agreement
on immediate action, between fundamentally irreconcilable
groups—and the Catholics and the Nonconformists in the Liberal
rank and file were never far from coming to blows. Party is a
civilizing thing: it has to unite many people, and overcome many
conflicts, before it can even begin to be divisive in turn itself.

## 5

The evidence gleaned from the pollbooks may serve to modify
some prevailing impressions. In the first place, in all types of town
and city, the electorate was predominantly involved in pre-
industrial types of activity. Even in Ashton, a cotton town *pur
sang*, only a sixth of voters were connected with the cotton industry.
The rank and file of both parties was drawn to an almost equal
extent from the lower middle class and the aristocracy of labour.
The suburban genteel vote did not exist. The *primum mobile* of the
Liberal party, in particular, was generally popular, in the sense of
coming from the *menu peuple*, not from an ascendancy of employers
and captains of industry, nor from proletarian masses working in
factories. The business and professional classes were numerically
small and half assimilated to the upper crust, and a long way below
these come what one can only call 'the people', who comprised the
great majority of politically articulate people in any town, and who
combined working-class and middle-class characteristics. There
are, then, only two great substantial classes, 'the people' and 'the
upper crust', to take into account; and each party was strong in
each class. Parties may have had their genesis in class, and their
function may have been to meet class needs, but the correlation
between class membership and party preference, though positive,
was too slight to have been of any predictive value for any particular group, occupation, locality, or person.

The business community was not a coherent entity, and it was
not especially committed to middle-class liberalism. It is necessary
to be quite specific as to what kind of business is meant, at what
time and place. In Wakefield, the ironfounders and worsted spin-

---

* Cf. the Liverpool election of 1835 for the Liberal vote of the only Rabbi
  recorded below.

ners tended to be Tory, the woolstaplers and manufacturers Liberal. In Warrington, in 1847, cotton was entirely Liberal, but the industry of the town as a whole was evenly divided. At Warwick, in 1831, the woollen interest supported reform by 23 votes to 1, while at Preston, in 1841, the manufacturers were divided equally between the parties, and their overlookers were Tory by a ratio of 3 to 2. In the East Midlands, the manufacturers were primarily conscious of being in conflict with the great landowners of the surrounding countryside, and thus retained their pristine virtue, e.g. the lace manufacturers of Nottingham in 1852 were Liberal by 2 to 1. But in towns like Liverpool and Bristol, the business community, less conscious of domination by the territorial aristocracy, and reacting against the popular radicalism of the 1830s, played the part of a 'force of order'. On the whole, the textile employers of Lancashire and the East Midlands were Liberal; the business and mercantile communities of the great provincial capitals, divided evenly, or became Tory in anxious times; and the small family businesses—builders, millers, and so on—of the market towns were Liberal. Whatever the exact formula may be, England never lacked Tory businessmen.

One of the most amiable innuendos in English history is the suggestion that political change was achieved through the enlightenment of the rich; that, in the happy days 'before the rise of Socialism', the rich were reasonably progressive in the narrow party sense, and that the educated among them in particular led the way forward to a better and higher state of things. Now in the narrow party and electoral sense, this is not really so. Political change was achieved by popular electoral ascendancy over a recalcitrant upper crust. Liberalism genuinely had to contend against a great weight of 'soundness', and, considering political orientation only and not policy, the victory of the people over their betters at the polls was the necessary cause of Victorian Liberalism. If I am led to state this somewhat stridently, it is because a certain school of persons, who never fail to refer to Gradgrind, have thought fit to argue that Victorian Liberalism was about the workers being passively misled by the bosses. However, the educated, in particular, when judged by the stereotyped historical judgements of the English liberal tradition, were wrong—wrong about democracy, about Protection, about slavery possibly—though there were always many who were right. Right and wrong here are intended not as absolute, but only as relative to what have become the dominant values of our political tradition; still, the strength of attachment to the Tory party shown by those possessing mental advantages at the very times when such an attachment was most imprudent, superfluous, or unattractive, may well be pondered over.* What there was acting for change among the rich—and their party preferences were of course far more evenly divided than today—came not from the advantages of education, but from the splendid panache of a political aristocracy, and from the social isolation of the usually badly educated commercial class. To do justice to the general electoral situation, it is necessary somehow to contemplate at once the existence, indeed the centrality, of force, power, coercion, defeat, in an almost military sense, between different groups, and the frequency with which the act of voting includes a claim to concern for some other group, which would by contemporary standards have been considered alien or hostile.

Equally, the masses were not like the *tricoteuses*, vengefully bent on the overthrow of all ascendancy, yet the long term effect of their checkered and complicated behaviour did tend in that direction. Again it is necessary to be specific as to groups. At Preston in 1841, weavers voted Liberal by 3 to 1, but spinners only by 11 to 9. The railwaymen of York in 1852 were Tory by 2 to 1, but railwaymen elsewhere were Liberal. At Norwich in 1830, the textile employees voted Liberal in just about the same proportion as their employers, but the Norwich labourers were Tory. At Oldham in the 1850s, the popular party, and especially the industrial workers, temporarily fought under the Tory label against the Liberal millowners. It was not in any way the essence of the behaviour of the

---

* A special case which tends strongly against the above argument should be recorded here. This is Gladstone's defeat in the Oxford University election of 1865. Gladstone was not defeated by the resident electors, about 250 in number, who voted for him by 155 to 89, including pairs on each side, but by new arrangements enabling the country clergy to vote by post. Many dons of course voted as Churchmen rather than as Liberals, Dr Pusey and Dr Routh for instance supporting Gladstone to the last. Yet even so a large majority of Oxford dons voted against a strong orthodox Conservative candidate in 1865. Sources: Noble, *Parliamentary Reformers' Manual* (1883), p. 30; J. Campbell, in *Oxford Magazine*, 9 November 1961; T. E. Kebbel, *Lord Beaconsfield and other Tory Memories* (1907), p. 305.

Similarly, we are told that in 1874 the masters at Harrow were 'Liberals almost to a man' (Lord Frederic Hamilton, *Here, There, and Everywhere*, 1921, p. 114). The reason why there is no real discrepancy here is of course that one would not expect Oxford dons and Harrow masters to behave in the same way as relatively well-educated people in the ordinary towns analysed below. Of more general relevance is the fact that even in 1906 all nine university seats remained Conservative.

masses to be hostile to those above them, merely the commonest form of it; and which groups among them did act like this, can only be ascertained, and not deduced.

6

It is now necessary to put into brief and condensed form the essentials of the relations between occupation and party preference. To do this, it is necessary to omit from the start certain elections, a substantial minority, where the fight was not on party grounds, or sociologically interesting motives were not given a clear turn. Where a Jewish candidate was standing (Maidstone 1841), where each village voted almost *en bloc* (Lincolnshire 1823), or where politics polarized about support or opposition to a landlord (Peterborough 1852), the voting patterns are of irreducibly particular interest. What can be generalized are the patterns in the majority of elections which were fought on party lines, which were and can be discussed in terms of class relations, and which had ideological overtones. (Party feeling is susceptible of numerical proof, e.g. at Yarmouth in 1830, only 12 votes out of 3,300 were not on a straight party ticket.) The following simplification of the empirical data was made by simple appraisal, rather than by statistical process, owing to the lack of any true principle for weighting and correlating different elections.

### Ratio of Liberal to Tory votes

| | Market town | Provincial metropolis | Industrial town |
|---|---|---|---|
| Gentlemen | 1 : 1 | 1 : 1 to 1 : 2 | 2 : 3 |
| Business | 3 : 2 | 1 : 1 to 1 : 2 | 2 : 1 to 1 : 1 |
| Professions | 2 : 3 | 1 : 2 | 1 : 2 |
| Shopkeepers | 1 : 1 to 2 : 1 | 1 : 1 to 2 : 1 | 1 : 1 to 2 : 1 |
| Craftsmen | 1 : 1 to 2 : 1 | 1 : 1 to 2 : 1 | 1 : 1 to 2 : 1 |
| Labourers | 2 : 3 | 2 : 3 | 1 : 1 |

These ratios are all rather low. The few really high ones recorded come from places where one particular craft was extremely concentrated, though not necessarily working in factories, and from the landed gentry in county constituencies. In the first category, the shoemakers of Northampton were for Reform in 1831 by about 5 to 1, being opposed by most of the gentlemen, lawyers, and publicans; in Norwich in 1830, the textile workers were for Reform by 2½ to 1, while the cordwainers were so only by 5 to 3; the

Leicester framework knitters voted Liberal by 4 to 1; the voting for Orator Hunt at Preston in 1830 was highest—6 to 1—among the most numerous group, the weavers, and much less among similar but smaller skilled groups like mechanics or spinners, who supported Hunt by only 2 to 1. (The same feature persisted at Preston in 1841.) The distinguishing feature in these cases is surely not any difference in the relations of production from those of the isolated, normally only mildly radical, craftsmen, but simply the change in consciousness produced by a literally physical solidarity. At the other end of the scale, the country gentlemen were Tory* by perhaps about 4 to 1, except in the great volte-face of 1830–2. Hence the curious feature of the apparent classlessness in voting at the top of the borough electorate may in fact result from deadlock between two counteracting patterns of conflict over authority, and not from absence of conflict at all; the two patterns being conflict for authority within the town, and conflict between the town hierarchy and the external authority of the landed interest. The second conflict, if perhaps more factitious, was more general and more overt. On the occasions when a Radical candidate did challenge the position of rank within a town, as with Orator Hunt at Preston, or the Chartists at Nottingham or Halifax, the upper crust closed its ranks with almost perfect discipline, and classlessness melted away overnight. But the existence of an external upper class outside the borough electorate, in conflict with the town community as a whole over political authority, is necessary, not to account for the existence of two parties within the town—the tendency of consensus to generate coalitions of fragmentary opposed interests is enough for that—but to explain why the consensual party should generally be Liberal.

## 7

The next point is to relate the typical voting pattern given above, to the social structure. In the first place, the political society, at least as enfranchised in the three types of constituency chiefly analysed, was pre-industrial. ('In industrial societies, nearly one out of every two citizens of such societies earns his living in industrial enterprises of production.'†) No group was linked to

---

* The best statistical evidence for their Toryism is the table on the Cambridge-shire election of 1868 in H. J. Hanham, *Elections and Party Management* (1959), p. 26.

† Dahrendorf, *Class and Class Conflict in Industrial Society* (1959), p. 142.

another by the cash nexus, or by the relations arising from production, except in a tenuous and indefinite way. (The labourers are no doubt a probable exception.) The characteristic relation was that of vendor and customer, not employer and employee. Conflict might emerge instantaneously, over a particular transaction, or reflectively, over jealousy of inequality, but not automatically and constantly, through the antagonism of differing groups competing for the rewards of the general flow of production in which they participated. There was no economic basis for conflict between regularly defined and constantly opposed groups, in the sense that if these ones were to have more, those must have correspondingly less. And, as has been shown, particular economic pressure groups were unusual. Therefore, by elimination, the basis of electoral conflict lay in the political order.

This is not to say that denominationalism, or beliefs about change, or some other immaterial entity, was the *primum mobile*. Electoral conflict was in fact primarily between groups, the hard cores of which were defined and constituted by economic categories, and which, though not in economic conflict except marginally (e.g. fiscally), developed from their economic dissimilarities, separate political consciousnesses and wills to authority. The economic element serves only to constitute the personnel involved on each side; the difference of interest, and the object of the struggle, are political, not economic.

The essential division was between distributed property (mainly urban) and concentrated property (mainly rural), between capitalist agriculture and distributist urban petty production and exchange, between an urban 'free peasantry' and the great capitalists who ruled the only real Marxian proletariat that England had, the labourers in husbandry. There were all shades and degrees of exceptions, undeniably: the cotton industry on the one hand and peasant districts like Cornwall or parts of the Fens on the other, for instance; but here it is only towns in general and the countryside in general that are intended. Hence the perennial schizophrenia of the radical ethic, hovering between two sets of unstated assumptions about social structure, seething at inequality yet cherishing property and individual achievement, and hence too the stability of the preoccupations which re-emerged in rank and file liberalism. Their tone goes back in English history through the pamphlets of the 'freeholder interest' in eighteenth-century county elections, to the plain speakers of the Commonwealth; and, among foreign analogies, from the contest of Luther with the Fuggers, to the populism of the prairies, the most expressive at least is Proudhon's quite untheoretical love of decent poverty as the cornerstone of justice.*

The *pièces justificatives* necessary to demonstrate what has been said about the relative concentration of ownership and units of production in agriculture and industry, and the implications as to the general occupational and electoral structure of the country, are omitted here, and the curious are referred to the bibliography for the scant information available. The relevant statistics are few, intricate, and defective, and rather than make a travesty of analysing the rather mysterious Victorian social structure *en passant*, what have been set forth here are really heads of proposals for imaginative reconstruction of a political system.

## 8

The *Annual Register* for 30 January 1869 describes the funeral of Ernest Jones, the Chartist and semi-Marxist agitator, as

one of the largest public funerals which has been seen in Manchester for some years. At the head of the procession were the executive of the United Liberal Party, and the executive of the Reform League. Several thousand persons joined the procession. The streets were lined with dense crowds. Following in some of the 50 carriages were the Mayor of Manchester; Sir Elkanah and Benjamin Armitage: Jacob Bright, M.P.: Beales, Odger, Howell: T. B. Potter, M.P. The pallbearers were Edward Hooson, Jacob Bright, Elijah Dixon, Edmond Beales, Ald. Heywood, T. B. Potter, Sir E. Armitage, F. Taylor, James Crossley, Rev. H. M. Steinthal, Mr H. Rawson, and Mr Thomasson.

These names, renowned in their day, included several millowners, including two or three very wealthy ones; one or two newspaper editors; the London radical orators; the Manchester civic élite; and the leaders of the working class in the co-operative, trade union and reform movements. And Ernest Jones was a close correspondent of Karl Marx ('mein lieber Jones'); in many ways,

---

* Even 'anti-Utopian' extreme radicals glowed at the thought of a property-owning democracy. See the speech by Ernest Jones, a radical closely connected with Karl Marx, reported in the *Birmingham Daily Post*, 27 November 1867: 'England's wealthiest Ballarat is England. Our true goldfields are golden fields of wheat. Back to the land. It is your only safeguard against the assaults of capital. Talk of confiscating wealth. I propose to give it a legion of additional defenders. It is a national regenerator. Give us a million peasant farmers.'

for a long time, himself a Communist; and the most able, spirited, and class conscious of the Chartist survivors—a kind of English Lassalle, in fact. And yet here he is, buried with kindness; the little town had seldom seen a costlier funeral. This kind of political behaviour—which is only *in parvo* what one finds throughout the Liberal movement—has sometimes understandably promoted the view that political man was different in 1869, more silly, more crafty, or more charitable, according to one's point of view.

It is the same with the voting studies carried out here. When one has finally reached typical ratios of preference for the chief groups, one finds they do not very obviously manifest any sociological meaning, written as it were on the face of the sun for all to see. The question is therefore to find what kind of ideas of class would fit the known facts, in the first place; and in the second place, afford some explanatory insight into why the facts are as they are.

In the first place, there is little correlation (though what there is, is more positive than negative) between voting and class in the colloquial sense, that is, class as stratum, the statistical category of people united by having certain objective criteria of stratification, not conscious of itself as such and not doing anything as such. In this sense, there is a weak, but general and detectable, form of class conflict, meaning conflict between objectively defined strata, between 'rich' and 'poor'. The trouble with the use of 'class' in this sense is that it defines what is at best a weak potentiality, a statistical probability, corresponding to nothing anyone ever felt, and that it leaves what actually did happen, the people who actually did vote together, as naked of conceptual mantle as before. Class as stratum then, class in the colloquial sense, cannot really be used to describe voting patterns, or to explain them.

Secondly, there is Marxian class, engaged in conscious struggle as such, and generated by the relations involved in production. 'Individuals form a class only in so far as they are engaged in a common struggle against another class.'* This deeply interesting definition cannot however be applied in an unsophisticated Marxist way to the matter in hand, on two grounds. In the first place, as already argued, the political situation of electors did not in general involve capitalism, factory production, a propertyless proletariat, or personal relations arising from the conditions of production. It was exactly the lack of any such relations which produced radicalism. In the second place, in the exceptional cases

* Marx, cited in Dahrendorf, *op. cit.* p. 134.

of industrial situations to which the Marxian formula might be analytically fitting, it is generally factually incorrect. This is, unity between masters and men was usually greatest in these areas; that when a state of acute class difference arose, it could dissolve into warm class collaboration again in a short time, as at Oldham in 1852 and 1865; and that when masters and men were on different sides, the masters were usually still to the left of other, more 'disinterested' sections of the rich and influential. Only in 1868, in the voting of some groups of railwaymen and labourers, does the beginning of a new, truly 'industrial' pattern begin to appear. Nor was collaboration* simply on the terms of the boss; the largest manufacturer in Halifax, Crossley, voted for the Chartist candidate, Ernest Jones, in the Halifax election of 1847. The Marxian idea of class, as deriving from the relations of capital and labour, is interesting in proportion as it shows what the situation was not like and what did not happen. It describes and interprets nothing.

Dahrendorf differs from Marx, not as regards the active, purposive, nature of class and class conflict, but over the need to refer to the character of the economic society to define class. 'Classes are neither primarily nor at all economic groupings.'† In fact, on his model, the conflicts of bourgeoisies and aristocracies were the great fundamental type of class conflict, not merely the overture to the real thing: while the conflict of capital and labour is relatively local, and the tendency to interpret class conflict in these terms, almost a culture trait.

Drawing in part on his terms and definitions, with modifications for difference of subject, I would say that the voting patterns can be satisfactorily interpreted in terms of class and class conflict, and perhaps have to be. Political conflict at rank and file level was mainly between classes (the exceptions enumerated above not being sufficient to affect the general point). *These classes were not strata of rich and poor as in the colloquial sense of class, nor capital and labour as in the simplest Marxian sense of class.* These classes did, however, resemble Marxian classes, in that they were operational collectivities, acting at national level to achieve or prevent general changes in the structure of the political order (including the Church), and in lesser degree, to change the kind of person in

---

* Another curiosity was the case of the old Owenite, Weston, who was on the inner committee of the First International in 1864, although he was a manufacturer (of handrails).

† Dahrendorf, *op. cit.* p. 139.

authority; and that they acted thus, not blindly or from their appetitive natures, but because they were conscious of what they wanted to do, because they saw their action as part of a natural class effort without which it would have been meaningless, and because they, on both sides, used a socially agreed interpretation of the political structure and its economic basis. (The high *visible* intelligibility of a society of market towns and stately homes must be borne in mind—the social system was, so to say, expounded in the streets. Bath and Brighton both caught radicalism of an especially plebeian kind.) Moreover, despite the natural scatter of opinions, an appreciable section of each class wanted total structural change in the political order on the one hand, total adherence to the ancient constitution, a term of the widest import, on the other. The totality of persons engaged in achieving, abetting, or frustrating this political transformation forms an *operational* collectivity; it corresponds to parts of various social strata, themselves not operational units; and it is not the mere numerical aggregate of small primary groups, since the reasons for which people voted in groups locally cannot be understood at any level below their understanding of the structure of the national society, and their sense of belonging without local mediation to a collectivity acting directly in relation to that structure. This totality, then, though it might be said pedantically that its name was an open question, vivid though the experience of it was, is surely the one to which the name of class can fitly be attached. It is a collectivity operating in politics at a general level, non-economic in that it aims at authority in the political order, only partly economic as regards how its personnel are constituted, and it is not a political party proper. Which term of discourse is so fit to label this great white whale as class, especially as we have seen that class lacks other adequate homes?

This would accord very well with the presence of an acute class sense in mid-Victorian political consciousness (i.e. *la vision dichotomique* of social structure was practically a matter of folk culture in areas that had never heard a loom creak), co-existing with relatively or even entirely 'classless' patterns of voting even in quite free and pure elections. This would also fit well the fact that the economic upper stratum in towns did not vote like one, but did vote like a middle group in a stratification by authority, in which the external aristocracy were, and behaved like, the top group.

Two points of refinement are necessary. First, one must distinguish between the nature of a struggle between classes for authority, and the struggle, which may be on a generous scale, between competing élites of 'Ins' and 'Outs' for office or for points of polity, within an unquestioned framework of aristocratic society. The two are quite different; but confusion arises because the 'Ins' and 'Outs' of the aristocratic élites were superimposed on the class struggle. The classes were not interested in the personal enjoyment or exercise of power, but in the relative distribution of authority between themselves. Secondly, while it is necessary to reject outright, at least at the level of definition, the idea that classes were economically constituted groups acting for economic motives to effect change in the economic order, one must recede from dramatic negation at the level of description, and admit that political class had an economic flavouring. What is relevant is that the belief that it was natural for the rich and poor to be on opposite sides, for economic reasons, was far more widespread than was such behaviour in real life. There was a kind of sixth sense that the distribution of property was a function of the distribution of political power, even when all explicit tradition of how society worked ignored or denied this. Hence, in the case of the Tory majority group among the landowners and the radical majority group among the *menu peuple*, political behaviour was influenced by a general agreement as to where their economic interest lay, by the tendency of politicians to address them as economically defined and engaged groups, and by their own explanation of their behaviour in terms of an economically constituted group. On the other hand, all this makes the behaviour of the minority groups in each stratum harder to explain. The obvious conclusion is that the knowing, mysterious sideways glance that people used to suggest the implications of politics for the economic order, did not stop people doing what they wanted to do and would have done anyway, on the basis of social relations and the stratification of political authority alone.

9

To the view set forth above of the centrality of class, in a certain sophisticated sense, in rank and file political orientation, may be opposed three limiting or modifying propositions. The first, a necessary and acceptable limitation, is that the ordinary political activity of the period belongs to an autonomous political culture and has still to be explained as such. Class was diluted by party, by events, by personality. It always needed incarnation in something of lesser generality which itself cannot be reduced to class terms. Class was largely irrelevant to the life of Parliament, the policy and preoccupations of the executive, or face to face politics in general. The real question of importance here is how class conflict could be retained for so long, endemic and in equilibrium, in the electoral system, with so little impingement on policy, or on the type of person in authority; the diversionary value of the electoral system, in focusing and resolving (if only by continued adjustments till the next election) structural conflicts at a safe distance from the world of political institutions and political culture, is suggested by this.

Secondly, it may be suggested that the word class as used here is not so much erroneous as tautologous, the conception intended being already well expressed by the more familiar idea of party. This is not so. Both class and party are indeed operational units, united by consciousness of themselves as such, rather than by organization; and of maximum comprehensiveness. There similarity ends and difference begins. Class is a homogeneous totality of those whose main aim is structural change in the political society; party is a heterogeneous alliance of people concerned to effect their own aims through the party. Party might in fact be made up of a core of 'class' and a fringe of 'interest groups' like the Catholic vote or the drink or West India interests; it might conceivably, as in Labour fundamentalism, be coterminous with class. But in fact the dissonance between party and class was much greater than one of fringes, for considerable sections in each party, entirely sound from a party point of view, were opposed to or had no interest in those ideas of political structure which animated the class-conscious sections within each party. This is especially true of the Whig leadership, of Disraeli, and of the Tory–Chartist working-class vote. Party and class are ideas of like order, but they are not of one nature.

Thirdly, there is the nominalist reproach against class, that political orientation is real enough for individuals and for small primary groups, but that classes, on the other hand, are just a mental convenience existing for the purposes of generalization and classification. This answers itself, for membership of an objectively existent class was in general integral to, and antecedently necessary for, individual political orientation. The existence of individual opinion, and the objective reality of the entity 'class' engendered by and yet also causing that opinion, stand or fall together. As for the 'small primary groups', those Panzer battalions of the new sociological approach, it is hard to think that they are the bricks of which the building is built. As far as one can tell, a Baptist shoemaker would probably be as close in political opinion to a Congregationalist tailor unrelated to him living in another town, as to a cousin of the same denomination and trade living in the same town. It follows consequentially that membership of a class entails membership of local groups, on the whole; but membership of a local group does not entail class membership. There is also monumental evidence, in the form of all political utterance from portentous speeches to cartoons and ballads, that people do typically see themselves as acting in a context of great generality (and, conversely, find it much harder to visualize their role in a situation 'they know from their own experience', like municipal elections).

10

Careful investigation of voting habits shows how well founded are many of the objections made against the idea of class (and especially against the idea that it is the raw material with which politicians have to work) by the sceptics and men of good will who have found it a monotonous simplification of the richness of human situations. One discovers a great flexibility of pattern and variety of data, and a wide penumbra of sleepy backwaters with a political life in which nothing is happening. Often it would be difficult, looking at analyses of the voting of each party in an election, to decide by any sociological criterion which was which. Then again, even in clearcut party battles fought with more than overtones of class, classlessness in party preference was vastly greater than today. The practical moral for the politician of the nineteenth century, had he concerned himself with analysing pollbooks, would have been that there is almost no quarter in which votes may not be sought and won, no interest so sharply hostile that it is not worth placating, that in short the electoral situation is profoundly plastic and responsive to political art.

On the other hand, political art cannot undo what is elemental; it cannot make a majority of those enjoying authority, vote for its diminution, nor a majority of those without it, habitually vote for their continued exclusion. Reason and education, and other things, produced Liberal landowners and Tory craftsmen in numbers: but never a secure majority of either. Whether or not class is irreducible, it was in fact not reduced. Almost regardless of circumstances, the majority of the poorer people would vote for different candidates from the majority of the richer people (even when both sides were liberal, the class split was obvious, as at Glasgow, Brighton, and Edinburgh). Class, not in the Marxian sense of economic class, nor in the colloquial sense of stratum, but class in the sense of a group contending over the structure of political authority, was the general ground of popular political orientation.

## II

## THE DISTRIBUTION OF CAPITAL
## AT DEATH: CAMBRIDGESHIRE 1848–57

This study is based on an examination of the grants of probate and administration made for all wills and intestacies occurring in Cambridgeshire (including Ely) in 1848–57 inclusive. These are to be found in the records of the four relevant courts, the Bishop's Court, the Archidiaconal Court, the Peculiar Court of Thorney, and the Prerogative Court of Canterbury* which had overlapping jurisdictions in the county up till the secularization of probate at the end of 1857. As over 90 per cent of entries give the occupation, or, in the case of women, the marital status, of the deceased, together with an indication of the amount left, they form a useful source for several problems in social history. Previous studies of capital distribution, such as those based on the death duties, have shown the distribution among socially unlocated holders. By using the probate records, it is possible to draw a general picture of social stratification, of the sectional distribution of capital between agriculture, manufacture and exchange, and of the internal capital structure within specific occupations, as well as dealing with the well-worn subject of simple inequality. The main features that emerge are so pronounced in Cambridgeshire, that it is hard not to think that a similar structure of ownership, differing only in degree, existed over a long period in the agricultural counties and market towns of much of England.† Three more general problems are therefore discussed: the conditions under which a capital structure of this type was compatible with economic growth, the motivation of individual economic action within such a structure, and the relation between popular political orientation in the towns and the system of ownership.

The statistics which follow are uncomplicated, but on four points a certain tolerance must be asked for. First, the category of 'gentlemen', which must have been a disguise for many of its

---

* I am indebted to Miss Peek of the Cambridge University Archives, and to the staff of the National Probate Registry, Somerset House, for instruction and guidance.

† The 1851 census divides the population of Cambridgeshire into 58,722 persons living 'in towns' and 133,172 persons living 'in the country parts'.

members who should properly have been placed in an earthier category, is irremediably impure. Secondly, grants of probate and administration were made only for one-tenth of all deaths, and this chapter proceeds on the assumption, made *ex silentio,* that those nine-tenths who do not reach the records died leaving little more than the clothes they stood up in, where they were not wives or minors. This is plausible, but the impossibility of recovering knowledge of working practice in these matters among the poor prevents a more positive basis than argument *ex silentio.* Thirdly, the distribution of capital at death is in certain cases not a good guide to the true distribution of capital among the living, e.g. it is fairly clear that widows would have held their capital for much shorter periods (and spinsters perhaps for longer periods) than the average holder of capital, and this would introduce a distortion into any analysis based on deaths. Fourthly, the sums at which estates were sworn are not proper valuations. It was sworn that an estate was 'under £450' or 'under £600', and it is this maximum figure which is used as the basis for computation. These maxima were always at certain conventional sums: £200, £300, £450, £600, £800, £1,000 and never at intermediate figures, i.e. there was no attempt at close valuation. Nevertheless, if an estate turned out larger or smaller than at first thought, the probate was carefully resworn, even for quite small changes: the matter was a serious one.

The figures which follow relate simply to the records, no attempt having been made to make adjustments for discrepancies between records and realities. The kinds of error in individual cases and quantities which the above remarks allow for are not sufficient to affect truths of proportion or the general tendency and implications of a multitude of instances.

More remarkable than the concentration of wealth among a few is the apparent complete absence of any effects among nine-tenths of male deaths:

|  | Total deaths 1848–57 | No. of persons leaving property |
|---|---|---|
| Male | 20,686 | 1,630 |
| Female | 19,797 | 694 |
|  | 40,483 | 2,324 |

As probate and administration were granted for sums as small as £5 (three months' subsistence for a labourer), it is probable that even when abatement is made for the wives and minors, whose ability to own property was legally restricted, among the deceased, most people at death left savings and property which were very low in relation to their annual income.

Even within the 5 per cent of deceased who had anything to leave there was extreme inequality of distribution. The 76 men and women leaving over £10,000, though only 2·6 per cent of those leaving property and 0·2 per cent of all deaths, left almost 50 per cent of the wealth. The top 1 per cent of persons dying (400 persons, about 17 per cent of those leaving property) left £3,309,000 out of £4,415,000, i.e. about 75 per cent.

Women left about 17 per cent of all capital, distributed as follows:

|  | No. of persons | Total amount (£) |
|---|---|---|
| Wives | 66 | 21,450 |
| Spinsters | 235 | 266,490 |
| Widows | 393 | 429,980 |
|  | 694 | 717,920 |

This sum, left by only 3½ per cent of female deceased, was nevertheless larger than the amount left by all males engaged in agriculture, in this predominantly rural county.

Among the men, the general inequality of distribution by persons corresponded to an unequal division between various sectors of economic activity:

|  | No. of persons | Amount left (£) |
|---|---|---|
| A. Gentlemen, clergy, academics | 291 | 2,326,000 |
| B. All other males | 1,339 | 1,371,000 |
| C. All males with specific occupations, less farmers and those in (A) above | 780 | 553,000 |
| Total, all males | 1,630 | 3,697,000 |

A more detailed table shows how little capital was needed for distribution, production, exchange, agriculture, and the small savings of employees, compared with the great quantity of wealth belonging to the genteel, which was not assigned to any specific economic role or function:

|  | No. | Total (£) | Median (£) |
|---|---|---|---|
| Gentlemen | 242 | 1,655,000 | 1,500 |
| Clergymen | 39 | 413,000 | 2,000 |
| Heads of Houses | 6 | 203,000 | 22,000 |
| Professors | 4 | 55,000 | 15,000 |

| | No. | Total (£) | Median (£) |
|---|---|---|---|
| Professions | 72 | 118,000 | 450 |
| Business | 97 | 174,000 | 800 |
| Farmers | 359 | 663,000 | 1,000 |
| Yeomen | 151 | 39,000 | 100 |
| Publicans | 48 | 15,000 | 200 |
| Shopkeepers | 128 | 129,000 | 300 |
| Craftsmen | 178 | 42,000 | 100 |
| Labourers | 53 | 6,000 | 50 |
| Mariners | 8 | 9,000 | 375 |
| Servants | 45 | 21,000 | 200 |
| Unstated | 200 | 155,000 | 300 |
| | 1,630 | 3,697,000 | |

The only considerable body of highly capitalized producers was in agriculture. There were two nuclei in farming communities, grouped about £200 and about £4,000 respectively. The former were in much the same position as the small urban producers. Capital was a by-product of income, a consequence of the need for a small reserve and for ownership of some essentials. For the large farmer, his capital was the cause of his income. (This agrarian capitalism, be it noted, quite outmatched in wealth and numbers its urban counterpart—builders, brewers, millers, and maltsters.) The distribution of wealth among farmers, according to the conventional fixed points at which estates were estimated, was as follows:

| Amount of estate | No. of persons | Total value (£) |
|---|---|---|
| £20 or under | 26 | 460 |
| £50 | 21 | 1,050 |
| £100 | 36 | 3,600 |
| £200 | 55 | 11,000 |
| £300 | 25 | 7,500 |
| £450 | 32 | 14,400 |
| £600 | 18 | 10,800 |
| £800 | 27 | 21,600 |
| £1,000 | 18 | 18,000 |
| £1,500 | 56 | 84,000 |
| £2,000–£9,000 | 102 | 393,000 |
| £10,000 and over | 5 | 58,000 |
| | 359 | 663,000 |

It is not clear whether the term 'yeoman' has any specific meaning, or whether, if it has, it refers to status, to being a freeholder, or to being a small cultivator of any kind above the rank of labourer. The latter seems most probable. If the structure of the yeomanry

is laid alongside that of the farmers, the economic chasm between
*petite culture* and capitalist high farming is still clearer:

| Amount of estate | No. of yeomen | Total value (£) |
|---|---|---|
| £20 and under | 42 | 655 |
| £50 | 24 | 1,200 |
| £100 | 28 | 2,800 |
| £200 | 18 | 3,600 |
| £300 | 9 | 2,700 |
| £450 | 9 | 4,050 |
| £600 | 4 | 2,400 |
| £800 | 6 | 4,800 |
| £1,000 | 2 | 2,000 |
| £1,500 | 7 | 10,500 |
| £2,000 and over | 2 | 4,000 |
| | 151 | 38,705 |

Disregarding marginal groups like labourers, servants, and
publicans, one finds a more egalitarian situation among shopkeepers and skilled workers and craftsmen. Apart from a group of
very substantial shopkeepers—such as booksellers, chemists,
drapers and wine merchants—the body of these people, such as
shoemakers, carpenters, grocers, butchers, bakers, tailors, left
effects amounting to about one to three years' income. (A craftsman's wage was about £50, taking one trade with another.) For
the craftsmen who were employees, not small masters, such a level
of savings in relation to income would be quite high by present-
day standards. But it must be remembered that an unknown number of craftsmen left practically nothing, and hence are not
recorded. The big shops apart, the shopkeepers were not on the
whole much better off than the skilled workers:

| | Shopkeepers | Skilled workers |
|---|---|---|
| £20 and under | 2 | 28 |
| £50 | 13 | 25 |
| £100 | 21 | 28 |
| £200 | 23 | 30 |
| £300 | 12 | 13 |
| £450 | 10 | 9 |
| £600–£800 | 11 | 5 |
| | | [£800–£1,000] |
| £1,000–£1,500 | 14 | 3 |
| | | [£1,500–£3,000] |
| £2,000–£8,000 | 20 | 4 |

The term 'gentlemen' is a net that catches many fish. But the
two most numerous strata, those leaving over £10,000, who were

landowning families like the Adeanes or Huddlestons, and those in the £2,000–£5,000 stratum, can reasonably be accepted as being generally free from 'trade' or from being merely pushing. The widows, like the shopkeepers and farmers, fall into two clusters, the widows of ordinary people, and the widows of gentlemen and rich farmers:

| | Gentlemen | Widows |
|---|---|---|
| £50 and under | 12 | 71 |
| £100 | 14 | 74 |
| £200 | 17 | 54 |
| £300 | 13 | 33 |
| £450 | 17 | 29 |
| £600 | 15 | 22 |
| £800 | 11 | 18 |
| £1,000 | 9 [£1,000 and | |
| £1,500 | 20    over]: | 90 |
| £2,000–£5,000 | 54 | |
| £5,001–£9,999 | 19 | |
| £10,000–£49,000 | 33 | |
| £50,000 and over | 8 | |
| | 242 | 391 |

Where in all this are the middle class? for by tradition they should be reasonably conspicuous in an ordinary English county in 1850. It is not hard so much to find them, as to think them important. There is a clear lower middle class of craftsmen and shopkeepers, a manual and retailing middle class, fairly numerous, poor and homogeneous. There are the lower levels of the gentry, people who could live off their capital invested in the funds, and the block of rich farmers. But the kind of middle class, to which a history-making role has been assigned, was not thought of as rudely demotic, or merely genteel, or specifically rural. What was in mind was business and the professions. In Cambridgeshire, at least, these people were not numerically or economically dominant. Between them, they amounted to 10 per cent of males leaving property, and they owned 8 per cent of property left by males. When listed in detail, they look still less like the dynamic behind the historical process:

| Business | No. | Amount (£) |
|---|---|---|
| Builders | 14 | 19,300 |
| Coal dealers | 4 | 5,100 |
| Carriers | 2 | 400 |
| Merchants | 10 | 35,900 |
| Ironfounders | 2 | 800 |

| Business | No. | Amount (£) |
|---|---|---|
| Coachmakers | 2 | 300 |
| Seedsmen | 3 | 7,100 |
| Upholsterer | 1 | 16,000 |
| Banker | 1 | 4,000 |
| Woolstapler | 1 | 18,000 |
| Millers | 24 | 26,870 |
| Coachbroker | 1 | 1,000 |
| Shipowner | 1 | 200 |
| Horse trainers | 4 | 16,320 |
| Brewers | 11 | 7,050 |
| Boatbuilders | 2 | 500 |
| Jobbers | 9 | 5,450 |
| Maltsters | 5 | 9,600 |
| | 97 | 173,890 |

| Professions, etc. | No. | Amount (£) |
|---|---|---|
| Bankers' Agent | 1 | 450 |
| Registrars | 2 | 1,050 |
| Dissenting Ministers | 7 | 3,250 |
| Clerks | 5 | 750 |
| Fellows | 4 | 11,500 |
| Gaol official | 1 | 200 |
| Tax collectors | 2 | 550 |
| Toll collectors | 2 | 200 |
| Curator, Botanic Gardens | 1 | 4,000 |
| Auctioneers | 3 | 8,500 |
| Organists | 2 | 2,000 |
| Librarian | 1 | 3,000 |
| Surgeons | 10 | 27,400 |
| Parish clerks | 2 | 250 |
| Civil engineers | 3 | 500 |
| Vet. | 1 | 1,500 |
| Lawyers | 7 | 39,500 |
| Pensioners | 2 | 300 |
| Schoolmasters | 6 | 2,370 |
| Officers | 8 | 9,350 |
| Workhouse masters | 2 | 400 |
| | 72 | 118,000 |

The capital structure drawn above was top-heavy; it concentrated capital away from those actively engaged in the normal processes of production and distribution towards those least likely to engage in local business. The actual figures given over-emphasize the situation, because they do not allow for the numbers of local businessmen calling themselves gentlemen, or for the participation of the gentry proper in agriculture. Nevertheless, much of the wealth of the county was relatively functionless in relation to the local economic situation, and had to be understood in terms of status and family endowment and provision. The position in Cambridgeshire in the 1850s would fit the hypothesis that the extreme concentration of wealth, not in the hands of entrepreneurs and captains of industry, but in the hands of widows, spinsters, rich farmers, clergymen, academics, squires and rentiers claiming gentility, created a permanent 'underconsumptionist' obstacle to economic growth under the English *ancien régime*. The causes which drew wealth out of the general flow, into the large savings of the genteel, were certain, perennial, and independent of individual initiative. The causes operating to draw the wealth of the rich back into circulation were occasional, variable and usually required positive action. These things being so, nothing would be more important in the historical economics of nineteenth-century England than to show the conversion of this type of capital structure, locally and usually an incubus, into an asset at national level, whether through the building of railways and canals, or through deficit-financed French wars acting rather like a public works programme. State activity, acting through the national debt, poor rates and taxes to bring underemployed wealth of this kind into play, was probably necessary at first to combine this type of capital structure with rapid economic growth.

It is important to notice that the concentration and social localization of capital did not take place for business reasons. Production and technique had nothing to do with it: it was a process taking place outside the daily economy, which was manned, on the whole, by independent small producers. The chief exceptions were among some of the farmers, shopkeepers and a few businesses like builders, where large property did correspond to large units of economic activity. But broadly, the kind of capitalism drawn above was not connected with a sense of economic role or vocation, was not concerned with entrepreneurship or production, which was carried on by different strata, and neither caused, nor was caused by, a business ethic. Indeed, so far as the owners of capital had a coherent social ethic, they repudiated all these things, and especially 'trade'. Those who carried on the normal economic life of Cambridgeshire needed singularly little of its total capital to do so; those who had most of the wealth of the county required as a mark of caste at least an outward non-participation in economic activity.

The extreme inequality of this society is better represented by a withdrawal of wealth to one side, away from daily life, rather than its imposition from above over daily life. In this way, a high degree of inequality had some curiously egalitarian consequences for the social ethic and political orientation of the ordinary person. For the productive situation especially in the towns, but also among the small farmers and yeomen, remained egalitarian, and was unaffected by inequality of ownership. The general experience almost conformed to 'the American dream'. With hard work and thrift, any yeoman, shopkeeper, carpenter or shoemaker might reach affluence as it was understood by the people he knew. A labour theory of value was quite appropriate to such a situation, as was a morality of sturdy independence, and a sense of the fitness of political democracy. The milieu of the townsman who was just rising, doubtless by merit, from poverty into small property, was self-explanatory without reference to the inequalities in the wider national life, however great these were objectively; for to these real and great inequalities, there was no corresponding experience of economic domination or conflict in daily urban life. Hence the puzzling features of Victorian popular radicalism (strong, incidentally, in Cambridge), with its ambivalence towards wealthy aristocrats and its preference for political over economic aims. The latter has generally been considered either irrational, or a product of insidious upper-class pressure. But the picture of social structure sketched above argues strongly against this. Victorian society achieved very great inequality at the top without affecting the fraternity, liberty and equality of the crucial stratum of the town population—the craftsmen, retailers, publicans and skilled employees and small masters. This was because the inequality lay almost entirely in the realm of functionally superfluous capital, while productive capital remained comparatively evenly distributed. In such circumstances, politics were centred on conflicts over authority in the town, in Parliament and in the Church, between two milieus not normally in economic conflict, but too far apart in daily life not to react to each other in a xenophobic way.

## III

# THE POLITICAL FEELINGS OF
# THE PEOPLE

In conclusion here is a psychological theory about the strange behaviour of 'the people' in modern English history. It starts from what is universally admitted in individual cases, that one person's needs may be chiefly material (money, housing, safety at work) and another's non-material (sociability, excitement, emotional satisfaction). Both needs are equally real and important and central to the action of those who have them. Can this simple individual distinction be generalized into a distinction of political psychology valid for large groups? In two cases at least, there are contrasting types of social situation inclusive enough to create a general psychological outlook among those they affect, irrespective of their 'personal character', which is submerged in public matters by their public, occupational function.

The social distinction which splits 'the people' broadly into two is between those who are institutionalized and given society by their work (mines, docks, large factories with *male* workers, labourers in Norfolk-type agriculture) and those whose work creates for them only an exiguous system of personal relations (petty producers, Cornish-type farmers,* retailers, tramping artisans, skilled craftsmen, small dealers). Nothing keeps people apart like small property.

---

* The contrast between the strength of Labour in rural Norfolk, and of the Liberal party in rural Cornwall, can be plausibly explained in terms of the local agrarian structure: it corresponds to the division between corn and grass, large farms and small farms, capitalist and peasant types of agriculture. See Hirsch, 'Size of Farm Holdings', *Farm Economist*, IX (1958), 87, for a map showing the strong east–west division in land ownership patterns. For Cornwall, see Daniell, *Cornwall* (1906), pp. 160–1, and Lawry, *J. Roy. Agric. Soc.* (1892). The average size of holdings in 1903 was:

|  |  |
|---|---|
| All England | 66·1 acres |
| Wales | 46·6 acres |
| Cornwall | 44·8 acres |

9,700 holdings out of 13,500 in Cornwall in 1903 were between 1 and 50 acres. It was a peasant society. Even in 1954 there were still no farms over 1,000 acres in the county, and in 1965 some 53 per cent of the 12,011 holdings were classified as 'part-time holdings'.

For the first group, their work carries with it membership of an essentially political, highly structured, situation, on the model of a school. Also their material interests are quite clear cut, and conflict over them follows the same lines of division as conflict about authority in the institutional situation. Because the emotional interest available for politics is fixed and in part absorbed for these people at local level, the carry-over from them into national politics consists of strong 'rationalist' demands (Taff Vale, Beveridge) for practical objects conceived in material terms, accompanied by weakly supported 'ideological' demands (clause 4), drastic in formulation, but with no weight of feeling or intention behind them.

For the second group, the individualists (whether employers, self-employed, or employees in a small enterprise), the situation is rather the reverse. Their material situation gives no clear lead. Their job does not array them immediately in conflict of authority with a superior. Their economic hopes are miscellaneous and shifting. Voluntary arrangements may suit them better than the Welfare State. General and collective betterment, they rightly fear, may cost them money. Yet, combined with antagonism to disturbance in their personal milieu, was a need to express the feelings naturally arising in the small man from contemplating the successful and the holders of power. Decent poverty of this type had very deep frustrations, but its social base precluded any economic programme, except economy. How was an outlet to be found for the political side of such people? Not in local voluntary associations, which, whether religious, prudential, or convivial, were combinations based on 'niceness' and were ill-suited to express sterner feelings. (Some of the apparent authoritarianism of the small town Radical —e.g. as to penal views or hatred of Rome—may be explained in this way. They were not inherently more aggressive than other people, but their position forced them into an unnatural 'niceness' in so many relations of life, e.g. to customers, that their patience broke more quickly than others, when it found a socially approved object to hate.) The only way for them to assert that they were as good as the holders of authority and of the means of enjoyment, was through national politics, and in national politics the really interesting thing would be the transfer of power from 'them' to 'us', and generally any symbolic reform which commuted the individual helplessness of the Radical voter into a sense of power over his betters. This demand reached national politics more fiercely because it was unabsorbed by being filtered through, and partly used in, a local situation.* This is what Liberalism was for, so far as the people were concerned, to enable them to have nationally, the satisfaction daily and local life denied to them. It was therefore not necessary that Liberal measures should benefit them: so long as they vexed the mighty, this was a sufficient reason for enthusiasm. What Gladstone was offering was emotional subsistence level—the possibility of participation, antagonism, struggle, commitment, eventual victory, a sense of power and domination—to people normally entirely subject to circumstances and to other people. The permanent issue behind Midlothian and Reform and Home Rule was what kind of people should have power, in whose name, and in accordance with whose ideas. Gladstone offered the psychic satisfaction of ruling to the ruled—not ruling over themselves, but ruling and overruling the traditional holders of authority, or large parts of them, which was much more gratifying. Gladstone offered this for what it was, and the people accepted it for what it was—a question of self-determination and of the union of hearts: not of bread. Nobody deluded anybody.

Now we have here two quite different styles of popular politics. On the one hand 'industrial' situations produce sharp, but institutionally self-contained, industrial conflicts, which overflow into national politics via a strong organization-based leadership, making strong practical demands, and drastic-sounding but really unsupported ideological and structural demands, at the national level.† On the other hand, people in 'individualist' situations— although probably in the same economic and self-assessed stratum —generate the opposite pattern of political behaviour. Here the occasion is the national elections, there is no antecedent or intermediate stage of local or institutional conflict, leadership acts through opinion not organization, and the practical programme is as tinkering as the ideological demands are fierce. Both situations

* This pent-up resentment of environment, overflowing into national ideological politics because there is no local outlet, occurs in the Communist vote in France and Italy today, in entirely non-industrial areas. Perugia and Siena, cities of small craftsmen, are Communist, Milan and Turin are not. The Communist vote in certain backward rural departments in France, e.g. Corrèze, is rather similar to the peasant anti-clericalism of such Liberal strongholds as North Cornwall and the Isle of Ely.

† The miners are a good example of this dichotomy. At a local level, they are bitter: half of all strikes in Britain are in coal mining. At parliamentary level, the miners' members of Parliament, from 1900 to the rise of Gaitskell, have been silent pillars of the Labour Right.

may derive something from the personal shortcomings of political personnel, or from the intellectual cramps of a received body of 'objective knowledge', but the pattern is too deep to come from anything but a difference in the area of unsatisfied basic needs between the 'industrial' and the 'individualist' sections of the people.

The relative validity and good faith of each type of popular politics is a question of numbers. To offer, as a novelty, the delights of solidarity and collective action to miners and dockers, who have it every day of their lives, would obviously be as out of place as to proselytize the self-employed (such as the Sheffield 'little masters') on employers' liability, or to preach housing policies to people whose existence turned on inhabiting one particular corner-shop, pub, or low-cost home workshop. What then were the people—were they 'individualists' or 'proletarians', more like miners or more like cobblers?

The statistics will not run to an exact answer. There are no reliable factory statistics* before the later 1890s. The occupational census returns fail to distinguish masters from men with any success. Nevertheless, the majority of 'individualists' over 'proletarians', indicated by all the imperfect data at our disposal for the period before 1900, is quite a large one. It is larger if only adult males are reckoned on each side, for women and children probably formed half the factory population.† In the nineteenth century many advanced industries, which to the traveller's eye must have seemed classic cases of large-scale enterprises where a capitalist employer was linked to undifferentiated wage labour by a cash nexus, were still holding to the forms of social organization associated with petty producers in dispersed crafts linked to a market by mercantile entrepreneurs. The Birmingham trades were riddled with cases of workmen employing their own workmen. 'The manufacturer, even if he had a large factory, usually delegated much of his authority to overhands, and had little to do with the actual productive process. He was, in truth, a factor who had gathered his dependent craftsmen into his own establishment.' In some cotton trades the same man could be employer and employee:

* On the question of reliability, see 'Report of the Departmental Committee on Factory Statistics', *Parl. Papers*, 1895, XIX, 583.

† See *Parl. Papers*, 1871, LXII, 164: Returns of all persons employed coming under all Factories and Workshops Acts (no distinction being made between factories and workshops):

| | |
|---|---|
| Total of all such persons for England | 2,006,000 |
| Total of whom males over 18 | 1,051,000 |

in the Sheffield crafts, the artisans were one week masters, next week employees, the next self-employed. Several coalfields also tried to organize mass production in the old small-scale groups through the butty system. In cotton, many mills were hired off, a floor or a loom at a time to very small operators, using their own labour. This obscure tendency of mass industry to go backwards to organization based on petty property and the creation of value by labour must have inhibited the growth of an employee mentality among workers. In Cornish mining, an important industry by world standards for most of the nineteenth century, the divergence from capitalist norms, through the practice by which groups of miners in effect rented mines and divided the profits, was even wider.*

The disparity in favour of pre-industrial life is further magnified when it is remembered that, for political purposes, what counted was the social structure, not in itself, but as distorted by an electoral régime which discounted concentrated industrial populations. (Before 1885 this electoral distortion was even greater.) If the psychological model used here is right, success in popular politics could only be had on Gladstonian lines, by recognizing that though the Radical voter did not want disturbance in his milieu, he found great vicarious excitement in identifying himself with an attack on authority, conducted as a public spectacle at national level. Gladstone created a national theatre for England as Verdi did for nineteenth-century Italy. To ask what the people hoped to get, say, from the election victory of 1880, is to ask the wrong question. What they primarily hoped to get was the election victory itself, as a visceral thrill, and as an assertion of their proper importance. Ulterior motives there were, but they were peripheral at popular level. The people went to the conflict like the Greeks went to the play. If the occupational aggregates are anything to go by, the political-psychological complexion and internal proportions of the population have changed little since 1850 (except by the enfranchisement of women). Change from small production to 'proletarian' types of production, and the decline in small property owners,† has been matched by a growth in white-collar employees.

* For Birmingham, see G. C. Allen, *The Industrial Development of Birmingham and the Black Country* (1929), p. 337; for Cornwall, see Warner, *A Tour through Cornwall* (1809), p. 229; and for a special case, see John Prest, *The Industrial Revolution in Coventry*.

† The number of publicans and beersellers in England and Wales fell from 113,000 in 1871 to 68,000 in 1964.

The psychic balance remains much the same.* The rural peasants have almost gone, but not the urban sources of the peasant mentality, or the general experience of domination in daily work, or the wide doubts as to the real advantage of politically won economic gains.

It is not too difficult to fit the change from Liberal to Labour, and the associated intensification of class attitudes, into this fairly stable occupational framework. It was not a question of changing distribution of occupations, so much as a remarkable difference in the ability of different groups to produce strong political institutions. With the stigma over the pubs, the chapels running to seed, and organizations like the National Union of Tobacconists hopelessly lightweight, great sections of the lower economic stratum were just not socially integrated enough to count. Also, an almost panic closing of the ranks against 'socialism' by the traditionally influential tended to make self-validating an initially false conception of what the change to Labour meant. The exaggeration of the change was due to special economic difficulties, interpreted by evolutionary pessimists imbued with a simple linear notion of historical change.

In fact, the Labour movement rose in an objective context not specially helpful to it, in a time of stable or declining relative employment in manual work in general and in manufacturing in particular. The situation was near enough to that of today (as pictured by revisionists) to suggest that the switch to a strongly 'proletarian' interpretation of the character of the manual workers was a subjective factor on both sides. Moreover, at that time the classical capitalism of the family firm was breaking up through the increasing differentiation of the labour force and the disintegration of the functions of the capitalist—processes often held to make for easing of conflict and 'post-capitalist' stability. Yet Labour *did* rise, and conflict *did* intensify. The reaction of the upper strata to practical demands for welfare through redistribution did differ sharply from their dealings with nineteenth-century demands for democratic participation. The twentieth-century conflict was more traumatic, and left less of a sense of flexible opportunism, of riding

* G. G. C. Routh, *Occupation and Pay in Great Britain, 1906–1960* (1965), states that while the proportion of manual workers fell from 81 to 70 per cent over 55 years, the proportion who were managers or proprietors has remained static over this period. Thus the figures hardly give a clear interpretative lead by themselves.

the storm, of fundamental ability to land on one's feet, than the change to a democratic franchise had produced in the politicians who carried it through.

But the issue raised by Labour was far less dangerous. The people seeing themselves as 'industrial masses'—rather forcedly—wanted what could well be given without general change in the political society. The people, typifying themselves as cobblers, had wanted to rule the Ascendancy of Church, land, and education, or at any rate to stop it ruling, even if it did this only by symbolic means (as with the disestablishment in 1868 of the Irish Church). Between Liberal and Labour the real revolutionary aim of English Jacobinism was lost sight of, and popular politics changed from being about power to being about bread. This change related directly to the *dominant conception* of social structure held by the people themselves and by political élites. This dominant conception changed in a way quite out of proportion to any changes in actual numbers in one group or another, and was much more over-drawn in favour of an 'industrial' interpretation of the people, than the Gladstonians had exaggerated their petty bourgeois and proprietary nature. One section of the people produced stable organization and striking leaders, the others were relatively void of institutional life, and people redrew their maps of the social structure accordingly, and incorrectly. The part was mistaken for the whole, and had in time to learn to speak for the whole and like the whole.

The method of change from Liberal to Labour was not by numbers, but, like the rise of Rome, due to weight of institutions. But the dropping of power as the central motive in popular politics was not just the replacement of an old idea by a new one, but corresponded very closely to the psychological needs created by the new supposedly dominant set of daily circumstances. There was a negative correlation between industrialization and revolution, considered from the point of view of popular contumacy and the probability of real change in the seat of power, and the type of person occupying it. There was a positive correlation between industrialization and revolution so far as the use of political power to benefit the poor at the expense of the rich goes. The latter criterion has been too much in favour at the expense of the political criterion. Both are very important. Each corresponds to the political psychology engendered by an archetypal occupational situation. Working with welfare as criterion, the Gladstonian Liberals were a pusillanimous prelude to Labour. Working with power and the total structure of society as terms of reference, the Liberals were much more drastic revolutionaries than Labour. To prefer the criterion of welfare is not only to neglect the extraordinary and lasting nineteenth-century achievement in the deliberate total structural change of the political society, but to foist a modern *Realpolitik* of bread, on men who needed politics chiefly to supply the circuses of their lives.

# IV

# NOTES ON THE MEANING OF THE OCCUPATIONAL CATEGORIES USED IN ANALYSIS

A fairly standard definition and classification of the significant occupational categories was evolved in preparing these tables. This classification had necessarily to be somewhat personal and arbitrary: also, there are in any case irreducible difficulties involved in using occupational descriptions which are based ultimately on the pleasant process of self-assessment of status. (Other causes of ambiguity, such as corruption or the same person holding several jobs, are not dealt with here, since they do not relate to the text of the pollbook.) A careful explanation of the procedure followed in compiling the tables is therefore important.

The first rule was to stick to the descriptions given in the pollbook, wherever possible; where the pollbook described a man as a 'banker', to write him down as a banker, and not otherwise. In many cases this procedure was followed unflinchingly. Only those described as merchants and grocers were set down as such; and mere 'corn merchants' and 'shopkeepers' were spurned. But this policy of no alteration to the classification given in the pollbook could not be followed to its limits. For instance, 'butchers' in the following tables includes those described as 'pork butchers', and 'gentlemen' includes those listed only as esquires. A measure of conflation or adulteration of categories was as necessary in some cases, as it would have been unfortunate in others. Also, in some cases the nature of the question asked dictated a different approach. There was little interest in the possible differences in voting between different grades of railwaymen and policemen, but much in the question how far the personnel of a railway or of a police force voted as a corps. In these and similar cases, where it is the general tendency of an institution that is at stake, the various grades of personnel were conflated into one category. The officers of the different services were also grouped together for convenience.

The normal practice (not always followed in the earlier analyses, since it was only reached *ambulando*) was as follows: 'Gentlemen' in the tables corresponds to 'gentlemen' and 'esquires' in the pollbooks. 'Officers' in the tables means all kinds of officers. 'Bankers' means simply bankers. 'Surgeons' includes those stated to be 'physician' or 'M.D.'. 'Lawyers' includes barristers, solicitors, and attorneys. Tailors are simply tailors, and carpenters do not include joiners. Grocers are grocers, but butchers may include pork butchers. Labourers do not include labouring men like navvies or bargemen, but only those described as labourers. The category of farmers may sometimes include a few yeomen. 'Cordwainers' includes shoemakers, bootmakers, and cobblers, but not cloggers, who are stated separately. Brewers are only brewers, and not maltsters. Beersellers include the synonymous beerhouse and alehouse keepers; publicans include victuallers and innkeepers. 'Merchants' means only merchants unqualified by any specific prefix. Manufacturers, equally, are those set down as such by the pollbook, where no information is given as to what they manufacture.

'Engineers' and 'firemen' carry an awkward double meaning in this period: the reader is left to decide whether they were really railwaymen or not. Still more awkward is the word 'clerk'. This can mean an Anglican clergyman, or it can mean a man who works in an office. Only the context can decide: office workers do not live in country vicarages. Apparently the terms 'clerk' and 'clergyman' always refer to an Anglican, and the term 'minister' always to a Nonconformist. Certainly, the voting patterns which emerge from such working assumptions strongly confirm their correctness. Most county pollbooks do not state the occupations of voters, but it is easy to pick out the names prefixed by 'Rev.', and thus to show the voting of Anglican clergy in the county elections. A few Nonconformist ministers may perhaps creep in to swell the apparent Liberal vote among the Anglican clergy. If so, this would only emphasize further the Toryism of the Church of England which stands out sufficiently already in the tables below.

Over a wide range of crafts and manufactures it is not possible to distinguish between master and man, capitalist and employee, retailer and craftsman, factory worker and domestic worker. This simply has to be accepted, for it is much more than a simple defect of information. Its real meaning is that although there were considerable differences of situation and of economic and technical function among skilled craftsmen and small entrepreneurs and retailers, there was nevertheless a feeling that people engaged in making the same kind of thing were the same kind of people. Emulation came into it, but it was hardly emulation that stopped

master shoemakers so calling themselves, just as much as wage-
earning shoemakers discarded the term of journeyman. Emulation
today does not make workers describe themselves as directors; and
if in the nineteenth century the pattern of self-description implies
that the social distance a shoemaker might move above and below
the normal shoemaker was not important to them, then probably
it was not objectively important either. The compilers of the
Census found this problem insoluble, and a Dr Ogle defended
their failure in an illuminating way:

It was suggested, as it had been suggested many times before, that the
employers should be distinguished from the employed...He could
assure Mr Booth that nobody was more anxious than those concerned in
the census that, were it possible, such a distinction should be made, and
special directions were given on the schedule that every worker should
state whether he was master or man: but it was all in vain: workmen
would not do anything of the kind. He believed that out of the 26
millions of people in England and Wales, there were not 1,000 who had
returned themselves as journeymen anything. A man called himself a
baker, whether he were a journeyman baker, or master baker, and so
with other trades: it was impossible to distinguish them.*

These remarks apply to the pollbooks as much as to the Census.
Only in Lancashire, and later in Yorkshire and Leicestershire, can
one distinguish with confidence between employer and employed.

Most of the tables which follow analyse only some of the many
occupations in each constituency. Necessity and reason alike
justify this. Wherever an unusual feature occurred, such as the
fullers in Exeter, the pinners in Gloucester, or the papermakers in
Maidstone, it was included for analysis, though it was necessarily
of little general significance. Secondly, some occupations, like
publicans, pilots, sweeps, or turnkeys, were analysed to try and uncover the effect of some trade question, legislation, or institutional
influence on voting. Thirdly, certain typical, widespread, fairly
numerous occupations were chosen as 'indicators' of class feeling
or its absence among a much wider body of men of whom they
were considered to be fairly representative. To have analysed more
constituencies completely might have enabled one to say more
exactly just what contingencies each election turned on, but it
would have been unlikely to uncover further abnormal or anomalous groups, and it would have added little to the data given below
for a study of political orientation. The 'indicators' chosen—or

* *Journal of the Royal Statistical Society* (June 1886), p. 438.

rather, which chose themselves—were usually bankers, merchants, manufacturers, clergy, surgeons, lawyers, and officers for the upper crust; shoemakers, tailors, weavers, grocers, butchers, for the craftsmen and tradesmen; and labourers, shipwrights, and mariners, where these occurred.

Far the most gnomic term is 'gentleman'. They are numerous and ubiquitous: they are usually Tory, but not nearly so much so as the clergy and the professions, and they may sometimes be chiefly Liberal. The 'gentleman' of the borough pollbooks is clearly of a different and lower order from the landed gentleman of the counties. For one thing, the urban 'gentleman' may be a Dissenter. For another, he may be in business—he might even be a shopkeeper beneath his broadcloth. The urban 'gentleman' is defined by the view from below, not from above; he is a gin'lman, a gent, but not quite a toff. He is nearer to the counting house than to the playing fields of Eton, but he does not really belong anywhere. Because it is such a ragbag of a category, the term 'gentleman' is very useful to us in tracing opinion among the urban well-to-do in general.

In towns like Leicester and Preston, those specifically textile occupations which hardly occur elsewhere were tabulated, though some among so many had to be omitted. In all towns, any occupations, whether of employer or employed, which seemed to involve factory production, mechanization, or capitalist forms of production, were taken note of—with disappointingly thin results for anyone seeking to get a grip on the political consequences of the Industrial Revolution. (In passing, it must be remarked how little political weight the great metal making and using industries had outside Sheffield and the Black Country.) If the tables below fail to contain many 'modern' industrial people, this is partly because of the maldistribution of the existing pollbooks, but it is chiefly because such people were not there. Probably they did not exist: but if they did, they did not have the vote. The absence of industrial people is not due to choice of the wrong categories. The following tables have their defects, but the principles upon which they have been analysed do provide data necessary for a general view of political orientation in this period. Refusal to make rough generalizations, on the basis of the evidence gathered below, would involve magnifying the admitted snags and untidiness of the data, into a sense of the mystery of the things which is rather out of place in dealing with 'beer, brawls, and bribery'.

# TABLES OF VOTING

# A. OCCUPATIONS ANALYSED BY CONSTITUENCIES*

### 1. The voting of Roman Catholic priests, 1832–72†

| Election | Leading Liberal | Leading Tory | Second Liberal | Second Tory |
|---|---|---|---|---|
| Beverley 1854 | 1 | 0 | — | — |
| Brighton 1841 | 1 | 0 | 1 | — |
| Bristol 1837 | 1 | 0 | 0 | — |
| Bristol 1841 | 2 | 0 | 0 | — |
| Bristol 1852 | 1 | 0 | — | — |
| Cambridge 1859 | 1 | 0 | 1 | 0 |
| Cambridge 1865 | 1 | 0 | 1 | 0 |
| Cambridge 1868 | 1 | 0 | 1 | 0 |
| Glasgow† 1832 | 1 | — | 1 | — |
| Ipswich 1847 | 1 | 0 | 0 | — |
| Ipswich 1857 | 1 | 0 | 0 | 0 |
| Ipswich 1859 | 1 | 0 | 0 | 0 |
| Ipswich 1865 | 0 | 1 | 0 | 1 |
| Leicester 1847 | 1 | 0 | 1 | 0 |
| Lindsey 1835 | 2 | 0 | 1 | — |
| Liverpool 1835 | 4 | 0 | 4 | 0 |
| Maidstone 1870 | 1 | 0 | — | — |
| Northampton 1831 | 1 | 0 | 1 | 0 |
| Oldham 1865 | 1 | 0 | — | — |
| Reading 1837 | 1 | 0 | 1 | — |
| Sandwich 1868 | 1 | 0 | 1 | — |
| Shrewsbury 1847 | 1 | 0 | 1 | — |
| Tamworth 1837 | 1 | 1 | 0 | — |

* The blank entries in this and the following tables may mean either that no third and fourth candidates were standing, or that, if they were, votes given for them were not tabulated by the present writer.
† In the Glasgow election of 1832, the Catholic bishop voted for the two successful Whig candidates.

### 2. The voting of organists, 1852–72

| Election | Leading Liberal | Leading Tory | Second Liberal | Second Tory |
|---|---|---|---|---|
| Beverley 1859 | 0 | 2 | — | 1 |
| Bristol 1852 | 0 | 3 | — | — |
| Cambridge 1859 | 0 | 3 | 0 | 3 |
| Cambridge 1863 | 0 | 3 | — | — |
| Cambridge 1865 | 0 | 3 | 0 | 3 |
| Cambridge 1866 | 0 | 2 | — | — |
| Cambridge 1868 | 0 | 5 | — | — |
| Ipswich 1852 | 1 | 1 | 0 | 0 |

*The voting of organists, 1852–72 (cont.)*

| Election | Leading Liberal | Leading Tory | Second Liberal | Second Tory |
|---|---|---|---|---|
| Ipswich 1857 | 1 | 1 | 1 | 1 |
| Ipswich 1859 | o | 1 | o | 1 |
| Leicester 1859 | o | 1 | 1 | — |
| Maidstone 1865 | o | 1 | — | — |
| Oldham 1865 | o | 1 | — | — |
| Rochester 1852 | o | 1 | o | 1 |
| Rochester 1856 | o | 1 | — | — |
| Rochester 1859 | o | 1 | o | 1 |
| Rochester 1868 | o | 1 | — | — |
| Shrewsbury 1868 | o | 1 | o | — |
| York 1852 | o | 1 | o | — |

### 3. The voting of sextons, 1852–72

| Election | Leading Liberal | Leading Tory | Second Liberal | Second Tory |
|---|---|---|---|---|
| Beverley 1854 | 1 | o | — | — |
| Bristol 1852 | o | 6 | — | — |
| Bury St Edmunds 1852 | 1 | 1 | o | — |
| Cambridge 1857 | o | 1 | o | 1 |
| Cambridge 1868 | o | 1 | o | 1 |
| Ipswich 1857 | o | 1 | o | 1 |
| Ipswich 1859 | o | 1 | o | 1 |
| Ipswich 1865 | o | 1 | o | 1 |
| Maidstone 1865 | o | 1 | — | — |
| Maidstone 1870 | o | 1 | — | — |
| Northampton 1852 | o | 2 | o | — |
| Sandwich 1868 | 1 | o | 1 | o |
| Shrewsbury 1868 | o | 1 | o | — |
| Southampton 1852 | o | 1 | o | 1 |

### 4. The voting of labourers, 1830–72

| Election | Leading Liberal | Leading Tory | Second Liberal | Second Tory |
|---|---|---|---|---|
| Abingdon 1830 | o | 1 | — | — |
| Ashton 1841 | 13 | 10 | — | — |
| Bedford 1841 | 56 | 46 | — | 46 |
| Bedford 1857 | 17 | 23 | — | — |
| Beverley 1840 | 25 | 37 | — | — |
| Beverley 1854 | 30 | 24 | — | — |
| Beverley 1859 | 53 | 36 | — | 25 |
| Bolton 1835 | 1 | 1 | o | — |
| Brighton 1841 | 29 | 16 | 19 | — |
| Bristol 1832 | 142 | 191 | 125 | — |
| Bristol 1837 | 108 | 140 | — | 112 |
| Bristol 1841 | 87 | 104 | — | 97 |

*The voting of labourers, 1830–72 (cont.)*

| Election | Leading Liberal | Leading Tory | Second Liberal | Second Tory |
|---|---|---|---|---|
| Bristol 1852 | 69 | 72 | — | — |
| Bury St Edmunds 1852 | 1 | 1 | — | 0 |
| Cambridge 1835 | 5 | 5 | 4 | — |
| Cambridge 1840 | 6 | 11 | — | — |
| Cambridge 1845 | 5 | 12 | — | — |
| Cambridge 1857 | 3 | 8 | 3 | 7 |
| Cambridge 1859 | 4 | 5 | 4 | 5 |
| Cambridge 1863 | 3 | 3 | — | — |
| Cambridge 1865 | 7 | 1 | 6 | 1 |
| Cambridge 1866 | 5 | 7 | — | — |
| Cambridge 1868 | 214 | 108 | — | — |
| Dover 1837 | 36 | 36 | — | 26 |
| Durham 1843 | 3 | 3 | — | — |
| Hereford 1832 | 14 | 21 | 13 | — |
| Hereford 1835 | 11 | 12 | 12 | — |
| Ipswich 1852 | 22 | 7 | 21 | 5 |
| Ipswich 1857 | 15 | 6 | 15 | 6 |
| Ipswich 1859 | 23 | 11 | 8 | 12 |
| Ipswich 1868 | 186 | 160 | — | — |
| Leicester 1847 | 17 | 30 | 17 | — |
| Leicester 1859 | 17 | 41 | 28 | — |
| Leicester 1861 | 11 | 62 | 4 | — |
| Lewes 1835 | 24 | 26 | 4 | — |
| Lewes 1837 | 14 | 17 | — | — |
| Lincoln 1835 | 9 | 38 | 6 | — |
| Lincoln 1841 | 11 | 42 | 10 | 40 |
| Lincoln 1848 | 25 | 33 | — | — |
| Liverpool 1835 | 89 | 60 | 76 | 54 |
| Loughborough 1830 | 6 | 4 | — | — |
| Maidstone 1841 | 15 | 55 | — | 50 |
| Maidstone 1857 | 33 | 58 | 33 | 57 |
| Maidstone 1865 | 65 | 82 | — | — |
| Northampton 1852 | 14 | 44 | 9 | — |
| Norwich 1830 | 10 | 23 | 7 | 21 |
| Nottingham 1852 | 9 | 29 | — | — |
| Reading 1841 | 3 | 1 | 3 | 1 |
| Rochdale 1857 | 3 | 2 | — | — |
| Rochester 1835 | 6 | 7 | 3 | — |
| Rochester 1852 | 18 | 17 | 18 | 17 |
| Rochester 1856 | 19 | 23 | — | — |
| Rochester 1859 | 16 | 18 | 16 | 18 |
| Rochester 1865 | 23 | 16 | 18 | — |
| Rochester 1868 | 180 | 116 | — | — |
| Sandwich 1852 | 2 | 21 | — | — |
| Sandwich 1859 | 14 | 19 | 11 | 17 |
| Sandwich 1868 | 119 | 102 | 128 | — |
| Shrewsbury 1837 | 19 | 16 | 17 | 15 |
| Shrewsbury 1868 | 131 | 147 | 85 | — |

*The voting of labourers, 1830–72 (cont.)*

| Election | Leading Liberal | Leading Tory | Second Liberal | Second Tory |
|---|---|---|---|---|
| Shropshire 1831 | 44 | 88 | 30 | 64 |
| Shropshire (North) 1832 | 45 | 54 | 29 | — |
| Tamworth 1837 | 28 | 46 | — | 27 |
| Tamworth 1841 | 27 | 47 | — | 23 |
| Warrington 1847 | 10 | 17 | — | — |
| York 1835 | 23 | 49 | 8 | — |
| York 1852 | 33 | 43 | 21 | — |

In 41 of the above cases the leading Tory received more votes than the leading Liberal; in 20 cases the leading Liberal received more votes.

### 5. The voting of shoemakers, 1830–72: sample cases from 'normal' elections

| Election | Leading Liberal | Leading Tory | Second Liberal | Second Tory |
|---|---|---|---|---|
| Ashton 1841 | 20 | 8 | — | — |
| Bedford 1841 | 28 | 36 | — | — |
| Bedford 1857 | 22 | 17 | — | — |
| Beverley 1840 | 33 | 56 | — | — |
| Beverley 1859 | 55 | 37 | 26 | — |
| Bristol 1832 | 99 | 125 | 129 | — |
| Bristol 1837 | 174 | 137 | — | 97 |
| Bristol 1841 | 210 | 136 | — | 105 |
| Bristol 1852 | 168 | 71 | — | — |
| Cambridge 1835 | 33 | 16 | 31 | — |
| Cambridge 1840 | 31 | 24 | — | — |
| Cambridge 1845 | 29 | 30 | — | — |
| Cambridge 1857 | 28 | 25 | 28 | 24 |
| Cambridge 1859 | 25 | 17 | 25 | 16 |
| Cambridge 1863 | 21 | 21 | — | — |
| Cambridge 1865 | 23 | 20 | 23 | 20 |
| Cambridge 1866 | 36 | 35 | — | — |
| Cambridge 1868 | 121 | 63 | — | — |
| Chatham 1857 | 25 | 18 | — | — |
| Chatham 1859 | 19 | 14 | — | — |
| Ipswich 1832 | 27 | 11 | 27 | 9 |
| Ipswich 1835 | 17 | 13 | 17 | 12 |
| Ipswich 1847 | 28 | 18 | 25 | 14 |
| Ipswich 1852 | 30 | 18 | 29 | 16 |
| Ipswich 1859 | 33 | 21 | 26 | 16 |
| Ipswich 1865 | 31 | 16 | — | — |
| Ipswich 1868 | 134 | 37 | — | — |
| Leeds 1834 | 27 | 8 | — | — |
| Leicester 1832 | 43 | 35 | 43 | — |
| Leicester 1847 | 62 | 44 | 62 | — |
| Leicester 1859 | 33 | 13 | 31 | — |
| Lewes 1837 | 27 | 18 | — | — |

*The voting of shoemakers, 1830–72 (cont.)*

| Election | Leading Liberal | Leading Tory | Second Liberal | Second Tory |
|---|---|---|---|---|
| Lewes 1841 | 29 | 18 | 26 | 26 |
| Maidstone 1857 | 37 | 30 | 34 | 29 |
| Maidstone 1859 | 42 | 21 | 41 | 21 |
| Maidstone 1865 | 41 | 30 | — | — |
| Northampton 1831 | 221 | 52 | 216 | — |
| Northamptonshire 1831 | 89 | 28 | 88 | 14 |
| Norwich 1830 | 125 | 88 | — | — |
| Oldham 1865 | 19 | 9 | — | — |
| Rochdale 1841 | 11 | 3 | — | — |
| Rochdale 1857 | 13 | 5 | — | — |
| Rochester 1835 | 25 | 29 | 23 | — |
| Rochester 1852 | 28 | 23 | 28 | 23 |
| Rochester 1856 | 29 | 17 | — | — |
| Rochester 1859 | 23 | 18 | 22 | 17 |
| Rochester 1865 | 19 | 11 | 17 | — |
| Rochester 1868 | 25 | 12 | — | — |
| Sandwich 1868 | 35 | 15 | 31 | — |
| Shrewsbury 1857 | 40 | 19 | — | — |
| Shrewsbury 1868 | 101 | 92 | 50 | — |
| Shropshire 1832 | 22 | 16 | — | 6 |
| Tamworth 1837 | 17 | 20 | — | 5 |
| Wakefield 1837 | 12 | 7 | — | — |
| Warrington 1847 | 9 | 4 | — | — |
| York 1835 | 127 | 124 | 104 | — |
| York 1852 | 94 | 96 | 80 | — |

## 6. The voting of butchers and grocers, 1830–72

N.B. Only those cases where there was a significant divergence of pattern are shown below.

| Election | Leading Liberal | Leading Tory | Second Liberal | Second Tory |
|---|---|---|---|---|
| Ashton 1841 | | | | |
| Butchers | 6 | 8 | — | — |
| Other retailers | 80 | 48 | — | — |
| Bedford 1841 | | | | |
| Butchers | 10 | 16 | — | — |
| Grocers | 11 | 10 | — | — |
| Bedford 1857 | | | | |
| Butchers | 11 | 10 | — | — |
| Grocers | 16 | 6 | — | — |
| Cambridge 1835 | | | | |
| Butchers | 6 | 17 | 3 | — |
| Grocers | 21 | 12 | 21 | — |

*The voting of butchers and grocers, 1830–72 (cont.)*

| Election | Leading Liberal | Leading Tory | Second Liberal | Second Tory |
|---|---|---|---|---|
| Cambridge 1840 | | | | |
| Butchers | 2 | 18 | — | — |
| Grocers | 19 | 15 | — | — |
| Cambridge 1845 | | | | |
| Butchers | 3 | 23 | — | — |
| Grocers | 26 | 17 | — | — |
| Cambridge 1857 | | | | |
| Butchers | 4 | 19 | 3 | 16 |
| Grocers | 25 | 17 | 23 | 16 |
| Cambridge 1859 | | | | |
| Butchers | 7 | 15 | 7 | 13 |
| Grocers | 21 | 20 | 21 | 20 |
| Cambridge 1863 | | | | |
| Butchers | 4 | 13 | — | — |
| Grocers | 21 | 12 | — | — |
| Cambridge 1865 | | | | |
| Butchers | 8 | 13 | 7 | 11 |
| Grocers | 34 | 13 | 31 | 13 |
| Cambridge 1866 | | | | |
| Butchers | 9 | 21 | — | — |
| Grocers | 43 | 21 | — | — |
| Cambridge 1868 | | | | |
| Butchers | 12 | 32 | — | — |
| Grocers | 53 | 22 | — | — |
| Chatham 1857 | | | | |
| Butchers | 13 | 20 | — | — |
| Grocers | 29 | 18 | — | — |
| Chatham 1859 | | | | |
| Butchers | 14 | 19 | — | — |
| Grocers | 28 | 20 | — | — |
| Dover 1833 | | | | |
| Butchers | 5 | 24 | — | — |
| Grocers | 15 | 17 | — | — |
| Dover 1837 | | | | |
| Butchers | 10 | 19 | — | 14 |
| Grocers | 24 | 15 | — | 11 |
| Halifax* 1847 | | | | |
| Butchers | 1 | 7 | 1 | 6 |
| All retailers | 82 | 63 | 79 | 55 |
| Leicester 1847 | | | | |
| Butchers | 23 | 36 | 23 | — |
| Grocers | 66 | 31 | 63 | — |

\* In the case of Halifax, the Whig candidate is counted as a Tory, and the two
Radical candidates counted as the Liberals.

*The voting of butchers and grocers, 1830–72 (cont.)*

| Election | Leading Liberal | Leading Tory | Second Liberal | Second Tory |
|---|---|---|---|---|
| **Liverpool 1832** | | | | |
| Butchers | 58 | 47 | 48 | 29 |
| Grocers | 53 | 19 | 42 | 10 |
| **Maidstone 1857** | | | | |
| Butchers | 13 | 22 | 11 | 20 |
| Grocers | 37 | 13 | 39 | 10 |
| **Northampton 1852** | | | | |
| Butchers | 21 | 29 | 18 | — |
| Grocers | 11 | 11 | 12 | — |
| **Northamptonshire 1831** | | | | |
| Butchers | 75 | 59 | 58 | 34 |
| Grocers | 60 | 24 | 52 | 15 |
| **Rochdale 1841** | | | | |
| Butchers | 14 | 11 | — | — |
| Grocers | 58 | 22 | — | — |
| **Rochdale 1857** | | | | |
| Butchers | 16 | 25 | — | — |
| Grocers | 71 | 37 | — | — |
| **Rochester 1852** | | | | |
| Butchers | 11 | 17 | 11 | 17 |
| Grocers | 22 | 12 | 22 | 12 |
| **Rochester 1856** | | | | |
| Butchers | 14 | 13 | — | — |
| Grocers | 19 | 9 | — | — |
| **Sandwich 1852** | | | | |
| Butchers | 2 | 15 | — | — |
| Grocers | 13 | 9 | — | — |
| **Sandwich 1859** | | | | |
| Butchers | 10 | 14 | 11 | 9 |
| Grocers | 21 | 8 | 21 | 8 |
| **Sandwich 1868** | | | | |
| Butchers | 10 | 21 | 11 | — |
| Grocers | 22 | 12 | 22 | — |
| **Shrewsbury 1857** | | | | |
| Butchers | 10 | 21 | — | — |
| Grocers | 36 | 10 | — | — |
| **Warrington 1847** | | | | |
| Butchers | 4 | 11 | — | — |
| Other retailers | 83 | 50 | — | — |

N.B. In some minor cases (Beverley 1859, Lewes 1841, Lincoln 1848), butchers were more Liberal than grocers. In some more important cases (Bristol 1841), they voted almost exactly alike. These exceptions however are sufficiently rare to make the selective table above quite a fair indication of the general picture.

*The voting of butchers and grocers, 1830–72 (cont.)*

It is curious to note a remarkable difference in suicide rates between the two occupations at this time:

Suicides among males of 25–65 years,
per million

| | |
|---|---|
| General average | 222 |
| Grocers | 218 |
| Butchers | 407 |

(Mulhall, *Dictionary of Statistics*, 4th ed., 1899, p. 552.)

## 7. The voting of gentlemen, 1830–72: some characteristic cases

| Election | Leading Liberal | Leading Tory | Second Liberal | Second Tory |
|---|---|---|---|---|
| Bedford 1857 | 24 | 22 | — | — |
| Bolton 1835 | 23 | 26 | 15 | — |
| Brighton 1841 | 42 | 23 | 33 | — |
| Bristol 1837 | 131 | 283 | 277 | — |
| Bristol 1852 | 127 | 225 | — | — |
| Cambridge 1835 | 50 | 41 | 50 | — |
| Cambridge 1845 | 47 | 33 | — | — |
| Cambridge 1857 | 42 | 51 | 38 | 48 |
| Cambridge 1866 | 37 | 61 | — | — |
| Cambridge 1868 | 61 | 78 | — | — |
| Chatham 1857 | 45 | 45 | — | — |
| Chatham 1859 | 45 | 33 | — | — |
| Dover 1833 | 46 | 46 | — | — |
| Ipswich 1832 | 45 | 29 | 43 | 25 |
| Ipswich 1852 | 46 | 67 | 41 | 64 |
| Ipswich 1865 | 86 | 81 | — | — |
| Ipswich 1868 | 118 | 100 | — | — |
| Lancaster 1865 | 17 | 25 | — | — |
| Leicester 1832 | 43 | 71 | 28 | — |
| Lewes 1841 | 21 | 24 | 21 | 24 |
| Liverpool 1832 | 128 | 84 | 107 | 61 |
| Maidstone 1832 | 35 | 29 | — | — |
| Maidstone 1859 | 32 | 46 | 31 | 49 |
| Maidstone 1865 | 38 | 45 | — | — |
| Maidstone 1870 | 41 | 50 | — | — |
| Northamptonshire 1831 | 223 | 169 | 205 | 117 |
| Norwich 1830 | 112 | 124 | 115 | 122 |
| Oldham 1865 | 7 | 34 | — | — |
| Rochdale 1841 | 6 | 22 | — | — |
| Rochester 1852 | 42 | 43 | 42 | 43 |
| Rochester 1856 | 47 | 32 | — | — |
| Rochester 1868 | 59 | 21 | — | — |
| Sandwich 1868 | 72 | 53 | 68 | — |
| Shrewsbury 1857 | 31 | 37 | — | — |
| Shrewsbury 1868 | 71 | 77 | 10 | — |
| Wakefield 1837 | 22 | 14 | — | — |
| Warrington 1847 | 13 | 14 | — | — |

## 8. The voting of publicans and beersellers, 1852-72

| Election | Leading Liberal | Leading Tory | Second Liberal | Second Tory |
|---|---|---|---|---|
| Bedford 1857 | | | | |
| Publicans | 22 | 21 | — | — |
| Bristol 1852 | | | | |
| Publicans | 118 | 71 | — | — |
| Beersellers | 108 | 32 | — | — |
| Cambridge 1857 | | | | |
| Publicans | 25 | 33 | 27 | 32 |
| Cambridge 1865 | | | | |
| Publicans | 40 | 41 | 39 | 39 |
| Cambridge 1866 | | | | |
| Publicans | 30 | 38 | — | — |
| Cambridge 1868 | | | | |
| Publicans | 41 | 40 | — | — |
| Chatham 1857 | | | | |
| Publicans | 38 | 58 | — | — |
| Chatham 1859 | | | | |
| Publicans | 41 | 56 | — | — |
| Ipswich 1852 | | | | |
| Publicans | 25 | 37 | 24 | 32 |
| Ipswich 1859 | | | | |
| Publicans | 39 | 78 | 13 | 76 |
| Ipswich 1865 | | | | |
| Publicans | 36 | 71 | — | — |
| Ipswich 1868 | | | | |
| Publicans | 15 | 71 | — | — |
| Beersellers | 10 | 19 | — | — |
| Leicester 1861 | | | | |
| Publicans | 29 | 28 | 2 | — |
| Maidstone 1857 | | | | |
| Publicans | 16 | 26 | 14 | 24 |
| Beersellers | 6 | 14 | 5 | 12 |
| Maidstone 1859 | | | | |
| Publicans | 17 | 25 | 16 | 26 |
| Beersellers | 7 | 17 | 7 | 17 |
| Maidstone 1865 | | | | |
| Publicans | 22 | 33 | — | — |
| Beersellers | 14 | 21 | — | — |
| Maidstone 1870 | | | | |
| Publicans | 19 | 25 | — | — |
| Beersellers | 5 | 19 | — | — |
| Oldham 1865 | | | | |
| Publicans | 41 | 80 | — | — |
| Beersellers | 30 | 74 | — | — |
| Rochdale 1857 | | | | |
| Publicans | 10 | 46 | — | — |
| Beersellers | 16 | 63 | — | — |

*The voting of publicans and beersellers, 1852–72 (cont.)*

| Election | Leading Liberal | Leading Tory | Second Liberal | Second Tory |
|---|---|---|---|---|
| Rochester 1852 | | | | |
| Publicans | 25 | 17 | 25 | 17 |
| Rochester 1868 | | | | |
| Beersellers | 11 | 8 | — | — |
| Publicans | 33 | 17 | — | — |
| Sandwich 1868 | | | | |
| Publicans | 46 | 48 | 45 | — |
| Shrewsbury 1857 | | | | |
| Publicans | 53 | 32 | — | — |
| Shrewsbury 1868 | | | | |
| Publicans | 57 | 65 | 9 | — |
| Beersellers | 17 | 19 | 7 | — |

### 9. The voting of pilots, 1830–72

| Election | Leading Liberal | Leading Tory | Second Liberal | Second Tory |
|---|---|---|---|---|
| Bristol 1837 | 1 | 3 | — | 0 |
| Bristol 1841 | 1 | 3 | — | 3 |
| Dover 1832 | 11 | 33 | 3 | 12 |
| Dover 1833 | 9 | 29 | — | — |
| Dover 1835 | 8 | 15 | — | 39 |
| Dover 1837 | 8 | 36 | — | 28 |
| Ipswich 1847 | 1 | 3 | 0 | 4 |
| Ipswich 1852 | 0 | 3 | 0 | 3 |
| Ipswich 1857 | 0 | 4 | 0 | 4 |
| Ipswich 1859 | 0 | 4 | 0 | 4 |
| Liverpool 1830 | 9 | 39 | — | — |
| Liverpool 1832 | 11 | 34 | 6 | 23 |
| Liverpool 1835 | 6 | 33 | 1 | 28 |
| Liverpool 1841 | 2 | 65 | 1 | 65 |
| Rochester 1835 | 2 | 1 | 2 | — |
| Rochester 1852 | 1 | 1 | 0 | 1 |
| Rochester 1856 | 0 | 1 | — | — |
| Rochester 1859 | 1 | 1 | 1 | 1 |
| Sandwich 1852 | 1 | 45 | — | — |
| Sandwich 1859 | 26 | 11 | 24 | 7 |
| Sandwich 1868 | 34 | 20 | 33 | — |
| Yarmouth 1832 | 6 | 11 | 6 | — |
| Yarmouth 1838 | 4 | 5 | — | — |
| Yarmouth 1841 | 2 | 8 | 2 | 8 |
| Yarmouth 1847 | 1 | 7 | 1 | 7 |

## 10. The voting of Dissenting ministers, 1830–47

| Election | Leading Liberal | Leading Tory | Second Liberal | Second Tory |
|---|---|---|---|---|
| Abingdon 1830 | 2 | 0 | — | — |
| Beverley 1840 | 2 | 0 | — | — |
| Beverley 1847 | 1 | 0 | 2 | — |
| Bolton 1832 | 3 | 0 | 3 | — |
| Bolton 1835 | 0 | 0 | 4 | 0 |
| Bolton 1837 | 4 | 1 | 4 | — |
| Brighton 1837 | 6 | 1 | 6 | — |
| Brighton 1841 | 3 | 2 | 3 | — |
| Bristol 1837 | 9 | 0 | — | 0 |
| Bristol 1841 | 14 | 0 | — | 0 |
| Cambridge 1835 | 2 | 0 | 2 | 0 |
| Cambridge 1840 | 1 | 0 | — | — |
| Cambridge 1845 | 5 | 0 | — | — |
| Dover 1832 | 1 | 0 | 1 | 0 |
| Dover 1833 | 1 | 0 | — | — |
| Dover 1835 | 1 | 1 | — | 0 |
| Dover 1837 | 1 | 0 | 0 | — |
| Durham 1832 | 1 | 0 | 1 | — |
| Hereford 1832 | 1 | 0 | 1 | — |
| Hereford 1835 | 2 | 0 | 2 | — |
| Ipswich 1832 | 3 | 0 | 2 | 0 |
| Ipswich 1835 | 3 | 0 | 3 | 0 |
| Ipswich 1847 | 8 | 0 | 8 | 0 |
| Leeds 1834 | 2 | 0 | — | — |
| Leicester 1832 | 5 | 0 | 5 | 0 |
| Leicester 1847 | 6 | 1 | 6 | — |
| Leicestershire 1830 | 13 | 4 | — | 2 |
| Lewes 1835 | 4 | 0 | 4 | 0 |
| Lewes 1837 | 4 | 1 | — | — |
| Lewes 1841 | 2 | 1 | 2 | 1 |
| Lindsey 1835 | 5 | 1 | 9 | — |
| Lindsey 1852 | 3 | 0 | — | 0 |
| Liverpool 1835 | 13 | 2 | 13 | 1 |
| Liverpool 1841 | 13 | 0 | 13 | 0 |
| Maidstone 1832 | 3 | 0 | — | — |
| Maidstone 1841 | 3 | 0 | — | 0 |
| Manchester 1839 | 8 | 0 | — | — |
| Northampton 1831 | 6 | 0 | 6 | 0 |
| Northamptonshire 1831 | 20 | 0 | 19 | 0 |
| Norwich 1830 | 2 | 0 | 1 | 0 |
| Preston 1841 | 4 | 0 | 3 | 0 |
| Reading 1837 | 4 | 0 | 4 | 0 |
| Reading 1841 | 2 | 1 | 2 | 1 |
| Shrewsbury 1837 | 3 | 0 | 3 | 0 |

*The voting of Dissenting ministers, 1830–47 (cont.)*

| Election | Leading Liberal | Leading Tory | Second Liberal | Second Tory |
|---|---|---|---|---|
| Shrewsbury 1847 | 1 | 0 | 0 | — |
| Shrewsbury 1868 | 8 | 0 | 6 | — |
| Tamworth 1841 | 1 | 0 | 0 | 0 |
| Tewkesbury 1831 | 1 | 0 | 2 | 0 |
| Tewkesbury 1841 | 3 | 0 | 3 | — |
| Wakefield 1837 | 1 | 0 | — | — |
| York 1835 | 3 | 0 | 3 | 0 |

## 11. The voting of Dissenting ministers, 1848–72

| Election | Leading Liberal | Leading Tory | Second Liberal | Second Tory |
|---|---|---|---|---|
| Beverley 1854 | 1 | 0 | — | — |
| Bristol 1852 | 14 | 1 | — | — |
| Bury St Edmunds 1852 | 3 | 3 | — | 0 |
| Cambridge 1857 | 2 | 0 | 2 | 0 |
| Cambridge 1859 | 2 | 0 | 2 | 0 |
| Cambridge 1865 | 3 | 0 | 2 | 0 |
| Cambridge 1868 | 6 | 0 | 6 | 0 |
| Chatham 1857 | 3 | 0 | — | — |
| Chatham 1859 | 1 | 0 | — | — |
| Ipswich 1852 | 6 | 0 | 6 | 0 |
| Ipswich 1857 | 7 | 0 | 7 | 0 |
| Ipswich 1859 | 7 | 0 | 4 | 0 |
| Ipswich 1865 | 9 | 0 | — | — |
| Ipswich 1868 | 9 | 0 | — | — |
| Leicester 1859 | 10 | 1 | 4 | 0 |
| Leicester 1861 | 14 | 2 | 1 | — |
| Maidstone 1853 | 6 | — | 0 | — |
| Maidstone 1857 | 2 | 0 | 2 | 0 |
| Maidstone 1859 | 3 | 0 | 3 | 0 |
| Maidstone 1865 | 7 | 0 | — | — |
| Maidstone 1870 | 7 | 0 | — | — |
| Nottingham 1852 | 5 | 2 | 0 | — |
| Oldham 1865 | 3 | 0 | — | — |
| Rochester 1852 | 1 | 0 | 1 | 0 |
| Rochester 1859 | 2 | 0 | 2 | 0 |
| Rochester 1865 | 1 | 0 | 1 | 0 |
| Rochester 1868 | 1 | 0 | — | — |
| Sandwich 1852 | 4 | 0 | — | — |
| Sandwich 1859 | 5 | 1 | 6 | 1 |
| Sandwich 1868 | 4 | 0 | 4 | — |
| York 1852 | 3 | 0 | 0 | — |

## 12. The voting of Dissenting ministers: specific denominations

| Election | Leading Liberal | Leading Tory | Second Liberal | Second Tory |
|---|---|---|---|---|
| Independent* ministers | | | | |
| Beverley 1854 | 1 | 0 | — | — |
| Manchester 1839 | 3 | 0 | — | — |
| Tewkesbury 1841 | 1 | 0 | 1 | 0 |
| Methodists | | | | |
| Cambridge 1868 | 2† | 0 | 2† | 0 |
| Liverpool 1832 | 0 | 1† | — | — |
| Bristol 1837 | 1 | 0 | — | 0 |
| Bristol 1841 | 1† | 0 | — | 0 |
| Bristol 1841 | 1 | 0 | — | 0 |
| Leeds 1834 | 1 | 0 | — | — |
| Leicester 1859 | 1 | 0 | 0 | 0 |
| Maidstone 1832 | 1† | 0 | — | — |
| Baptist preachers, ministers | | | | |
| Bristol 1841 | 1 | 0 | — | 0 |
| Leicester 1859 | 1 | 1 | 0 | 0 |
| Manchester 1839 | 2 | 0 | — | — |
| Tewkesbury 1841 | 2 | 0 | 2 | — |
| Cambridge 1868 | 2 | 0 | 2 | 0 |
| Unitarian ministers | | | | |
| Manchester 1839 | 3 | 0 | — | — |
| Presbyterian ministers | | | | |
| Rochester 1868 | 1 | 0 | — | — |

\* I.e. Congregationalist, presumably.      † Wesleyan.

## 13. 'The Political Sentiments of Wesleyans', 1841(?)* (extract)

'We continue to cherish the hope of being able to ascertain the political sentiments of our Wesleyan brethren as evinced by their votes at elections for the boroughs and counties in which they possess the elective franchise. From time to time the kindness of correspondents has enabled us to state in what way Wesleyan voters have in particular places disposed of their suffrages. We have been at the pains of collecting these accounts and of registering the results which they disclose in a tabular form. These returns comprise 29 cities and boroughs, and 7 county districts, of which 4 belong to the West Riding of Yorkshire. They exhibit, as nearly as can be ascertained, the number of Wesleyan electors in each place, and the manner in which they voted at the last Election.

| Place | Total no. of Wesleyan Voters | Voted Liberal | Voted Tory | Split Votes | Abstained |
|---|---|---|---|---|---|
| Durham | 23 | 21 | 2 | 0 | 0 |
| Kendal | 15 | 14 | 0 | 0 | 1 |
| Salisbury | 53 | 47 | 1 | 0 | 5 |

\* This excerpt from the *Wesleyan Chronicle* is to be found in *The League*, vol. 1, no. 44 (27 July 1844), p. 720. The reference was given me by Dr Brian Harrison, Fellow of Nuffield College, Oxford.

*'The Political Sentiments of Wesleyans'* (*cont.*)

| Place | Total no. of Wesleyan Voters | Voted Liberal | Voted Tory | Split Votes | Abstained |
|---|---|---|---|---|---|
| Leicester | 66 | 60 | 6 | 0 | 0 |
| Exeter | 90 | 85 | 3 | 2 | 0 |
| Rochester | 74 | 44 | 18 | 7 | 5 |
| Plymouth | 73 | 60 | 10 | 3 | 0 |
| Lancaster | 33 | 27 | 2 | 2 | 2 |
| Rochdale | 130 | 105 | 15 | 0 | 10 |
| Aylesbury | 30 | 11 | 17 | 0 | 2 |
| Newport, I.o.W. | 52 | 36 | 15 | 0 | 1 |
| Bury St Edmunds | 25 | 17 | 6 | 0 | 2 |
| Canterbury | 45 | 27 | 10 | 4 | 4 |
| Norwich | 80 | 63 | 12 | 0 | 3 |
| Oxford | 82 | 58 | 14 | 4 | 6 |
| Stroud | 46 | 32 | 1 | 0 | 13 |
| Taunton | 34 | 22 | 8 | 0 | 4 |
| Halifax | 81 | 49 | 21 | 5 | 6 |
| Thetford | 16 | 9 | 0 | 7 | 0 |
| Frome | 33 | 20 | 10 | 0 | 3 |
| Worcester | 61 | 52 | 6 | 3 | 0 |
| Northampton | 113 | 87 | 19 | 4 | 3 |
| Maidstone | 41 | 25 | 16 | 0 | 0 |
| Derby | 63 | 51 | 9 | 0 | 3 |
| Kidderminster | 24 | 17 | 2 | 0 | 5 |
| Leeds (Bramley township) | 117 | 86 | 20 | 0 | 11 |
| Yarmouth | 111 | 84 | 10 | 1 | 16 |
| Ludlow | 22 | 14 | 7 | 0 | 1 |
| Banbury | 31 | 21 | 7 | 0 | 3 |
| Mildenhall | 25 | 24 | 0 | 1 | 0 |
| Wednesbury | 48 | 34 | 12 | 1 | 1 |
| Settle | 12 | 11 | 0 | 0 | 1 |
| Dent, Yorks. | 29 | 10 | 14 | 0 | 5 |
| Addingham, Yorks. | 27 | 20 | 4 | 0 | 3 |
| Oulton, Yorks. | 16 | 7 | 7 | 2 | 0 |
| Bury, Lancs. | 24 | 20 | 4 | 0 | 0 |
| Total | 1843 | 1370 | 308 | 46 | 119 |

...We ourselves, however, shall not rest satisfied until we are able to present our readers with a table showing how the Wesleyans have voted in each borough and county of the United Kingdom. Our friends are therefore earnestly entreated to supply us as quickly as possible with the needful information.'

(*Wesleyan Chronicle*)

# B. CONSTITUENCIES ANALYSED BY OCCUPATIONS

## The Abingdon election of 30 July 1830

The pollbook is in the Bodleian Library.

Result: Maberly, Whig    159
Maitland, Tory    94

| All voters | Maberly | Maitland | All voters | Maberly | Maitland |
|---|---|---|---|---|---|
| Clergymen | 1 | 1 | Cordwainers | 8 | 3 |
| Surgeons | 4 | 1 | Ironfounders | 0 | 2 |
| Gentlemen | 11 | 8 | Sheriff's officer | 0 | 1 |
| Bakers | 10 | 8 | Parish clerk | 0 | 1 |
| Dissenting ministers | 2 | 0 | Labourer | 0 | 1 |
| Lawyer | 1 | 0 | Miller | 0 | 2 |
| Victuallers | 20 | 15 | Tailors | 6 | 1 |
| Butchers | 9 | 1 | Farmer | 1 | 0 |
| Grocers | 6 | 3 | Banker | 1 | 0 |
| Carpenters | 3 | 1 | Others | 76 | 45 |

## The Ashton-under-Lyne election of 1841

The pollbook is in Ashton-under-Lyne Public Library.

Result: Hindley, Charles   Liberal    303
Harrop, Jonah   Conservative   254

| All voters | Harrop | Hindley | All voters | Harrop | Hindley |
|---|---|---|---|---|---|
| I. Gentlemen | 7 | 5 | V. Cottonmasters | 4 | 9 |
| Legal | 5 | 1 | Overlookers | 3 | 7 |
| Medical | 4 | 4 | Textile | 34 | 33 |
| Official | 7 | 1 | workers | | |
| Other professionals | 13 | 14 | VI. Small business | 6 | 18 |
| | | | Ironfounders | 2 | 3 |
| II. Publicans | 22 | 11 | Clerks | 8 | 4 |
| Beersellers | 20 | 13 | | | |
| Brewer | 1 | 0 | VII. Metal, | 12 | 9 |
| III. Butchers | 8 | 6 | engineering | | |
| Other shopkeepers | 48 | 80 | Tailors | 4 | 6 |
| | | | Shoemakers | 8 | 20 |
| | | | Building crafts | 10 | 16 |
| IV. Labourers, etc. | 10 | 13 | Other artisans | 5 | 9 |

| Summary | | Conservative | Liberal |
|---|---|---|---|
| I. | Gentlemen, Professions | 36 | 25 |
| II. | Drink | 43 | 24 |
| III. | Retailers | 56 | 86 |
| IV. | Labourers | 10 | 13 |
| V. | Cotton | 41 | 49 |
| VI. | Small business | 16 | 25 |
| VII. | Artisans | 39 | 60 |

## The Aylesbury election of May 1831

The pollbook, which is in the Institute of Historical Research, gives the occupations of the electors of Aylesbury town only, and not of the electors from the surrounding hundreds who made up the bulk of the constituency.

|  |  |  |
|---|---|---|
| Result: Wm. Rickford | 983 |
| Lord Nugent | 604 |
| Lord Kirkwall | 508 |

Rickford and Nugent were the Reform candidates. Kirkwall was the nominee of Lords Chandos and Buckingham, who also ordered their faggot voters to support Rickford in the hope of excluding Nugent.

| Selected categories | Nugent | Rickford | Kirkwall |
|---|---|---|---|
| Gentlemen | 7 | 9 | 3 |
| Clergymen | 2 | 2 | 0 |
| Minister | 1 | 1 | 0 |
| Surgeons | 3 | 2 | 0 |
| Attorney | 0 | 1 | 1 |
| Victuallers | 7 | 14 | 7 |
| Grocers | 5 | 7 | 1 |
| Butchers | 6 | 12 | 6 |
| Tailors | 12 | 15 | 4 |
| Cordwainers | 20 | 27 | 12 |
| Labourers | 23 | 46 | 25 |

## The Banbury election of 1847

The pollbook is in the Bodleian Library.

|  |  |  |
|---|---|---|
| Result: H. W. Tancred, Liberal | 226 |
| J. Macgregor, Conservative | 164 |

| Selected categories | Tancred | Macgregor |
|---|---|---|
| Grocers | 7 | 6 |
| Butchers | 7 | 6 |
| Tailors | 10 | 5 |
| Shoemakers | 12 | 1 |
| Lawyers | 6 | 4 |
| Gentlemen | 14 | 6 |
| Farmers | 4 | 13 |
| Surgeons | 2 | 3 |
| Dissenting ministers | 2 | 1 |
| Banker | 1 | 0 |
| Saddlers | 3 | 2 |
| Sexton | 1 | 0 |
| Police officer | 0 | 1 |

## The Bath election of 1847

The pollbook is in the Bodleian Library.

Result: Lord Ashley, Conservative 1,278
Lord Duncan, Liberal 1,228
J. A. Roebuck, Radical 1,093

### Voters A–Z

| Selected categories | Roebuck | Duncan | Ashley |
|---|---|---|---|
| R.C. priest | 1 | 1 | 0 |
| Sweeps | 1 | 1 | 7 |
| Unitarian ministers | 1 | 2 | 0 |
| Clergymen | 2 | 3 | 44 |
| Surgeons | 10 | 20 | 48 |
| Beersellers | 26 | 24 | 5 |
| Labourers | 18 | 21 | 14 |
| Army | 4 | 5 | 20 |
| Navy | 5 | 7 | 11 |
| Bankers | 0 | 4 | 4 |
| Saddlers | 2 | 2 | 8 |
| Postboys | 0 | 1 | 3 |

### Voters A–J inclusive only*

| Selected categories | Roebuck | Duncan | Ashley |
|---|---|---|---|
| Grocers | 25 | 24 | 14 |
| Butchers | 18 | 21 | 14 |
| Policemen | 2 | 3 | 4 |
| Gentlemen | 49 | 65 | 91 |
| Victuallers | 24 | 27 | 15 |
| Tailors | 27 | 28 | 16 |
| Wesleyan preacher | 1 | 1 | 0 |
| Shoemakers | 24 | 28 | 18 |

\* I.e. half the electorate.

## The Bedford election of 1841

The pollbook is in Bedford Public Library.

Result: F. Polhill, Conservative 433
Capt. Henry Stuart, Conservative 421
W. H. Whitbread, Liberal 410

Votes analysed were *only* (*a*) the 349 plumpers for Whitbread, and (*b*) the 393 who split between Polhill and Stuart.

| | | Liberal | Con-servative | | | Liberal | Con-servative |
|---|---|---|---|---|---|---|---|
| I. | Gentlemen | 8 | 16 | | Officials | 3 | 2 |
| | Farmers | 6 | 7 | | Teachers and clergy | 3 | 10 |
| II. | Legal | 2 | 3 | | | | |
| | Medical | 8 | 7 | | Other professions | 5 | 4 |
| | Military | 1 | 5 | | | | |
| | Clerks | 5 | 11 | III. | Miscellaneous | 9 | 8 |

*The Bedford election of 1841 (cont.)*

| | Liberal | Con-servative | | | Liberal | Con-servative |
|---|---|---|---|---|---|---|
| IV. Publicans | 13 | 15 | | Bakers | 16 | 10 |
| | | | | Butchers | 10 | 16 |
| V. Millers and maltsters | 2 | 4 | | Others | 17 | 16 |
| Merchants | 4 | 5 | VII. | Servants | 14 | 18 |
| Banker | 1 | 1 | | Labourers | 56 | 46 |
| Builder | 0 | 1 | VIII. | Building | 38 | 44 |
| Brewers | 4 | 9 | | Metal | 18 | 23 |
| | | | | Shoemakers | 28 | 36 |
| VI. Grocers | 11 | 10 | | Tailors | 23 | 17 |
| Drapers | 14 | 12 | | Others | 26 | 36 |

Summary:

| | | Liberal | Conservative |
|---|---|---|---|
| I. | Gentlemen | 14 | 23 |
| II. | Professions | 27 | 42 |
| III. | Miscellaneous | 9 | 8 |
| IV. | Publicans | 13 | 15 |
| V. | Business | 11 | 20 |
| VI. | Retail | 68 | 64 |
| VII. | Labour | 70 | 64 |
| VIII. | Crafts | 133 | 156 |

## The Bedford election of 1857

The pollbook is in Bedford Public Library.

| Result: Samuel Whitbread, Liberal | 452 |
|---|---|
| Thos. Barnard, Liberal | 435 |
| Wm. Stuart, Conservative | 376 |
| E. T. Smith, Conservative | 176 |

Votes analysed were (a) the 399 votes split between Whitbread and Barnard and (b) plumpers for Stuart (136), for Smith (5), and splitters for Stuart and Smith (164)—in all 305 Tory voters analysed.

| | | Liberal | Con-servative | | | Liberal | Con-servative |
|---|---|---|---|---|---|---|---|
| I. | Gentlemen | 24 | 22 | V. | Brewers | 5 | 9 |
| | Farmers | 7 | 6 | | Builders | 5 | 6 |
| II. | Legal | 3 | 5 | | Banker | 1 | 0 |
| | Medical | 3 | 6 | | Millers and maltsters | 8 | 3 |
| | Military | 4 | 6 | | Small mfr. | 1 | 1 |
| | Clerks | 6 | 15 | | Coal merchants | 5 | 3 |
| | Teachers and clergy | 10 | 5 | | Merchants | 5 | 6 |
| | Miscellaneous | 10 | 5 | VI. | Railway employees | 5 | 0 |
| | Officials | 6 | 1 | | Labourers | 17 | 23 |
| | Musicians | 0 | 2 | | Servants | 15 | 3 |
| III. | Miscellaneous | 13 | 10 | | | | |
| IV. | Publicans | 22 | 21 | | | | |

*The Bedford election of 1857 (cont.)*

|       |          | Liberal | Con-servative |        |           | Liberal | Con-servative |
|-------|----------|---------|---------------|--------|-----------|---------|---------------|
| VII.  | Grocers  | 16      | 6             | VIII.  | Building  | 31      | 28            |
|       | Drapers  | 22      | 2             |        | Metal     | 21      | 19            |
|       | Butchers | 11      | 10            |        | Shoemakers| 22      | 17            |
|       | Bakers   | 16      | 8             |        | Tailors   | 26      | 9             |
|       | Others   | 22      | 16            |        | Others    | 35      | 27            |

| Summary |               | Liberal | Conservative |
|---------|---------------|---------|--------------|
| I.      | Gentlemen     | 31      | 28           |
| II.     | Professions   | 42      | 45           |
| III.    | Miscellaneous | 13      | 10           |
| IV.     | Publicans     | 22      | 21           |
| V.      | Business      | 30      | 28           |
| VI.     | Labour        | 37      | 26           |
| VII.    | Retail        | 87      | 42           |
| VIII.   | Craftsmen     | 135     | 100          |

## The Beverley election of 31 July 1830

The pollbook is in the Guildhall Library.*

Result: Henry Burton, Whig     1,065
        Daniel Sykes, Whig       739
        Capel Cure, Tory         657

Capel Cure was an Essex country gentleman, and Daniel Sykes, formerly an iron merchant in Hull, had become its Recorder.

| Selected categories | Burton | Sykes | Cure |
|---------------------|--------|-------|------|
| Innkeepers          | 23     | 14    | 17   |
| Cordwainers         | 113    | 52    | 78   |
| Mariners            | 27     | 12    | 20   |
| Gentlemen           | 40     | 36    | 20   |
| Butchers            | 45     | 50    | 23   |
| Grocers             | 27     | 25    | 6    |
| Shipwrights         | 15     | 9     | 7    |
| Farmers             | 24     | 30    | 6    |
| Labourers           | 39     | 19    | 21   |
| Surgeons            | 6      | 4     | 5    |
| Parish clerk        | 1      | 2     | 1    |
| Shipowner           | 0      | 1     | 0    |
| Banker              | 0      | 1     | 0    |
| Weavers             | 15     | 5     | 7    |
| Merchants           | 3      | 5     | 3    |
| Watermen            | 3      | 1     | 3    |
| Gaolers             | 2      | 1     | 1    |
| Sexton              | 0      | 0     | 1    |
| Clergymen           | 1      | 0     | 1    |

* This refers throughout to the Guildhall Library in the City of London.

### The Beverley election of 1840

The pollbook is in the Guildhall Library.

Result: Sackville Lane Fox, Conservative    556
Thomas Murray, Liberal    410

| Selected categories | Murray | Fox |
| --- | --- | --- |
| Solicitors | 4 | 5 |
| Surgeons | 4 | 4 |
| Farmers | 11 | 48 |
| Butchers | 19 | 20 |
| Grocers | 6 | 9 |
| Mariners | 8 | 7 |
| Shoemakers | 33 | 56 |
| Labourers | 25 | 37 |
| Watermen | 1 | 4 |
| Dissenting ministers | 2 | 0 |
| Relieving officer | 0 | 1 |

### The Beverley election of 1847

The pollbook is in Manchester Public Library.

Result: S. L. Fox, Peelite    543
J. Towneley, Liberal    542
Sir I. Goldsmid, Liberal    257

| Selected categories | Towneley | Goldsmid | Fox |
| --- | --- | --- | --- |
| Gentlemen | 15 | 11 | 40 |
| Solicitors | 2 | 1 | 5 |
| Surgeons | 2 | 0 | 3 |
| Clergymen | 1 | 1 | 3 |
| Parish clerk | 1 | 0 | 1 |
| Butchers | 19 | 6 | 20 |
| Wesleyan minister | 0 | 0 | 1 |
| Dissenting ministers | 1 | 2 | 0 |
| Farmers | 21 | 6 | 48 |

### The Beverley election of 1854

The pollbook is in the Guildhall Library.

Result: Hon. Arthur Gordon, Liberal    493
G. W. Hastings, Conservative    192

| Selected categories | Gordon | Hastings |
| --- | --- | --- |
| Gentlemen | 18 | 10 |
| Solicitors | 0 | 1 |
| Surgeons | 2 | 0 |
| Farmers | 17 | 7 |
| Butchers | 10 | 2 |
| Grocers | 9 | 3 |

*The Beverley election of 1854 (cont.)*

| Selected categories | Gordon | Hastings |
|---|---|---|
| Mariners | 7 | 2 |
| Shoemakers | 41 | 16 |
| Labourers | 30 | 24 |
| Railwayman | 1 | 0 |
| Sexton | 1 | 0 |
| Registrar | 1 | 0 |
| R.C. priest | 1 | 0 |
| Independent minister | 1 | 0 |

## The Beverley by-election of 1857

The pollbook is in Manchester Public Library.

Result: Henry Edwards, Conservative    579
William Wells, Liberal    401

| Selected categories | Wells | Edwards |
|---|---|---|
| Gentlemen | 12 | 51 |
| Solicitors | 1 | 4 |
| Surgeons | 2 | 2 |
| Clergymen | 0 | 3 |
| Farmers | 23 | 37 |
| Gaoler | 1 | 0 |

## The Beverley election of 1859

The pollbook is in the Guildhall Library.

Result: Ralph Walters, Liberal    605
Henry Edwards, Conservative    539
J. R. Walker, Conservative    435
E. A. Glover, Liberal-Conservative    54

| Selected categories | Walters | Edwards | Walker |
|---|---|---|---|
| Solicitors | 0 | 5 | 3 |
| Surgeons | 3 | 2 | 1 |
| Clergy | 0 | 3 | 3 |
| Farmers | 17 | 36 | 31 |
| Butchers | 16 | 5 | 5 |
| Grocers | 12 | 15 | 12 |
| Mariners | 12 | 12 | 9 |
| Shoemakers | 55 | 37 | 26 |
| Labourers | 53 | 36 | 25 |
| Railwaymen | 2 | 1 | 0 |
| Gentlemen | 21 | 51 | 43 |
| Sexton | 1 | 0 | 0 |
| Organists | 0 | 2 | 1 |
| Dissenting ministers | 3 | 1 | 1 |

## The Birmingham Liberal caucus in 1880

The apparently socially exclusive character of the Birmingham radical caucus is strongly suggested by this analysis of activists in the Market Hall Ward. Materials also exist for a social analysis of Edgbaston Ward party, but this was not pursued as the essential point about the gentility of radicalism is better made in relation to the very mixed and not specially genteel Market Hall Ward in the town centre.

Members representing the Ward on the City Executive Committee, and also Ward Executive Committee:

President. A merchant
Treasurer. A merchant
Secretary. A merchant
Businessman
Ironmonger
Accountant and estate agent

Ward representatives on the '800' (the caucus): 50 persons

| | | | |
|---|---|---|---|
| Businessmen and merchants | 4 | Bootmaker | 1 |
| Coal merchants | 2 | Pawnbroker | 1 |
| Solicitors | 4 | Silk mercer | 1 |
| Accountants | 3 | Drapers | 2 |
| Stockbroker | 1 | Saddler | 1 |
| Auctioneer | 1 | Master decorator | 1 |
| Maltster | 1 | Master tailors | 2 |
| Estate agent | 1 | Wholesale baker | 1 |
| Doctor | 1 | Antique dealer | 1 |
| Grammar school teachers* | 2 | Publican | 1 |
| Law stationer | 1 | Hotelier | 1 |
| Watchmaker | 1 | Manager, Coffee House Co. | 1 |
| Ironmonger | 1 | Occupation not discoverable | 13 |

* One of these was a clergyman.

Sources: *Birmingham Liberal Association, Market Hall Ward. List of officers*, etc. (1880) (Birmingham Public Library, reference no. 72349), and *Birmingham Directory*, 1880.

## The Bolton election of 1835

The pollbook is in the Guildhall Library.

Result: Wm. Bolling, Conservative 633
Peter Ainsworth, Liberal 590
Robert Torrens, Liberal 343

| Selected categories | Ainsworth | Torrens | Bolling |
|---|---|---|---|
| Beersellers | 32 | 5 | 29 |
| Surgeons | 9 | 7 | 15 |
| Spinners | 14 | 11 | 30 |
| Cloggers | 12 | 6 | 4 |
| Publicans | 40 | 15 | 46 |
| Weavers | 10 | 4 | 9 |
| Tailors | 12 | 5 | 10 |
| Grocers | 10 | 5 | 7 |

*The Bolton election of 1835 (cont.)*

| Selected categories | Ainsworth | Torrens | Bolling |
|---|---|---|---|
| Farmers | 15 | 2 | 16 |
| Butchers | 13 | 12 | 13 |
| Ironfounders | 9 | 1 | 13 |
| Manufacturers | 44 | 41 | 37 |
| Labourer | 1 | 0 | 1 |
| Gentlemen | 23 | 15 | 26 |
| Bleachers | 3 | 3 | 6 |
| Paper makers | 2 | 1 | 1 |
| Machine makers | 1 | 0 | 2 |
| Shoemakers | 10 | 7 | 12 |
| Overlookers | 2 | 3 | 7 |
| Manager | 1 | 0 | 1 |
| Spindle makers | 3 | 0 | 3 |
| Foundrymen | 1 | 0 | 2 |
| Solicitors | 6 | 5 | 12 |
| Collier | 1 | 0 | 1 |
| Mechanics | 2 | 1 | 6 |
| Clergymen | 2 | 0 | 3 |
| Sizers | 3 | 0 | 1 |
| Cotton dealers | 2 | 1 | 3 |
| Calenderer | 1 | 0 | 1 |
| Boilermakers | 0 | 2 | 4 |
| Coalmasters | 0 | 0 | 8 |
| Dissenting ministers | 0 | 4 | 0 |
| Moulder | 0 | 1 | 1 |
| Banker | 0 | 0 | 1 |
| Warper | 1 | 1 | 0 |

## The Boston election of 1852

The pollbook is in the Bodleian Library.

Result: Heathcote, Liberal 547
Cabbell, Conservative 490
J. A. Hankey, Liberal 436
T. Hankey, Liberal 146
Adams, Conservative 19

| Selected categories | Heathcote | J. Hankey | T. Hankey | Cabbell |
|---|---|---|---|---|
| Railwaymen | 6 | 11 | 6 | 4 |
| Shoemakers | 25 | 10 | 4 | 29 |
| Policemen | 2 | 1 | 0 | 2 |
| Pilots | 4 | 5 | 1 | 2 |
| Wesleyan minister | 0 | 0 | 0 | 1 |
| Sexton | 1 | 0 | 0 | 1 |
| Bankers | 3 | 1 | 1 | 2 |
| Baptist minister | 0 | 1 | 1 | 0 |
| Anglican clergy | 1 | 0 | 0 | 2 |
| Independent minister | 1 | 1 | 0 | 0 |

According to the pollbook, 'since the Reform Act little personal influence has prevailed'.

### The Brighton election of 1832

The pollbook, which is in the Guildhall Library, takes the form of a single alphabetical list.

Result: I. N. Wigney, Liberal          873
G. Faithfull, Liberal          722
Capt. Pechell, R.N., Liberal          613
Wm. Crawford, Liberal          391
Sir A. J. Dalrymple, Conservative   32

#### Voters A–D inclusive only

|  | Wigney | Faithfull | Pechell | Crawford |
|---|---|---|---|---|
| Gentlemen | 26 | 17 | 36 | 26 |

#### Voters A–Z

| Selected categories | Wigney | Faithfull | Pechell | Crawford |
|---|---|---|---|---|
| Clergy | 0 | 0 | 12 | 10 |
| Officers | 1 | 0 | 11 | 5 |
| Sexton | 1 | 0 | 0 | 1 |
| Dissenting ministers | 4 | 3 | 1 | 2 |
| Carpenters | 52 | 63 | 21 | 14 |
| Butchers | 30 | 25 | 17 | 10 |
| Shoemakers | 36 | 36 | 7 | 8 |
| Grocers | 53 | 48 | 15 | 9 |
| Surgeons | 5 | 1 | 31 | 25 |
| Saddlers | 5 | 2 | 4 | 5 |
| Beersellers | 5 | 11 | 2 | 3 |
| Mariners | 2 | 1 | 1 | 0 |
| Publicans | 30 | 19 | 17 | 3 |
| Bankers | 0 | 1 | 2 | 2 |
| Labourers | 10 | 10 | 5 | 2 |
| Police | 2 | 1 | 1 | 0 |

### The Brighton election of 1835

The pollbook is in the Library of the Society of Genealogists.

Result: Capt. G. R. Pechell, Liberal          961
I. W. Wigney, Liberal          523
Sir Adolphus Dalrymple, Cons.          483
Geo. Faithfull, Liberal          467

| Selected categories | Pechell | Wigney | Faithfull | Dalrymple |
|---|---|---|---|---|
| Anglican clergy | 12 | 2 | 0 | 11 |
| Parish clerks | 2 | 0 | 0 | 2 |
| Sexton | 1 | 0 | 0 | 1 |
| Dissenting ministers | 0 | 5 | 4 | 1 |
| Officers | 7 | 3 | 0 | 3 |
| Surgeons | 29 | 9 | 1 | 17 |
| Lawyers | 16 | 5 | 4 | 10 |
| Gentlemen | 200 | 107 | 47 | 112 |
| Cordwainers | 18 | 10 | 18 | 10 |
| Carpenters | 34 | 18 | 46 | 12 |
| Beersellers | 11 | 1 | 7 | 2 |

## The Brighton election of 1837

The pollbook is in the Institute of Historical Research.

Result: Capt. G. R. Pechell, R.N., Liberal    1,083
Sir Adolphus J. Dalrymple, Bt., Cons.   819
I. N. Wigney, Liberal      801
Geo. Faithfull, Liberal      183

| Selected categories | Pechell | Wigney | Faithfull | Dalrymple |
|---|---|---|---|---|
| Clergymen | 5 | 3 | 1 | 18 |
| Parish clerk | 1 | 0 | 0 | 1 |
| Sexton | 1 | 0 | 0 | 1 |
| Dissenting ministers | 6 | 6 | 0 | 1 |
| Bankers | 2 | 1 | 0 | 3 |
| Officers | 5 | 3 | 0 | 8 |
| Surgeons | 18 | 9 | 1 | 19 |
| Organist | 1 | 0 | 0 | 1 |
| Butchers | 32 | 21 | 4 | 31 |
| Grocers | 46 | 44 | 14 | 30 |
| Carpenters | 62 | 40 | 17 | 42 |
| Fishermen | 3 | 2 | 1 | 2 |
| Mariners | 5 | 2 | 0 | 5 |
| Labourers | 12 | 4 | 4 | 12 |

| Plumps | | Splits | |
|---|---|---|---|
| Wigney | 39 | Wigney and Pechell | 616 |
| Pechell | 30 | Wigney and Dalrymple | 102 |
| Dalrymple | 268 | Wigney and Faithfull | 44 |
| Faithfull | 51 | Pechell and Dalrymple | 399 |
| | | Pechell and Faithfull | 38 |
| | | Dalrymple and Faithfull | 50 |

## The Brighton election of 1841

The pollbook, which is in the Guildhall Library, takes the form of a single alphabetical list.

Result: Pechell, Liberal     1,443
Wigney, Liberal     1,235
Dalrymple, Conservative 872
C. Brooker, Liberal    19

Voters A–D inclusive only

| | Pechell | Wigney | Dalrymple |
|---|---|---|---|
| Gentlemen | 42 | 33 | 23 |

Voters A–Z

| Selected categories | Pechell | Wigney | Dalrymple |
|---|---|---|---|
| Ministers | 3 | 3 | 2 |
| Clergy | 6 | 6 | 21 |
| Sexton | 0 | 0 | 1 |
| Butchers | 46 | 44 | 26 |
| Grocers | 56 | 50 | 23 |
| Carpenters | 91 | 71 | 43 |

*The Brighton election of 1841 (cont.)*

Voters A–Z (*cont.*)

| Selected categories | Pechell | Wigney | Dalrymple |
|---|---|---|---|
| Saddlers | 8 | 9 | 5 |
| Officers | 5 | 5 | 5 |
| Surgeons | 17 | 15 | 20 |
| Labourers | 29 | 19 | 16 |
| Bankers | 0 | 0 | 2 |
| R.C. priest | 1 | 1 | 0 |
| Police | 2 | 2 | 2 |
| Parish clerk | 1 | 0 | 1 |

### The Bristol election of 30 July–5 August 1830

The pollbook is in the Institute of Historical Research.

Result: R. Hart Davis (probably Ministerialist)    5,012
James Evan Baillie (West India interest Whig)    3,377
Edward Protheroe (anti-slavery and Reform)    2,840
Jas. Acland (Radical)    25

| Selected categories excluding out-voters* | Davis | Protheroe | Baillie |
|---|---|---|---|
| Colliers | 13 | 2 | 17 |
| Subsacrist | 1 | 0 | 0 |
| Organists | 2 | 2 | 1 |
| Cathedral almsmen | 2 | 0 | 2 |
| Dissenting ministers | 0 | 2 | 0 |
| Anglican clergy | 19 | 5 | 16 |
| Victuallers | 47 | 25 | 24 |
| Merchants | 42 | 20 | 29 |
| Mariners | 84 | 28 | 85 |
| Cordwainers | 265 | 133 | 174 |
| Labourers | 271 | 121 | 198 |
| Shipwrights | 128 | 16 | 127 |

Davis: plumps    183
   and Baillie    2,900
   and Protheroe    1,929
   5,012

Baillie: plumps    460
   and Davis    2,900
   and Protheroe    15
   and Acland    2
   3,377

Protheroe: plumps    873
   and Davis    1,929
   and Baillie    15
   and Acland    23
   2,840

Acland: and Protheroe    23
   and Baillie    2
   25

* Out-voters were about one-sixth of the electorate.

*The Bristol election of 1830 (cont.)*

The pollbook quotes Charles Pinney as saying in support of J. E. Baillie, the pro-slavery Whig: 'Gentlemen, the present Election differs in principle and public importance from any that has previously occurred in this city. So great is the difference, that the old party names are either forgotten, or in disuse, and for the first time, a new distinction has taken place. Slavery and Anti-Slavery is now the cry, instead of Whig and Tory...I believe I do not exaggerate when I assert that ⅝ of the whole trade of Bristol depend on the West Indies.'

## The Bristol election of December 1832

The pollbook is in the Institute of Historical Research, and lists the occupations of freemen voters only.

Result: Sir Richard Vyvyan, Conservative    3,709
J. E. Baillie, Liberal    3,159
Edward Protheroe, Liberal    3,030
John Williams, Liberal    2,741

| Freemen only: selected categories | Baillie | Protheroe | Williams | Vyvyan |
|---|---|---|---|---|
| Colliers | 5 | 16 | 16 | 5 |
| Surgeons | 7 | 2 | 2 | 12 |
| Organists | 1 | 1 | 1 | 1 |
| Subsacrist | 0 | 0 | 0 | 1 |
| Cathedral almsmen | 1 | 0 | 0 | 2 |
| Parish clerk | 1 | 0 | 0 | 1 |
| Clergy | 11 | 1 | 1 | 13 |
| Merchants | 34 | 9 | 6 | 31 |
| Grocers | 16 | 10 | 10 | 21 |
| Mariners | 62 | 20 | 19 | 67 |
| Shipwrights | 86 | 30 | 25 | 79 |
| Labourers | 142 | 125 | 108 | 191 |
| Cordwainers | 99 | 129 | 112 | 125 |

## The Bristol election of 1837

The pollbook is in the Institute of Historical Research.

Result: P. W. S. Miles, Conservative    3,838
Hon. F. H. F. Berkeley, Liberal    3,212
Wm. Fripp, Conservative    3,156

| Selected categories | Berkeley | Miles | Fripp |
|---|---|---|---|
| Pilots | 1 | 3 | 0 |
| Colliers | 17 | 14 | 5 |
| Bankers | 2 | 8 | 8 |
| Lamplighters | 3 | 2 | 2 |
| Sextons | 1 | 3 | 3 |
| Clergy | 0 | 11 | 11 |
| Police | 2 | 5 | 6 |
| Weavers | 9 | 9 | 5 |

*The Bristol election of 1837 (cont.)*

| Selected categories | Berkeley | Miles | Fripp |
|---|---|---|---|
| Dissenting ministers | 8 | o | o |
| Organists | o | 2 | 2 |
| Methodist minister | 1 | o | o |
| R.C. priest | 1 | o | o |
| Parish clerk | o | 1 | 1 |
| Shipbuilders | 4 | 6 | 5 |
| Chorister | o | 1 | 1 |
| Gentlemen | 131 | 283 | 277 |
| Merchants | 16 | 74 | 74 |
| Lawyers | 27 | 54 | 55 |
| Surgeons | 22 | 54 | 55 |
| Shoemakers | 174 | 137 | 97 |
| Shipwrights | 25 | 84 | 69 |
| Grocers | 72 | 55 | 46 |
| Mariners | 22 | 42 | 31 |
| Labourers | 108 | 140 | 112 |

## The Bristol election of 1841

The pollbook is in the Institute of Historical Research.

| Result: | P. W. S. Miles, Conservative | 4,193 |
|---|---|---|
| | Hon. F. H. F. Berkeley, Liberal | 3,739 |
| | Wm. Fripp, Conservative | 3,684 |

| Selected categories | Berkeley | Miles | Fripp |
|---|---|---|---|
| Bankers | 3 | 8 | 7 |
| Gravedigger | 1 | o | o |
| Parish clerks | 1 | 3 | 2 |
| Harbourmaster | o | 1 | 1 |
| Methodist preacher | 1 | o | o |
| Wesleyan minister | 1 | o | o |
| R.C. priests | 2 | o | o |
| Organists | o | 6 | 6 |
| Baptist preacher | 1 | o | o |
| 'Itinerant preacher' | 1 | o | o |
| Subsacrist | o | 1 | 1 |
| Verger | o | 1 | 1 |
| Sextons | o | 9 | 9 |
| 'Clerks', Rev., etc. | 1 | 11 | 11 |
| The Dean of Bristol | 1 | o | o |
| Chorister | o | 1 | 1 |
| Dissenting ministers | 11 | o | o |
| Sweeps | 5 | 4 | 3 |
| Coal miners | 22 | 6 | 4 |
| Weavers | 4 | 3 | 4 |
| Officers | 4 | 15 | 15 |
| Lamplighters | 1 | 6 | 6 |
| Watermen | o | 5 | 5 |
| Mariners | 9 | 23 | 17 |

*The Bristol election of 1841 (cont.)*

| Selected categories | Berkeley | Miles | Fripp |
|---|---|---|---|
| Police, all ranks | 3 | 10 | 14 |
| 'Captains' | 2 | 8 | 9 |
| Postmen | 0 | 2 | 2 |
| Sailmakers | 6 | 12 | 9 |
| Boatbuilders | 4 | 2 | 1 |
| Almsmen | 4 | 1 | 0 |
| Pilots | 1 | 3 | 3 |
| Merchants | 17 | 69 | 66 |
| Lawyers | 25 | 77 | 77 |
| Surgeons | 24 | 58 | 57 |
| Victuallers | 139 | 141 | 109 |
| Beersellers | 51 | 34 | 25 |
| Carpenters | 160 | 116 | 103 |
| Shoemakers | 210 | 136 | 105 |
| Shipwrights | 51 | 91 | 70 |
| Grocers | 83 | 76 | 69 |
| Butchers | 83 | 73 | 61 |
| Labourers | 87 | 104 | 97 |

## The Bristol election of 1852

The pollbook is in the Institute of Historical Research.

Result: F. H. F. Berkeley, Liberal          4,642
W. H. G. Langton, Liberal          4,489
F. A. M'Geachy, Conservative     3,648

There was little cross-voting.

The following analysis of selected categories omits 180 out-voters in Gloucester and Somerset.

| Selected categories | Berkeley | M'Geachy |
|---|---|---|
| Gentlemen | 127 | 225 |
| Military and naval officers | 5 | 18 |
| Barristers | 0 | 3 |
| Surgeons and physicians | 30 | 50 |
| Bankers | 3 | 6 |
| Share brokers | 4 | 7 |
| Victuallers | 118 | 71 |
| Beersellers | 108 | 32 |
| Shoemakers | 168 | 71 |
| Labourers | 69 | 72 |
| Anglican clergy* | 3 | 56 |
| Dissenting ministers | 14 | 1 |
| R.C. priest | 1 | 0 |
| Sextons | 0 | 6 |
| Organists | 0 | 3 |
| Gravediggers | 0 | 2 |
| Sweeps | 3 | 6 |
| Bargeman | 0 | 1 |

* The Dean of Bristol voted Liberal, as in 1841.

## The Bury St Edmunds election of 1852

The pollbook is in the Guildhall Library.

Result: Earl Jermyn, Conservative    493
J. Stuart, Ministerialist    328
E. Bunbury, Liberal    319

| Selected categories | Bunbury | Stuart | Jermyn |
|---|---|---|---|
| Solicitors | 7 | 7 | 12 |
| Surgeons | 1 | 8 | 9 |
| Farmers | 2 | 7 | 7 |
| Parish clerks | 0 | 1 | 1 |
| Butchers | 2 | 6 | 1 |
| Grocers | 2 | 6 | 7 |
| Shoemakers | 9 | 3 | 7 |
| Labourers | 1 | 0 | 1 |
| Police | 2 | 1 | 2 |
| Newspaper owner | 1 | 0 | 1 |
| Sheriff's officer | 1 | 0 | 1 |
| Corn inspector | 1 | 0 | 0 |
| Tobacco manufacturer | 1 | 0 | 0 |
| Relieving officer | 0 | 1 | 1 |
| Sexton | 1 | 0 | 1 |
| Willow manufacturer | 1 | 0 | 0 |
| Ministers | 3 | 0 | 3 |
| Tax gatherer | 1 | 0 | 1 |
| Ironfounders | 1 | 1 | 2 |
| Registrar | 1 | 0 | 1 |

## The Cambridge Borough election of 1835

The pollbook is in the Guildhall Library.

Result: Spring Rice, Liberal    736
George Pryme, Liberal    693
J. L. Knight, Conservative    688

| Selected categories | Rice | Pryme | Knight |
|---|---|---|---|
| Gentlemen | 50 | 44 | 41 |
| Solicitors | 10 | 11 | 9 |
| Surgeons | 10 | 11 | 8 |
| Farmers | 1 | 1 | 8 |
| Grocers | 21 | 21 | 12 |
| Butchers | 6 | 3 | 17 |
| Servants | 7 | 8 | 24 |
| College servants | 34 | 34 | 68 |
| Publicans | 59 | 52 | 56 |
| Clergy | 7 | 6 | 10 |
| Labourers | 5 | 4 | 5 |
| Shoemakers | 33 | 31 | 16 |
| Gaolers | 0 | 0 | 2 |
| Sheriff's officers | 1 | 1 | 2 |
| Dissenting ministers | 2 | 2 | 0 |

## The Cambridge Borough election of 1840

The pollbook is in the Guildhall Library.

Result: Sir A. C. Grant, Conservative 736
Thomas Starkie, Liberal 651

| Selected categories | Starkie | Grant |
|---|---|---|
| Solicitors | 8 | 8 |
| Surgeons | 9 | 8 |
| Farmers | 1 | 6 |
| Butchers | 2 | 18 |
| Grocers | 19 | 15 |
| Labourers | 6 | 11 |
| College servants | 24 | 69 |
| Servants | 5 | 7 |
| Publicans | 36 | 37 |
| Gentlemen | 31 | 47 |
| Clergy | 4 | 7 |
| Shoemakers | 31 | 24 |
| Parish clerks | 0 | 3 |
| Dissenting minister | 1 | 0 |
| Police | 3 | 0 |

## The Cambridge Borough election of 1845

The pollbook is in the Guildhall Library.

Result: Fitzroy Kelly, Conservative 746
Shafto Adair, Liberal 729

| Selected categories | Adair | Kelly |
|---|---|---|
| Solicitors | 9 | 14 |
| Surgeons | 6 | 7 |
| Farmers | 3 | 7 |
| Butchers | 3 | 23 |
| Grocers | 26 | 17 |
| Labourers | 5 | 12 |
| College servants | 10 | 66 |
| Servants | 14 | 41 |
| Publicans | 48 | 29 |
| Gentlemen | 47 | 33 |
| Clergy | 4 | 7 |
| Shoemakers | 29 | 30 |
| Dissenting ministers | 5 | 0 |
| Organists | 1 | 2 |
| Parish clerks | 0 | 2 |
| Turnkey | 0 | 1 |
| Machine maker | 0 | 1 |
| Ironfounders | 3 | 1 |
| Sheriff's officer | 0 | 1 |
| Relieving officers | 1 | 1 |

## The Cambridge Borough election of 1857

The pollbook is in the Guildhall Library.

Result: K. Macaulay, Conservative     769
A. Steuart, Conservative     735
Shafto Adair, Liberal     729
John Hibbert, Liberal     702

| Selected categories | Adair | Hibbert | Macaulay | Steuart |
|---|---|---|---|---|
| Solicitors | 9 | 8 | 15 | 16 |
| Surgeons | 5 | 5 | 11 | 11 |
| Farmers | 2 | 0 | 8 | 7 |
| Butchers | 4 | 3 | 19 | 16 |
| Grocers | 25 | 23 | 17 | 16 |
| Railwaymen | 1 | 1 | 1 | 1 |
| Labourers | 3 | 3 | 8 | 7 |
| Servants | 16 | 17 | 27 | 25 |
| College servants | 11 | 7 | 55 | 48 |
| Publicans | 25 | 27 | 33 | 32 |
| Gentlemen | 42 | 38 | 51 | 48 |
| Clergy | 6 | 6 | 11 | 10 |
| Shoemakers | 28 | 28 | 24 | 25 |
| Dissenting ministers | 2 | 2 | 0 | 0 |
| Lodging-house keepers | 0 | 0 | 5 | 5 |
| Relieving officers | 1 | 1 | 1 | 1 |
| Serjeant at mace | 1 | 1 | 0 | 0 |
| Sexton | 0 | 0 | 1 | 1 |

## The Cambridge Borough election of 1859

The pollbook is in the Guildhall Library.

Result: K. Macaulay, Conservative     752
A. Steuart, Conservative     748
F. Mowatt, Liberal     669
Hon. E. T. Twistleton, Liberal     682

| Selected categories | Mowatt | Twistleton | Macaulay | Steuart |
|---|---|---|---|---|
| Surgeons | 5 | 7 | 11 | 11 |
| Farmers | 2 | 2 | 10 | 10 |
| Butchers | 7 | 7 | 15 | 13 |
| Grocers | 21 | 21 | 20 | 20 |
| Labourers | 4 | 4 | 5 | 5 |
| Railwaymen | 2 | 2 | 4 | 4 |
| Clergymen | 2 | 3 | 12 | 12 |
| Shoemakers | 25 | 25 | 16 | 17 |
| Dissenting ministers | 2 | 2 | 0 | 0 |
| Organists | 0 | 0 | 3 | 3 |
| Professors | 0 | 0 | 3 | 3 |
| Engineers | 2 | 2 | 0 | 0 |

*The Cambridge Borough election of 1859 (cont.)*

| Selected categories | Mowatt | Twistleton | Macaulay | Steuart |
|---|---|---|---|---|
| Sheriff's officer | o | o | 1 | 1 |
| Serjeant at mace | 1 | 1 | o | o |
| R.C. priest | 1 | 1 | o | o |
| Parish clerks | o | o | 2 | 2 |
| Editor of *Cambridge Chronicle* | o | o | 1 | 1 |
| Lodginghouse keepers | o | o | 2 | 2 |

## The Cambridge Borough election of 1863

The pollbook is in the Guildhall Library.

Result: Powell, Conservative  708
Fawcett, Liberal  627

| Selected categories | Fawcett | Powell |
|---|---|---|
| Surgeons | 6 | 13 |
| Farmers | o | 5 |
| Butchers | 4 | 13 |
| Grocers | 21 | 12 |
| Labourers | 3 | 3 |
| Railwaymen | o | 2 |
| Clergy | 2 | 8 |
| Shoemakers | 21 | 21 |
| Saddlers | 1 | 4 |
| Robemakers | 9 | 6 |
| Gasmen | 2 | o |
| Organists | o | 3 |
| Tobacco manufacturer | 1 | o |
| Engineers | 2 | o |
| University marshal | o | 1 |
| Lodging-house keepers | 1 | 4 |
| Serjeant at mace | 1 | o |
| Registrar | 1 | o |
| Sheriff's officer | o | 1 |
| Commercial travellers | 3 | o |
| Parish clerk | o | 1 |
| Professors | o | 2 |
| Curator | o | 1 |
| Librarians | 1 | 1 |

## The Cambridge Borough election of 1865

The pollbook is in the Guildhall Library.

Result: Forsyth, Conservative 762
Powell, Conservative 760
Torrens, Liberal 726
Christie, Liberal 725

| Selected categories | Torrens | Christie | Forsyth | Powell |
|---|---|---|---|---|
| Solicitors | 8 | 8 | 15 | 15 |
| Surgeons | 4 | 5 | 15 | 14 |
| Farmers | 1 | 1 | 6 | 5 |
| Butchers | 7 | 8 | 11 | 13 |
| Grocers | 34 | 31 | 13 | 13 |
| Railwaymen | 2 | 2 | 6 | 6 |
| Labourers | 6 | 7 | 1 | 1 |
| Servants | 14 | 14 | 24 | 25 |
| College servants | 17 | 17 | 70 | 74 |
| Publicans | 41 | 40 | 39 | 39 |
| Clergymen | 4 | 4 | 20 | 19 |
| Dissenting ministers | 2 | 3 | 0 | 0 |
| Shoemakers | 23 | 23 | 20 | 20 |
| Organists | 0 | 0 | 3 | 3 |
| Tobacco manufacturer | 1 | 1 | 0 | 0 |
| Librarians | 2 | 2 | 0 | 0 |
| Relieving officers | 2 | 2 | 0 | 0 |
| Parish clerks | 0 | 0 | 2 | 2 |
| Cricketers | 0 | 0 | 3 | 3 |
| Professors | 0 | 0 | 4 | 5 |
| Gaoler | 0 | 0 | 1 | 1 |
| Curators | 0 | 0 | 2 | 2 |
| Ironfounder | 1 | 1 | 0 | 0 |
| Chimney sweeps | 0 | 0 | 2 | 3 |
| Lodging-house keepers | 0 | 0 | 3 | 3 |
| R.C. priest | 1 | 1 | 0 | 0 |
| Town crier | 1 | 1 | 0 | 0 |
| Engineers | 2 | 2 | 0 | 0 |

## The Cambridge Borough election of 1866

The pollbook is in Cambridge University Library.

Result: John Eldon Gorst, Conservative 774
Lt.-Col. R. R. Torrens, Liberal 755

Virtually all voters are shown below.

| | | Torrens | Gorst | | Torrens | Gorst |
|---|---|---|---|---|---|---|
| I. | Gentlemen | 37 | 61 | Agents | 5 | 2 |
| | Farmers | 2 | 6 | Military | 0 | 2 |
| II. | Medical | 3 | 19 | Officials | 13 | 4 |
| | Legal | 7 | 16 | Clerks | 26 | 28 |

*The Cambridge Borough election of 1866 (cont.)*

| | | Torrens | Gorst | | | Torrens | Gorst |
|---|---|---|---|---|---|---|---|
| | Teachers | 4 | 4 | Booksellers | | 10 | 18 |
| | Clergy | 7 | 25 | Hairdressers | | 3 | 6 |
| | Musicians | 4 | 10 | Milkmen | | 6 | 10 |
| | Librarians | 2 | 1 | Jewellers | | 1 | 1 |
| | Organists | 0 | 2 | Bakers | | 38 | 20 |
| | Miscellaneous professions | 13 | 22 | Hardware | | 10 | 5 |
| | | | | Chemists | | 8 | 9 |
| III. | Publicans | 30 | 38 | Butchers | | 9 | 21 |
| IV. | Servants | 14 | 37 | Fruiterers | | 8 | 6 |
| | College servants | 23 | 76 | Tobacconists | | 8 | 2 |
| | Railway employees | 1 | 6 | VII. | Building craftsmen | 31 | 29 |
| | Labourers | 5 | 7 | Metalworkers | | 35 | 31 |
| | | | | Shoemakers | | 36 | 35 |
| V. | Brewers | 19 | 6 | Tailors | | 71 | 30 |
| | Builders | 21 | 18 | Furniture makers | | 22 | 15 |
| | Bankers | 2 | 3 | Painters | | 4 | 7 |
| | Millers | 13 | 5 | Printers | | 25 | 11 |
| | Maltsters | 2 | 1 | Luxury craftsmen | | 3 | 8 |
| | Small manufacturers | 4 | 1 | Leather workers | | 9 | 2 |
| | Coal merchants | 3 | 2 | Coach builders | | 10 | 4 |
| | Merchants | 17 | 13 | Hatters | | 1 | 4 |
| | Hoteliers | 0 | 4 | Sweeps | | 0 | 2 |
| VI. | Grocers | 43 | 21 | Bookbinders | | 3 | 8 |
| | Drapers | 45 | 12 | Other craftsmen | | 9 | 5 |
| | Wine | 10 | 8 | | | | |
| | Fishmongers | 9 | 2 | VIII. | Miscellaneous | 10 | 28 |

| Summary: | | Liberal | Conservative |
|---|---|---|---|
| I. | Gentlemen and farmers | 39 | 67 |
| II. | Professions | 84 | 135 |
| III. | Publicans | 30 | 38 |
| IV. | Labour | 43 | 126 |
| V. | Business | 81 | 53 |
| VI. | Retailers | 208 | 141 |
| VII. | Craftsmen | 259 | 191 |
| VIII. | Miscellaneous | 10 | 28 |

## The Cambridge Borough election of 1868

The pollbook is in Cambridge University Library.

Result: Col. R. R. Torrens, Liberal    1,879
W. Fowler, Liberal    1,857
F. S. Powell, Conservative    1,436
John E. Gorst, Conservative    1,389

The votes analysed were those which were cast for two Liberals or two Tories. Cross voting, or plumping for a single candidate, was omitted from the analysis. The figures therefore are not quite complete, for the totals of split votes were 1,843 in the case of Liberals (out of total votes of 1,879 and 1,857 for their men) and 1,382 for the Tories (out of total polls of 1,436 and 1,389).

| All voters | Liberal | Con-servative | | | Liberal | Con-servative |
|---|---|---|---|---|---|---|
| I.   Gentlemen | 61 | 78 | VI. | Craftsmen and skilled workers | | |
| Farmers | 3 | 13 | | Leather | 13 | 5 |
| | | | | Luxury | 12 | 9 |
| II.   Professional and commercial | | | | Hatters | 2 | 7 |
| Legal | 10 | 19 | | Painters | 45 | 29 |
| Medical | 7 | 22 | | Furniture | 42 | 25 |
| Clergy | 13 | 34 | | Printers | 46 | 17 |
| Officials | 12 | 10 | | Tailors | 176 | 51 |
| Musicians | 5 | 8 | | Shoemakers | 121 | 63 |
| Organists | 0 | 5 | | Metal | 118 | 62 |
| Teachers | 8 | 12 | | Building | 207 | 85 |
| Librarians | 2 | 4 | | craftsmen | | |
| Military | 0 | 4 | | Coach- | 12 | 9 |
| Agents and | 7 | 6 | | builders | | |
| Brokers | | | | Bookbinders | 8 | 10 |
| Clerks | 54 | 39 | | Minor crafts | 7 | 14 |
| Miscellaneous | 13 | 32 | | Sweeps | 0 | 7 |
| III.   Publicans | 41 | 40 | VII. | Retailers | | |
| | | | | Wine | 10 | 7 |
| IV.   Labour | | | | Fish | 5 | 4 |
| Labourers | 214 | 108 | | Tobacco | 4 | 3 |
| Railwaymen | 75 | 15 | | Milk | 10 | 16 |
| Servants | 65 | 120 | | Hardware | 23 | 11 |
| College | 25 | 115 | | Chemists | 7 | 11 |
| servants | | | | Bakers | 44 | 28 |
| | | | | Booksellers | 9 | 19 |
| V.   Business | | | | Green- | 8 | 7 |
| Hoteliers | 0 | 2 | | grocers | | |
| Brewers | 18 | 16 | | Jewellers | 7 | 1 |
| Builders | 24 | 23 | | Drapers | 51 | 14 |
| Maltsters | 9 | 1 | | Grocers | 53 | 22 |
| Millers | 23 | 3 | | Hairdressers | 4 | 7 |
| Coal mer- | 9 | 5 | | Butchers | 12 | 32 |
| chants | | | | | | |
| Merchants | 36 | 19 | VIII. | Miscellaneous | 39 | 57 |
| Bankers | 2 | 1 | | | | |
| Small manu- | 8 | 2 | | | | |
| facturers | | | | | | |

*The Cambridge Borough election of 1868 (cont.)*

'Miscellaneous' included the following. Tories: lamplighter, students, 9 cricketers, carter, cabman, stablekeeper, undertaker, pianotuner, billiards-keeper, artist, photographer, lodging-house keeper, sexton, moneylender, hawker, eating-house keeper. Liberals: pieman, drover, cattledealer, money-lender, carter, pianotuner, chiropodist, horsekeeper, eating-house and lodging-house keepers, watermen, ten firemen and seven hawkers, artist, photographer. All the hoteliers, organists, cricketers, students, lamplighters, billiards-keepers, sweeps, and military men were Tories. All the firemen and Dissenting clergy were Liberal.

| Summary: | | Liberal | Conservative |
|---|---|---|---|
| I. | Gentlemen and farmers | 64 | 91 |
| II. | Professional and commercial | 131 | 195 |
| III. | Publicans | 41 | 40 |
| IV. | Labour | 379 | 359 |
| V. | Business | 129 | 72 |
| VI. | Craftsmen and skilled workers | 809 | 393 |
| VII. | Retailers | 247 | 182 |
| VIII. | Miscellaneous | 39 | 57 |

## The Cambridge Borough Election of 1868

### Tenders

The Cambridge pollbook for 1868 in the Guildhall Library has an appendix listing votes tendered by members of the University, etc., pending a legal decision. 'The right of members of the University to vote as lodgers under the Representation of the People Act, 1867, being at the time of the Election the subject of an appeal in the Court of Common Pleas, the following Members of the University tendered their votes, pending the decision of the Court.'

| | Torrens (Liberal) | Fowler (Liberal) | Powell (Con-servative) | Gorst (Con-servative) |
|---|---|---|---|---|
| Students | 3 | 3 | 34 | 35 |
| Clerks in holy orders | 0 | 0 | 3 | 3 |
| Scholars | 0 | 0 | 3 | 3 |
| Fellows | 0 | 0 | 9 | 9 |
| Lecturers | 0 | 0 | 1 | 1 |
| Gentlemen | 0 | 0 | 1 | 1 |
| Barrister | 1 | 1 | 0 | 0 |

## The Cambridge University election of 1831

*The Times* for 9 May 1831 contains on page 3 this item, which is reproduced as it stands:

'One of the weekly papers maintains that the electors of Cambridge "come from no particular class, and are of no particular professions". An examination of the pollbook will soon dissipate this error...The numbers subjoined are not given as altogether accurate, but may be relied on within a few, and show pretty

*The Cambridge University election of 1831 (cont.)*

plainly in what "particular class and professions" Messrs. Goulburn and Peel have found their majorities.

|  | Clergy | Laity | Total |
|---|---|---|---|
| Goulburn | 570 | 236 | 806 |
| Peel | 573 | 232 | 805 |
| Cavendish | 323 | 307 | 630 |
| Palmerston | 309 | 301 | 610' |

According to *The Times* for 19 May 1831, the professors of the University of Cambridge were distinctly for Reform. Fifteen voted for Palmerston and Cavendish, and only 6 for Goulburn and Peel.

## The Carlisle elections of 1865 and 1868

The following electors in Carlisle were employed by the London and North Western Railway:

In 1865 30:    of whom 27 voted Tory.
In 1868 154:    of whom 136 voted Tory.

The following voters were employees of the North Eastern Railway:

In 1868 45:    of whom 27 voted Liberal;
of whom 8 voted Tory.

The Tory candidate for Carlisle was a director of the London and North Western Railway; the chairman of the North Eastern line had been a Liberal M.P. for Whitby.

Sources: *Parl. Papers 1868–9*, VIII, 367–8, qq. 9359, 9393, 9398.

## The Chatham election of 1857

The pollbook is in the Guildhall Library.

Result: Col. Sir Frederick Smith, Conservative    672
W. G. Romaine, Liberal    643

| Selected categories | Romaine | Smith |
|---|---|---|
| Anglican clergy | 0 | 6 |
| Dissenting ministers | 3 | 0 |
| Bankers | 0 | 2 |
| Farmers | 4 | 7 |
| Policemen | 4 | 4 |
| Pensioners | 5 | 7 |
| Brewers | 0 | 4 |
| Victuallers | 38 | 58 |
| Tailors | 19 | 13 |
| Shoemakers | 25 | 18 |
| Grocers | 29 | 18 |
| Butchers | 13 | 20 |
| Carpenters | 11 | 16 |
| Mariners | 12 | 1 |
| Sailmakers | 3 | 2 |
| Gentlemen | 45 | 45 |
| Army, Navy, Marines | 16 | 15 |
| Shipwrights | 31 | 39 |
| Dockyard | 82 | 104 |

## The Chatham election of 1859

The pollbook is in the Guildhall Library. For about 50 voters, no occupation was stated.

Result: Maj.-Gen. Sir F. Smith, Conservative    713
         A. J. Otway, Liberal                    652

| Selected categories | Otway | Smith |
|---|---|---|
| Anglican clergy | 0 | 6 |
| Dissenting ministers | 1 | 0 |
| Bankers | 2 | 2 |
| Farmers | 3 | 6 |
| Policemen | 5 | 2 |
| Pensioners | 6 | 9 |
| Brewers | 0 | 3 |
| Victuallers | 41 | 56 |
| Beersellers | 0 | 3 |
| Tailors | 19 | 14 |
| Shoemakers | 19 | 14 |
| Grocers | 28 | 20 |
| Butchers | 14 | 19 |
| Carpenters | 13 | 15 |
| Mariners | 10 | 4 |
| Sailmakers | 3 | 3 |
| Gentlemen | 45 | 33 |
| Army, Navy, Marines | 16 | 19 |
| Shipwrights | 35 | 31 |
| Dockyard | 85 | 119 |

## The Chester election of 1859

The pollbook is in Chester Public Library.

Result: Earl Grosvenor, Liberal               1,464
         Humberston, Liberal-Conservative      1,110
         Salisbury, Radical                      708

### Breakdown of the 708 Radical voters

A. £10 householders

| 'Householders' | 133 |
|---|---|
| Publicans | 15 |
| Shopkeepers | 79 |
| Craftsmen | 13 |
| Brewers, ironfounders, farmer, dealers | 8 |
| Doctor, teacher, solicitors | 4 |
|  | 252 |

B. Freemen voters

| I. Shopkeepers | 33 |
|---|---|
| Bakers | 19 |
| II. Shoemakers | 35 |
| Tailors | 24 |
| Building craftsmen | 48 |

| Wood workers | 62 |
|---|---|
| Metal workers | 36 |
| Printers | 15 |
| Leather workers | 14 |
| Other craftsmen | 47 |

| III. Gentlemen | 6 |
|---|---|
| Brewer, builders, shipbuilder, ironfounders, hop merchant, coachmakers | 17 |
| Architect, auctioneer, accountant | 3 |
| IV. Clerks | 16 |
| Labourers | 40 |
| Others | 41 |

*The Chester election of 1859 (cont.)*

Summary of the Radical vote

| | |
|---|---:|
| £10 householders | 252 |
| Freemen | |
| I. Retailers | 52 |
| II. Craftsmen | 281 |
| III. Upper crust | 26 |
| IV. Miscellaneous | 97 |
| | 708 |

## The Chichester election of 2–4 August 1830

The pollbook is in the Guildhall Library.

Result: Lord George Lennox    643
John Smith    527
C. Sinclair Cullen    219

Smith and Cullen both claimed to be for Reform and for Civil and Religious Liberty. Cullen was an Anglican, and pledged himself to support any measure of reform, however sweeping, to reduce taxation, and to abolish negro slavery. Lennox had no platform, but claimed to be independent of all parties. According to *Dod*, however, Lennox supported the Reform Bills and generally acted with the Whigs for several years, before returning to the Tories.

| Selected categories | Lennox | Cullen | Smith |
|---|---|---|---|
| Clergymen | 11 | 0 | 7 |
| Chorister | 1 | 0 | 1 |
| Organist | 1 | 0 | 1 |
| Vergers | 3 | 0 | 3 |
| Unitarian minister | 0 | 1 | 0 |
| Freemen | 28 | 1 | 9 |
| Corporators | 18 | 0 | 12 |
| Drapers | 9 | 3 | 7 |
| Butchers | 18 | 10 | 13 |
| Grocers | 19 | 14 | 16 |
| Publicans | 23 | 3 | 21 |
| Labourers | 41 | 10 | 50 |
| Carpenters | 24 | 14 | 15 |
| Woolsorters | 5 | 1 | 3 |
| Gentlemen | 43 | 10 | 31 |
| Tailors | 20 | 7 | 17 |
| Shoemakers | 29 | 13 | 29 |
| Surgeons | 9 | 1 | 7 |
| Bankers | 6 | 0 | 5 |

## The Chichester election of 2–3 May 1831

The pollbook is in the Guildhall Library.

Result: Lord Arthur Lennox　　665
John Abel Smith　　　　388
Sir Godfrey Webster, Bt.　306

| Selected categories | Lennox | Webster | Smith |
|---|---|---|---|
| Clergymen | 8 | 0 | 6 |
| Organist | 1 | 0 | 1 |
| Precentor | 1 | 0 | 1 |
| Verger | 1 | 0 | 1 |
| Unitarian minister | 1 | 1 | 0 |
| Freemen | 12 | 4 | 8 |
| Corporators | 16 | 1 | 12 |
| Drapers | 12 | 4 | 9 |
| Butchers | 22 | 12 | 9 |
| Grocers | 23 | 13 | 12 |
| Publicans | 21 | 7 | 14 |
| Labourers | 46 | 27 | 30 |
| Carpenters | 30 | 23 | 11 |
| Gentlemen | 52 | 12 | 41 |
| Shoemakers | 36 | 20 | 19 |
| Surgeons | 8 | 0 | 6 |
| Tailors | 24 | 14 | 10 |
| Bankers | 3 | 1 | 1 |

## The Colchester election of 30 March 1831

The pollbook is in the Guildhall Library.

Result: William Mayhew, Whig　604
Sir Wm. Curtis, Tory　　490

### Resident voters only

| Selected categories | Curtis | Mayhew |
|---|---|---|
| Aldermen | 7 | 1 |
| Common Councilmen | 12 | 0 |
| Gentlemen | 10 | 6 |
| Farmers | 4 | 1 |
| Cordwainers | 15 | 24 |
| Labourers | 23 | 14 |
| Weavers | 2 | 0 |
| Ironfounders | 0 | 4 |
| Serjeants at mace | 3 | 0 |
| Town crier | 1 | 0 |
| Parish clerk | 1 | 0 |
| Mayor | 1 | 0 |
| Silk weavers | 1 | 5 |
| Tinplate worker | 0 | 1 |

### Voters resident outside Colchester

| Selected categories | Curtis | Mayhew |
|---|---|---|
| Weavers and silk weavers | 13 | 21 |
| Silk manufacturers | 0 | 1 |

## The Dover election of July–August 1830

The pollbook is in the Institute of Historical Research.

Result: C. Poulett Thompson, Reformer     992
Sir John Rae Reid, Tory     986
John Halcomb, Tory     748

Reid had the interest of the Lord Warden. Halcomb was a Tory barrister and the son of a coach proprietor, and stood for Dover as an Anti-Catholic candidate.

The figures in the first table are based on an analysis of the whole pollbook for the categories concerned. The figures in the second are based on an analysis of about half the pollbook.

| Selected categories | Thompson | Reid | Halcomb |
|---|---|---|---|
| Officers | 6 | 13 | 1 |
| Sextons | 2 | 2 | 0 |
| Surgeon | 7 | 10 | 1 |
| Pilots | 41 | 62 | 18 |
| Dissenting ministers | 1 | 0 | 2 |
| Butchers | 10 | 18 | 26 |
| Grocers | 23 | 13 | 24 |

| Selected categories | Thompson | Reid | Halcomb |
|---|---|---|---|
| Gentlemen | 36 | 42 | 22 |
| Victuallers | 18 | 13 | 20 |
| Carpenters | 25 | 28 | 23 |
| Cordwainers | 25 | 14 | 22 |
| Tailors | 23 | 20 | 12 |
| Mariners | 42 | 41 | 38 |
| Labourers | 18 | 23 | 22 |

## The Dover election of December 1832

The pollbook is in the Institute of Historical Research.

Result: C. P. Thompson, Liberal     713
Sir J. R. Reid, Conservative     644
John Halcomb, Conservative     523
Capt. Stanhope, R.N., Liberal     498

Freemen only:

| selected categories | Thompson | Stanhope | Reid | Halcomb |
|---|---|---|---|---|
| Officers | 3 | 2 | 3 | 0 |
| Surgeons | 1 | 1 | 5 | 1 |
| Dissenting minister | 1 | 1 | 0 | 0 |
| Parish clerks | 0 | 0 | 2 | 0 |
| Sexton | 1 | 0 | 1 | 0 |
| Pilots | 11 | 3 | 33 | 12 |
| Grocers | 12 | 11 | 8 | 13 |
| Butchers | 8 | 5 | 11 | 23 |

| Plumps | | Splits | |
|---|---|---|---|
| Thompson | 28 | Thompson and Reid | 173 |
| Reid | 200 | Thompson and Halcomb | 53 |
| Halcomb | 191 | Thompson and Stanhope | 459 |
| Stanhope | 5 | Reid and Halcomb | 258 |
| | | Reid and Stanhope | 13 |
| | | Halcomb and Stanhope | 21 |

## The Dover by-election of 1833

The pollbook is in the Institute of Historical Research.

Result: John Halcomb, Conservative     734
Capt. Stanhope, R.N., Liberal     665

Freemen only:

| selected categories | Stanhope | Halcomb |
|---|---|---|
| Gentlemen | 46 | 46 |
| Clergymen | 0 | 1 |
| Sexton | 1 | 0 |
| Parish clerks | 0 | 2 |
| Surgeons | 1 | 5 |
| Policemen | 1 | 1 |
| Officers | 2 | 2 |
| Dissenting minister | 1 | 0 |
| Innkeepers | 23 | 42 |
| Pilots | 9 | 29 |
| Tailors | 33 | 24 |
| Carpenters | 29 | 24 |
| Butchers | 5 | 24 |
| Grocers | 15 | 17 |
| Mariners | 54 | 58 |
| Cordwainers | 26 | 26 |

## The Dover election of 1835

The pollbook is in the Institute of Historical Research.

Result: J. M. Fector, Conservative     908 (a Dover man)
Sir J. R. Reid, Conservative     782
E. R. Rice, Liberal     761

Freemen only:

| selected categories | Rice | Fector | Reid |
|---|---|---|---|
| Anglican clergyman | 0 | 0 | 1 |
| Sexton | 0 | 1 | 1 |
| Parish clerks | 0 | 2 | 2 |
| Officers | 1 | 4 | 3 |
| Surgeons | 0 | 5 | 5 |
| Dissenting ministers | 1 | 1 | 0 |
| Innkeepers | 27 | 43 | 36 |
| Butchers | 11 | 19 | 19 |
| Grocers | 20 | 21 | 17 |
| Pilots | 8 | 15 | 39 |

| Plumps | | Splits | |
|---|---|---|---|
| Fector | 25 | Fector and Reid | 549 |
| Reid | 110 | Fector and Rice | 336 |
| Rice | 302 | Reid and Rice | 126 |

### The Dover election of 1837

The pollbook is in the Institute of Historical Research.

Result: E. R. Rice, Liberal 854
Sir J. R. Reid, Conservative 829
J. M. Fector, Conservative 742

Freemen only:

| selected categories | Rice | Reid | Fector |
|---|---|---|---|
| Pilots | 8 | 36 | 28 |
| Policemen | 3 | 10 | 9 |
| Parish clerks | o | 2 | 2 |
| Surgeons | o | 5 | 5 |
| Solicitors | o | 3 | 3 |
| Dissenting minister | 1 | o | o |
| Harbour master | o | 1 | o |
| Sexton | 1 | 1 | o |
| Anglican clergyman | o | 1 | 1 |
| Gaoler | o | 1 | 1 |
| Officers | o | 2 | 2 |
| Butchers | 10 | 19 | 14 |
| Grocers | 24 | 11 | 15 |
| Cordwainers | 29 | 24 | 15 |
| Mariners | 61 | 49 | 32 |
| Labourers | 36 | 36 | 26 |

| Plumps | | Splits | |
|---|---|---|---|
| Rice | 536 | Rice and Reid | 194 |
| Reid | 39 | Rice and Fector | 126 |
| Fector | 20 | Reid and Fector | 596 |

| Polled | | Unpolled | |
|---|---|---|---|
| Freemen | 1,060 | Freemen | 102 |
| £10 Electors | 451 | £10 Electors | 64 |
| | 1,511 | | |

### The Dublin City elections of 1857, 1859 and 1865

The candidates in the elections of 1857 and 1859 were:

| | 1857 | 1859 |
|---|---|---|
| Grogan (G), Conservative | 3,767 | 4,251 |
| Vance (V), Conservative | 3,711 | 4,224 |
| Brady (B), Liberal | 3,405 | 3,976 |
| Reynolds (R), Liberal | 3,348 | — |
| McCarthy (McC), Liberal | — | 3,881 |

The candidates in 1865 were:

| | |
|---|---|
| Guinness (G), Conservative | 4,739 |
| Pim (P), Liberal | 4,653 |
| Vance (V), Conservative | 4,073 |

*The Dublin City elections of 1857, 1859 and 1865 (cont.)*

I. The voting of builders

There were 43 builders on the register altogether. These voted as follows:

| No. of builders | 1857 | 1859 | 1865 |
|:---:|:---:|:---:|:---:|
| 18 | G V | G V | G V |
| 5 | R B | B McC | P |
| 2 | — | — | P |
| 4 | — | — | G V |
| 3 | R B | B McC | G P |
| 2 | — | — | G P |
| 2 | — | — | V |
| 1 | G V | G V | — |
| 3 | — | G V | G V |
| 1 | G V | — | G P |
| 1 | — | — | V P |
| 1 | G B | G V | G V |
| 43 | | | |

II. The voting of particular surnames

DONNELLY: 13 of these voted: of whom 11 voted some form of: R B, B McC, P.

MURPHY: There were 92 Murphys voting. Almost without exception they voted some form of R B, B McC, P.

WHELAN: There were 16 Whelans voting.

| | 1857 | 1859 | 1865 |
|:---:|:---:|:---:|:---:|
| 14 | R B | B McC | P |
| 1 | B | B McC | G P |
| 1 | — | — | V G |

| M'EVOY: | 1857 | 1859 | 1865 |
|:---:|:---:|:---:|:---:|
| 7 | R B | B McC | P |
| 2 | — | B McC | P |
| 1 | — | B McC | — |

| M'GRATH: | 1857 | 1859 | 1865 |
|:---:|:---:|:---:|:---:|
| 5 | R B | B McC | P |
| 1 | R B | B McC | — |

DUNNE: 54 Dunnes are given. In 11 cases, occupations are stated: these all voted some combination of G V, G V, G V. Of the 43 whose occupation is not given, 29 are some combinations of R B, B McC, P. There were 6 Patrick Dunnes, all voting some form of R B, B McC, P.

*The Dublin City elections of 1857, 1859 and 1865 (cont.)*

III.  The pollbook being very large, only certain sections of it were transcribed and sent to me. The analysis below is of about 2,500 voters whose names began with M, Mc, Mac, M', O and O', C and D, and A and part of B.

| | 1857 | | | | 1859 | | | | 1865 | | |
| --- | --- | --- | --- | --- | --- | --- | --- | --- | --- | --- | --- |
| | G | V | R | B | G | V | B | McC | G | V | P |
| Rev. Dr Cullen | 0 | 0 | 1 | 1 | 0 | 0 | 0 | 0 | 0 | 0 | 1 |
| Clergymen | 25 | 25 | 2 | 2 | 34 | 34 | 5 | 5 | 36 | 34 | 12 |
| Gentlemen | 66 | 63 | 11 | 13 | 73 | 73 | 12 | 12 | 98 | 96 | 20 |
| Surgeons | 17 | 17 | 5 | 8 | 17 | 17 | 5 | 5 | 26 | 22 | 11 |
| Lawyers | 45 | 44 | 6 | 8 | 65 | 64 | 12 | 10 | 60 | 63 | 14 |
| Minor professions | 12 | 11 | 1 | 1 | 15 | 15 | 2 | 2 | 28 | 28 | 2 |
| Merchants | 17 | 17 | 7 | 7 | 22 | 22 | 7 | 7 | 16 | 22 | 12 |
| Clerks | 6 | 6 | 0 | 0 | 11 | 11 | 0 | 0 | 26 | 30 | 3 |
| Yeomen | 12 | 12 | 1 | 1 | 15 | 14 | 3 | 2 | 13 | 15 | 4 |
| Druggists | 6 | 6 | 0 | 0 | 7 | 7 | 0 | 0 | 7 | 8 | 1 |
| Grocers, chandlers | 11 | 11 | 5 | 5 | 14 | 14 | 8 | 7 | 19 | 15 | 12 |
| Drapers, hosiers | 8 | 8 | 0 | 0 | 10 | 10 | 0 | 0 | 6 | 9 | 0 |
| Jewellers, etc. | 7 | 7 | 2 | 3 | 5 | 5 | 4 | 4 | 7 | 6 | 4 |
| Brassfounders | 7 | 7 | 1 | 1 | 8 | 8 | 3 | 3 | 10 | 11 | 6 |
| Housepainters | 6 | 6 | 1 | 1 | 6 | 6 | 0 | 0 | 9 | 9 | 1 |
| Furniture workers | 11 | 11 | 6 | 6 | 12 | 12 | 6 | 6 | 16 | 17 | 7 |
| Printers | 19 | 19 | 2 | 2 | 21 | 22 | 5 | 4 | 21 | 23 | 8 |
| Weavers, tailors | 10 | 9 | 3 | 2 | 11 | 10 | 2 | 1 | 12 | 11 | 6 |
| Tanners | 3 | 3 | 0 | 0 | 3 | 3 | 0 | 0 | 3 | 3 | 0 |
| Plumbers | 3 | 3 | 0 | 0 | 3 | 3 | 0 | 0 | 6 | 6 | 1 |
| Shoemakers | 9 | 9 | 1 | 1 | 6 | 6 | 2 | 2 | 10 | 10 | 2 |
| General unskilled | 12 | 12 | 27 | 26 | 12 | 13 | 27 | 26 | 19 | 17 | 39 |

## The Durham City election of 1832

The pollbook is in the Guildhall Library.

Result: W. C. Harland, Liberal     439
W. R. C. Chaytor, Liberal     403
Hon. A. Trevor, Conservative     383

| Freemen and householders: selected categories | Harland | Chaytor | Trevor |
| --- | --- | --- | --- |
| Anglican clergy | 5 | 3 | 15 |
| Verger | 0 | 0 | 1 |
| Organist | 0 | 0 | 1 |
| Choristers | 0 | 0 | 2 |
| Dissenting minister | 1 | 1 | 0 |
| Mayor of Durham | 1 | 1 | 0 |
| Town clerk of Durham | 1 | 1 | 0 |
| Pitmen | 2 | 2 | 5 |

## The Durham City by-election of 1843

The pollbook is in the Institute of Historical Research.

Result:           John Bright, Thos. Purvis,
                      Liberal   Conservative

| | Bright | Purvis |
|---|---|---|
| Freemen | 284 | 230 |
| £10 Householders | 204 | 180 |
| | 488 | 410 |

For all the householders, and for about one-fifth of the freemen voters, no particulars of occupations were given. All the other freemen voters appear in the table below:

| Selected categories | Bright | Purvis |
|---|---|---|
| Surgeon | 0 | 1 |
| Solicitors | 2 | 0 |
| Innkeeper | 1 | 0 |
| Butchers | 8 | 5 |
| Grocers | 2 | 0 |
| Drapers | 2 | 6 |
| Shoemakers | 28 | 22 |
| Leather crafts | 18 | 10 |
| Painters | 6 | 8 |
| Tailors | 29 | 10 |
| Masons | 25 | 22 |
| Plumbers | 7 | 6 |
| Ropers | 9 | 2 |
| Smiths | 8 | 3 |
| Weavers | 4 | 0 |
| Wood workers | 33 | 26 |
| Pitmen | 4 | 1 |
| Labourers | 3 | 3 |
| Others | 15 | 11 |

The Anglican clergy voted as ten-pound householders as follows:

| | Bright | Purvis | Abstained |
|---|---|---|---|
| Anglican clergy | 1 | 13 | 6 |

## The Durham (North) election of 1868

The pollbook is in Cambridge University Library.

Result:  G. Elliot, Conservative      4,649
           Sir H. Williamson, Liberal   4,011
           I. L. Bell, Liberal      3,822

Voting of clergy

| For Williamson | 20 |
|---|---|
| For Bell | 19 |
| For Elliot | 68 |
| Abstained | 9 |

## The Durham (South) election of 1868

The pollbook is in Cambridge University Library.

Result: J. W. Pease, Liberal     4,321
    F. E. B. Beaumont, Liberal  4,021
    C. F. Surtees, Conservative  3,726
    Hon. G. R. Hamilton-Russell,
     Conservative     3,215

Voting of clergy
 For Pease   6
 For Beaumont  5
 For Surtees  84
 For Russell  84
 Abstained   26 (mostly living outside the county)

## The Edinburgh election of 1852

The pollbook is in the Guildhall Library.

Result: Macaulay, Liberal     1,872
   Cowan, Liberal     1,754
   Provost Maclaren, Liberal  1,559
   Bruce, Conservative   1,066
   Campbell, Liberal-Conservative 626

| Selected categories | Macaulay | Cowan | Provost Maclaren | Campbell | Bruce |
|---|---|---|---|---|---|
| Manufacturers | 4 | 3 | 4 | 1 | 0 |
| Merchants | 59 | 73 | 42 | 27 | 29 |
| Surgeons | 35 | 29 | 11 | 9 | 13 |
| Writers | 40 | 33 | 8 | 5 | 29 |
| Shoemakers | 37 | 33 | 46 | 15 | 14 |
| Grocers | 60 | 58 | 56 | 19 | 19 |
| Clergy and ministers | 6 | 16 | 13 | 9 | 11 |
| Bankers | 4 | 14 | 1 | 9 | 11 |
| Police | 2 | 1 | 1 | 0 | 1 |
| Railwaymen | 1 | 1 | 0 | 0 | 0 |

## The Essex (East) election of 1868

The pollbook is in the Guildhall Library. It does not give occupations, but clergymen can be identified by their prefix.

Result: James Round, Conservative  2,861
   S. B. Ruggles-Brise, Conservative 2,816
   Sir T. B. Western, Liberal   2,224
   Sir T. N. Abdy, Liberal    2,134

| | Western | Abdy | Round | Brise |
|---|---|---|---|---|
| Clergy | 12 | 12 | 176 | 177 |

## The Exeter election of April 1831

The pollbook is in the Guildhall Library.

Result: Wentworth Buller, Whig 753
Buck, Tory 548
Divett, Whig 379

Resident voters only:*

| selected categories | Buller | Buck | Divett |
|---|---|---|---|
| Gentlemen | 37 | 30 | 17 |
| Shoemakers | 15 | 10 | 9 |
| Weaver | 1 | 0 | 1 |
| Labourers | 3 | 3 | 3 |
| Clergy | 7 | 13 | 3 |
| Vergers | 0 | 3 | 0 |
| Lay vicars | 2 | 2 | 0 |
| Surgeons | 7 | 9 | 0 |
| Fullers | 32 | 26 | 11 |
| Wool and worsted manufacturers | 3 | 4 | 1 |
| Parish clerks | 2 | 3 | 0 |
| Town crier | 1 | 1 | 0 |
| Aldermen | 3 | 3 | 0 |
| Serjeants at mace | 1 | 3 | 0 |
| Governor of workhouse | 1 | 1 | 0 |
| Sheriff's officers | 2 | 2 | 0 |
| Dissenting minister | 1 | 0 | 1 |
| Fringe manufacturer | 1 | 1 | 0 |
| Starch manufacturer | 1 | 1 | 0 |

* This excludes out-voters.

## The Glasgow election of 1832

The pollbook is in Manchester Public Library.

Result: James Ewing 3,214
James Oswald 2,838
Sir D. K. Sandford 2,168
John Crawfurd 1,850
John Douglas 1,340
Joseph Dixon 995

| Selected categories | Ewing | Oswald | Sandford | Crawfurd | Dixon | Douglas |
|---|---|---|---|---|---|---|
| Ministers* | 28 | 7 | 6 | 7 | 2 | 6 |
| Surgeons | 57 | 47 | 48 | 43 | 13 | 33 |
| Manufacturers | 203 | 158 | 99 | 80 | 41 | 24 |
| Merchants | 474 | 310 | 144 | 126 | 131 | 46 |
| Cotton merchants | 13 | 17 | 2 | 5 | 1 | 0 |
| Cotton spinners | 13 | 13 | 0 | 2 | 0 | 1 |

* The Rev. Dr Ralph Wardlaw plumped for Ewing. The R.C. bishop voted for Ewing and Oswald.

*The Glasgow election of 1832 (cont.)*

| Selected categories | Ewing | Oswald | Sandford | Crawfurd | Dixon | Douglas |
|---|---|---|---|---|---|---|
| Weavers | 23 | 28 | 81 | 39 | 16 | 65 |
| Brewers | 9 | 6 | 8 | 2 | 4 | 5 |
| Victuallers | 38 | 46 | 47 | 37 | 23 | 25 |
| Grocers | 105 | 114 | 140 | 95 | 41 | 79 |
| Shoemakers | 48 | 41 | 51 | 40 | 16 | 32 |
| Farmers | 12 | 15 | 1 | 5 | 1 | 2 |

The *Annual Register* commented on this election: 'In Glasgow...a strong but unsuccessful battle was fought for Radicalism. It selected for its members an accomplished and moderate-minded merchant, and gave him for his colleague a practised Whig.'

### The Grantham election of 1865

The pollbook is in the Bodleian Library.

Result: Thorold, Conservative  432
Welby, Conservative  404
Tollemache, Liberal  315

| Selected categories | Tollemache | Thorold | Welby |
|---|---|---|---|
| Grocers | 13 | 12 | 11 |
| Butchers | 17 | 10 | 12 |
| Shoemakers | 16 | 8 | 6 |
| Surgeons | 4 | 6 | 7 |
| Farmers | 12 | 33 | 32 |
| Railwaymen | 0 | 3 | 3 |
| Organist | 1 | 0 | 0 |
| R.C. priest | 1 | 0 | 0 |
| Clergymen | 1 | 5 | 6 |
| Sexton | 0 | 1 | 1 |
| Wesleyan minister | 0 | 1 | 1 |

### The Halifax election of 1847

The pollbook is in Manchester Public Library.

Result: Henry Edwards, Conservative  511
Sir C. Wood, Whig  507
E. Miall, Radical  351
E. Jones, Chartist  280

#### I. Drink

| | Jones | Miall | Wood | Edwards |
|---|---|---|---|---|
| Spirit merchants | 0 | 1 | 7 | 7 |
| Publicans | 8 | 7 | 27 | 30 |
| Brewer | 0 | 0 | 0 | 1 |
| Beersellers | 3 | 3 | 6 | 8 |
| Coopers | 0 | 0 | 2 | 2 |

*The Halifax election of 1847 (cont.)*

### II. Upper crust and dependants

|  | Jones | Miall | Wood | Edwards |
|---|---|---|---|---|
| Gentlemen | 1 | 2 | 9 | 13 |
| Solicitors | 1 | 1 | 10 | 13 |
| Doctors | 1 | 1 | 11 | 12 |
| Clergy | 3 | 3 | 4 | 4 |
| Architects | 0 | 0 | 2 | 2 |
| Surveyors | 0 | 0 | 4 | 4 |
| Schoolmasters | 2 | 3 | 1 | 2 |
| Clerks | 0 | 1 | 3 | 3 |
| Farmers | 2 | 1 | 3 | 4 |
| Sexton | 0 | 0 | 1 | 1 |
| Gardeners | 0 | 0 | 1 | 3 |
| Other respectables* | 5 | 7 | 24 | 26 |

* Registrar, dentist, relieving officer, accountant, artists, inspector, bank manager, vet., insurance agents, stockbrokers, bailiffs, auctioneers, music teachers, designers, opticians.

### III. Textiles, all classes

|  | Jones | Miall | Wood | Edwards |
|---|---|---|---|---|
| Cardmakers | 4 | 8 | 12 | 8 |
| Dyers | 7 | 6 | 7 | 7 |
| Manufacturers | 7 | 15 | 22 | 15 |
| Woolstaplers | 2 | 8 | 19 | 13 |
| Carpet weaver | 1 | 1 | 0 | 0 |
| Cloth dresser | 0 | 0 | 1 | 0 |
| Worsted spinners | 1 | 2 | 2 | 1 |

### IV. Business, except textiles

|  | Jones | Miall | Wood | Edwards |
|---|---|---|---|---|
| Organbuilders | 0 | 0 | 2 | 2 |
| Coachmakers | 0 | 0 | 2 | 2 |
| Corn millers and dealers | 7 | 7 | 10 | 8 |
| Ironfounders | 0 | 0 | 5 | 5 |
| Merchants | 1 | 1 | 8 | 8 |
| Others | 2 | 4 | 7 | 4 |

### V. Crafts

|  | Jones | Miall | Wood | Edwards |
|---|---|---|---|---|
| Watchmakers | 2 | 1 | 6 | 3 |
| Light metal crafts | 7 | 9 | 7 | 3 |
| Leather | 6 | 11 | 11 | 7 |
| Building trades | 4 | 5 | 3 | 5 |
| Blacksmiths | 2 | 2 | 1 | 1 |
| Machine makers | 6 | 6 | 3 | 2 |
| Cloggers | 6 | 4 | 2 | 2 |
| Tailors | 10 | 8 | 6 | 4 |
| Shoemakers | 4 | 6 | 9 | 7 |

*The Halifax election of 1847 (cont.)*

### V. Crafts (*cont.*)

|  | Jones | Miall | Wood | Edwards |
|---|---|---|---|---|
| Woodworkers | 5 | 9 | 11 | 11 |
| Printers | 3 | 3 | 2 | 2 |
| Plumbers | 2 | 2 | 2 | 4 |
| Others* | 4 | 9 | 2 | 6 |

\* Cork, basket, button, rope trades, carver, gilder.

### VI. Shopkeepers

|  | Jones | Miall | Wood | Edwards |
|---|---|---|---|---|
| Grocers and general | 37 | 37 | 22 | 19 |
| Hatters | 3 | 3 | 2 | 2 |
| Booksellers | 3 | 3 | 5 | 5 |
| Drapers | 14 | 17 | 9 | 7 |
| Tobacconists | 1 | 1 | 2 | 2 |
| Butchers | 1 | 1 | 6 | 7 |
| Hairdressers | 6 | 5 | 5 | 3 |
| Furniture | 2 | 3 | 1 | 0 |
| Milkman | 1 | 1 | 0 | 0 |
| Druggists | 3 | 2 | 6 | 5 |
| Clothes brokers | 3 | 3 | 1 | 2 |
| Ironmongers | 3 | 4 | 3 | 2 |
| Pawnbrokers | 2 | 2 | 1 | 1 |

### VII. Unclassified*

| Jones | Miall | Wood | Edwards |
|---|---|---|---|
| 78 | 102 | 158 | 180 |

Summary:

|  | Jones | Miall | Wood | Edwards |
|---|---|---|---|---|
| I. Drink | 11 | 11 | 42 | 48 |
| II. Upper crust | 10 | 12 | 48 | 61 |
| III. Textiles | 22 | 40 | 63 | 44 |
| IV. Other business | 10 | 12 | 34 | 29 |
| V. Crafts | 59 | 75 | 65 | 57 |
| VI. Shopkeepers | 79 | 82 | 63 | 55 |
| VII. Unclassified | 78 | 102 | 158 | 180 |

\* I.e. occupations not stated in the pollbook.

Reg. no. of Electors   1,022

| Edwards: | plumps | 108 |
|---|---|---|
|  | and Wood | 370 |
|  | and Miall | 19 |
|  | and Jones | 14 |
| Wood: | plumps | 60 |
|  | and Edwards | 370 |
|  | and Miall | 59 |
|  | and Jones | 14 |
| Miall: | plumps | 26 |
|  | and Jones | 245 |
| Jones: | plumps | 3 |
|  | and Miall | 245 |

## The Hereford City election of 1826

The pollbook is in the Institute of Historical Research.

Result: The Rt. Hon. John Somers, Viscount Eastnor, Tory 667
           E. B. Clive, Whig                      453
           R. Blakemore, Tory               437

| Selected categories | Clive | Eastnor | Blakemore |
|---|---|---|---|
| Gentlemen | 73 | 129 | 75 |
| Clergymen | 13 | 35 | 25 |
| Officers | 5 | 11 | 5 |
| Surgeons | 3 | 6 | 4 |
| Victuallers | 33 | 42 | 31 |
| Farmers | 31 | 29 | 14 |
| Tailors | 26 | 33 | 19 |
| Shoemakers | 25 | 36 | 27 |
| Grocers | 12 | 15 | 4 |
| Butchers | 9 | 16 | 11 |
| Weavers | 2 | 8 | 6 |
| Labourers | 26 | 36 | 25 |

## The Hereford City election of 1832

The pollbook is in the Institute of Historical Research.

Result: E. B. Clive, Liberal        392
      Robert Biddulph, Liberal    380
      R. Blakemore, Conservative   245

Freemen and £10 householders:

| selected categories | Clive | Biddulph | Blakemore |
|---|---|---|---|
| Gentlemen | 38 | 37 | 19 |
| Clergymen | 6 | 6 | 14 |
| Officers | 2 | 2 | 2 |
| Surgeons | 2 | 2 | 1 |
| Farmers | 16 | 17 | 3 |
| Victuallers | 16 | 12 | 17 |
| Beersellers | 1 | 2 | 0 |
| Grocers | 26 | 27 | 4 |
| Butchers | 12 | 11 | 9 |
| Tailors | 21 | 21 | 15 |
| Shoemakers | 13 | 14 | 15 |
| Lawyers | 5 | 6 | 6 |
| Weavers | 1 | 1 | 2 |
| Labourers | 14 | 13 | 21 |
| Dissenting minister | 1 | 1 | 0 |
| Verger | 0 | 0 | 1 |
| Sexton | 0 | 0 | 1 |

### The Hereford City election of 1835

The pollbook is in the Institute of Historical Research.

Result: E. B. Clive, Liberal      457    Plumps:   4
Robt. Biddulph, Liberal     435            3
R. Blakemore, Conservative   426        301

Freemen voters:

| selected categories | Clive | Biddulph | Blakemore |
|---|---|---|---|
| Gentlemen | 30 | 23 | 23 |
| Clergymen | 9 | 8 | 19 |
| Officers | 3 | 3 | 5 |
| Surgeon | 0 | 0 | 1 |
| Solicitors | 12 | 9 | 11 |
| Farmers | 12 | 11 | 8 |
| Grocers | 9 | 9 | 2 |
| Butchers | 6 | 5 | 8 |
| Tailors | 12 | 11 | 13 |
| Victuallers | 11 | 12 | 28 |
| Weavers | 0 | 0 | 4 |
| Labourers | 8 | 8 | 8 |

£10 householders:

| selected categories | Clive | Biddulph | Blakemore |
|---|---|---|---|
| Gentlemen | 20 | 21 | 7 |
| Clergymen* | 7 | 6 | 7 |
| Officers | 2 | 1 | 2 |
| Surgeons | 7 | 6 | 1 |
| Solicitors | 6 | 6 | 3 |
| Bankers | 1 | 1 | 0 |
| Farmers | 18 | 15 | 7 |
| Grocers | 15 | 16 | 4 |
| Butchers | 5 | 7 | 9 |
| Tailors | 14 | 8 | 10 |
| Victuallers | 4 | 5 | 9 |
| Labourers | 3 | 4 | 4 |
| Verger | 0 | 0 | 1 |
| Dissenting ministers | 2 | 2 | 0 |

\* The Dean of Hereford voted for Blakemore.

### The Herefordshire election of 1868

The pollbook is in the Guildhall Library. It does not give occupations.

Result: Sir H. Croft, Conservative    3,351
Sir J. R. Bailey, Conservative   3,341
M. Biddulph, Liberal         2,273
Thomas Blake, Liberal       1,878

| | Biddulph | Blake | Croft | Bailey |
|---|---|---|---|---|
| Clergy | 15 | 7 | 61 | 61 |

### The Hertfordshire election of December 1832

The pollbook is in the Guildhall Library. It does not state occupations.

Result: Sir J. S. Sebright, Bart, Liberal    2,154
        N. Calvert, Liberal    2,141
        Viscount Grimston, Conservative    2,074
        R. Alston, Liberal    2,007

|  | Sebright | Calvert | Alston | Grimston |
|---|---|---|---|---|
| Clergy | 25 | 27 | 20 | 64 |

### The Huddersfield election of 1834

The pollbook is in Huddersfield Public Library.

Result: John Blackburne, K.C., Liberal    234
       Michael T. Sadler, Conservative    147
       Capt. Joseph Wood, Liberal    108

| All voters | Wood | Blackburne | Sadler |
|---|---|---|---|
| Merchants and manufacturers | 10 | 44 | 20 |
| Woolstaplers | 0 | 11 | 16 |
| Cloth drawers | 0 | 4 | 0 |
| Cloth dressers | 0 | 15 | 8 |
| Innkeepers and beersellers | 22 | 16 | 5 |
| Farmers | 7 | 8 | 13 |
| Tailors | 5 | 3 | 3 |
| Shoemakers | 5 | 0 | 4 |
| Corn dealers | 2 | 0 | 3 |
| Butchers | 3 | 2 | 2 |
| Ironmongers | 2 | 0 | 3 |
| Leather trades | 1 | 8 | 1 |
| Maltsters | 1 | 0 | 5 |
| Grocers | 23 | 14 | 6 |
| Druggists | 0 | 3 | 2 |
| Drapers, hatters | 10 | 2 | 4 |
| Clergy | 0 | 0 | 3 |
| Attorneys | 0 | 8 | 5 |
| Surgeons | 0 | 6 | 2 |
| Yarn dealers | 0 | 5 | 1 |
| Ironfounders | 0 | 2 | 0 |
| Dyers | 0 | 7 | 1 |
| Joiners, painters, masons, plasterers | 1 | 15 | 4 |
| Plumbers, glaziers | 0 | 4 | 0 |
| Miscellaneous | 17 | 51 | 34 |

The 1834 pollbook contains these remarks:

'Who does Lawyer Blackburne represent? Why, not the men of Huddersfield, under the haggard form of a few dead body-bill doctors, factory-mongers, Mushroom Merchants, and their Myrmidons, who are instinctively against the

*The Huddersfield election of 1834 (cont.)*

people, as the shark is against the herring...However, that these Sharks of Society may be known, in order to be avoided as much as possible, the following "List of Voters" is published, so that every Patriot may distinguish his Friend from his Enemy.'

'They [£10 voters] have a second time set aside the man of your choice. Yes; and they glory in the deed. If these new Boroughmongers will have the power exclusively, let them enjoy their trade after the same Reforming fashion. Touch their POCKETS, and their spurious INDEPENDENCE will lick the dust...by this you will conquer. Remember, and never forget, that *labour* is the only earthly handmaid of wealth, power, and safety. You, the unrepresented, are the BEES: let the DRONES take care of themselves till they learn to whom the hive belongs...'

### The Huddersfield election of 1837

The pollbook is in Huddersfield Public Library.

Result: Edward Ellice, jun., Liberal    340
Richard Oastler, Conservative    290

| All voters | Edward Ellice, jun. | Oastler |
|---|---|---|
| Merchants and manufacturers | 51 | 24 |
| Banker | 0 | 1 |
| Attorneys | 7 | 6 |
| Surgeons | 7 | 4 |
| Magistrates | 0 | 2 |
| Farmers | 7 | 51 |
| Ironfounders, machine makers | 6 | 0 |
| Sir J. Ramsden's agents | 6 | 0 |
| Innkeepers, etc. | 25 | 38 |
| Spirit merchants | 4 | 4 |
| Grocers | 21 | 20 |
| Corn dealers | 2 | 3 |
| Tailors | 7 | 5 |
| Shoemakers, cloggers | 5 | 11 |
| Drapers, hatters | 14 | 10 |
| Druggists | 5 | 1 |
| Butchers | 6 | 4 |
| Booksellers, stationers | 4 | 4 |
| Masons, painters, joiners, plasterers | 19 | 9 |
| Woolstaplers | 13 | 20 |
| Tinner, brazier, ironmongers | 5 | 6 |
| Hairdressers | 1 | 3 |
| Heald and slay makers | 2 | 2 |
| Cloth dressers and drawers | 28 | 13 |
| Clothes dealers | 2 | 4 |
| Coopers | 1 | 3 |
| Dyers | 11 | 2 |
| Leather crafts | 5 | 0 |
| Clock and watch makers | 4 | 0 |
| Miscellaneous | 56 | 40 |

*The Huddersfield election of 1837 (cont.)*

The 1837 pollbook concludes with this message:

'In the above list you may behold your opponents in their true colours:— there are the determined supporters of Bastiles and bad government in all its shapes... Is it for this we have formed an Anti-Poor Law Association? Is it for this we have organized the surrounding Hamlets for the purpose of making every possible resistance to the introduction of the "Starvation Law"?... Thus they despise the poor and send their enemies to Parliament, to make laws for their further oppression... it is neither your duty nor your interest to support them; but directly the reverse. The WAY to their brains is through their pockets —FIND IT.'

### The Hull election of 29–30 July 1830

The pollbook is in the Guildhall Library.

Result: G. Schonswar, Tory     1,564
W. B. Wrightson, Whig   1,213
T. G. Burke, Whig          869

Schonswar was an Alderman and former Mayor of Hull, a Justice of the Peace and Deputy Lieutenant for the East Riding.

Voters A–D inclusive only

|  | Wrightson | Burke | Schonswar |
|---|---|---|---|
| Mariners | 23 | 37 | 43 |
| Shipwrights | 21 | 32 | 35 |

Voters A–Z

| Selected categories | Wrightson | Burke | Schonswar |
|---|---|---|---|
| Cordwainers | 36 | 30 | 45 |
| Officers | 2 | 2 | 4 |
| Merchants | 20 | 6 | 57 |
| Butchers | 30 | 29 | 32 |
| Grocers | 10 | 5 | 10 |
| Pilots | 3 | 2 | 11 |
| Shipbuilders | 1 | 0 | 4 |
| Victuallers | 10 | 6 | 10 |
| Gaoler | 0 | 0 | 1 |
| Town clerk | 0 | 0 | 1 |
| Surgeons | 3 | 0 | 5 |
| Sexton | 0 | 0 | 1 |
| Mayor's officers | 1 | 0 | 3 |
| Shipowners | 3 | 0 | 2 |
| Police | 1 | 0 | 1 |
| Beadle | 0 | 0 | 1 |
| 'Commodore of the pilots' | 0 | 0 | 1 |

### The Huntingdon election of 1832

The pollbook is in the Institute of Historical Research.

Result: Col. F. Peel, Conservative   177
F. Pollock, Conservative   171
Capt. Duberly, Liberal   128
E. Maltby, Liberal   94

| Selected categories | Duberly | Peel |
|---|---|---|
| Gentlemen | 13 | 17 |
| Doctor | 1 | 0 |
| Solicitors | 2 | 4 |
| Teachers | 2 | 3 |
| Servants | 2 | 16 |
| Surveyor | 1 | 0 |
| Builders | 1 | 1 |
| Brewers | 4 | 2 |
| Merchants* | 7 | 15 |
| Publicans | 9 | 14 |
| Shoemakers | 5 | 12 |
| Tailors† | 11 | 6 |
| Building crafts‡ | 16 | 27 |
| Metal crafts§ | 4 | 7 |
| Minor crafts** | 22 | 21 |
| Grocers | 4 | 7 |
| Druggist | 1 | 1 |
| Jeweller | 1 | 0 |
| Ironmongers | 1 | 2 |
| Drapers | 3 | 2 |
| Butchers | 5 | 7 |
| Bakers | 9 | 9 |
| Coachmaker | 1 | 0 |

State of the poll

| | Liberal | | Conservative | |
|---|---|---|---|---|
| | Duberly | Maltby | Peel | Pollock |
| Huntingdon Old Electors (Burgesses) | 5 | 4 | 61 | 62 |
| Huntingdon electors newly enfranchised | 59 | 49 | 73 | 71 |
| Godmanchester electors | 64 | 41 | 43 | 38 |

   * Includes millers, corn factors, wholesalers.
   † Includes glovers.
   ‡ Includes woodworkers and painters.
   § Includes watchmakers.
 ** Includes cottagers and handymen.

## The Ipswich election of 1832

The pollbook is in Manchester University Library.

Result: Morrison, Liberal 594
Wason, Liberal 593
E. Goulburn, Conservative 308
Fitzroy Kelly, Conservative 265
C. Mackinnon, Conservative 94

| Selected categories | Morrison | Wason | Goulburn | Kelly | Mackinnon |
|---|---|---|---|---|---|
| Gentlemen | 45 | 43 | 29 | 25 | 11 |
| Lawyers | 5 | 5 | 9 | 7 | 5 |
| Physicians | 5 | 5 | 4 | 4 | 0 |
| Dissenting ministers | 3 | 2 | 0 | 0 | 0 |
| Brewers | 7 | 7 | 0 | 0 | 0 |
| Publicans | 30 | 31 | 10 | 10 | 3 |
| Farmers | 8 | 8 | 16 | 14 | 2 |
| Grocers | 15 | 17 | 11 | 11 | 0 |
| Butchers | 14 | 14 | 5 | 5 | 0 |
| Shoemakers | 27 | 27 | 11 | 9 | 1 |
| Shipwrights | 4 | 4 | 3 | 3 | 0 |
| Mariners | 29 | 29 | 11 | 10 | 4 |

## The Ipswich election of 1835

The pollbook is in Manchester University Library.

Result: Morrison, Liberal 542
Wason, Liberal 533
Broke, Conservative 454
Holmes, Conservative 434

| New Constituency | | Old Constituency | |
|---|---|---|---|
| Morrison | 393 | Morrison | 149 |
| Wason | 385 | Wason | 148 |
| Broke | 291 | Broke | 163 |
| Holmes | 274 | Holmes | 160 |

| Selected categories | Morrison | Wason | Broke | Holmes |
|---|---|---|---|---|
| Gentlemen | 50 | 50 | 66 | 66 |
| Lawyers | 3 | 3 | 13 | 10 |
| Physicians | 8 | 6 | 5 | 3 |
| Dissenting ministers | 3 | 3 | 0 | 0 |
| Brewers | 4 | 4 | 1 | 1 |
| Publicans | 21 | 21 | 21 | 21 |
| Beersellers | 3 | 3 | 0 | 0 |
| Farmers | 4 | 3 | 19 | 18 |
| Grocers | 17 | 17 | 13 | 11 |
| Butchers | 12 | 12 | 14 | 11 |
| Shoemakers | 17 | 17 | 13 | 12 |
| Shipwrights | 4 | 4 | 1 | 1 |
| Mariners | 39 | 38 | 21 | 20 |
| Master mariners | 4 | 4 | 0 | 0 |
| Parish clerk | 0 | 0 | 1 | 1 |
| Sweep | 0 | 0 | 1 | 1 |

### The Ipswich election of 1847

There are two pollbooks covering this election, one in Manchester University Library, the other in the Institute of Historical Research.

Result: J. C. Cobbold, Tory    829
H. E. Adair, Liberal    708
Capt. Gladstone, Tory    661
H. Vincent, Radical    546

The following table is based on the pollbook in Manchester University Library.

| Selected categories | Vincent | Adair | Cobbold | Gladstone |
|---|---|---|---|---|
| Gentlemen | 17 | 33 | 54 | 48 |
| Bankers | 1 | 1 | 3 | 2 |
| Lawyers | 2 | 6 | 12 | 12 |
| Physicians | 4 | 7 | 15 | 12 |
| Dissenting ministers | 8 | 8 | 0 | 0 |
| R.C. priest | 0 | 1 | 0 | 0 |
| Brewers | 8 | 8 | 3 | 3 |
| Publicans and beersellers | 17 | 30 | 55 | 46 |
| Farmers | 6 | 7 | 34 | 32 |
| Grocers | 29 | 31 | 14 | 10 |
| Butchers | 10 | 16 | 20 | 19 |
| Shoemakers | 25 | 28 | 18 | 14 |
| Shipwrights | 9 | 7 | 8 | 6 |
| Mariners | 23 | 27 | 22 | 20 |
| Master mariners | 0 | 2 | 2 | 1 |
| Pilots | 0 | 1 | 4 | 3 |
| Railwaymen | 1 | 1 | 5 | 3 |
| Parish clerk | 0 | 0 | 1 | 0 |
| Organists | 0 | 1 | 2 | 1 |

The following analysis is based on the pollbook in the Institute of Historical Research.

Composition of Vincent's vote

| Plumps | 52 |
|---|---|
| and Adair | 453 |
| and Cobbold | 29 |
| and Gladstone | 12 |

I. Respectables

| Gentlemen | 42 |
|---|---|
| Shipbuilders | 4 |
| Merchants, etc. | 26 |
| Brewers | 8 |
| Surgeons | 4 |
| Banker | 1 |
| Builders | 4 |
| Dissenting ministers | 8 |
| Police officer | 1 |
| Coachmakers | 4 |
| Schoolmasters | 3 |
| Shipowner | 1 |
| Maltsters | 4 |
| Commercial professions | 22 |
| Farmers | 6 |
| | 138 |

II. Trade

| Shopkeepers | 119 |
|---|---|
| Milkmen | 4 |
| Publicans | 10 |
| Beersellers | 8 |
| | 141 |

*The Ipswich election of 1847 (cont.)*

III. Crafts

| | |
|---|---|
| Shoemakers | 24 |
| Tailors | 29 |
| Building, etc. | 19 |
| Metal crafts | 29 |
| Shipwrights | 9 |
| Minor crafts | 37 |
| Mariners | 21 |

| | |
|---|---|
| Woodworkers | 53 |
| | 221 |

IV. Others

| | |
|---|---|
| Cordwainers and servants | 13 |
| Labourers | 24 |
| Miscellaneous | 7 |
| | 44 |

## The Ipswich election of 1852

The pollbook is in the Institute of Historical Research.

Result: J. C. Cobbold, Conservative 810
H. E. Adair, Liberal 784
S. Bateson, Conservative 727
T. B. Hobhouse, Liberal 725

| Selected categories | Adair | Hobhouse | Cobbold | Bateson |
|---|---|---|---|---|
| Clergymen | 3 | 1 | 12 | 11 |
| Parish clerk | 0 | 0 | 1 | 1 |
| Organist | 1 | 0 | 1 | 0 |
| Dissenting ministers | 6 | 6 | 0 | 0 |
| Gentlemen | 46 | 41 | 67 | 64 |
| Lawyers | 7 | 5 | 17 | 16 |
| Surgeons | 6 | 5 | 15 | 14 |
| Bankers | 3 | 3 | 2 | 2 |
| Farmers | 11 | 9 | 35 | 31 |
| Publicans | 25 | 24 | 37 | 32 |
| Beersellers | 6 | 5 | 5 | 3 |
| Brewers | 8 | 7 | 3 | 3 |
| Mariners | 21 | 21 | 32 | 32 |
| Shipwrights | 7 | 6 | 8 | 7 |
| Pilots | 0 | 0 | 3 | 3 |
| Butchers | 19 | 18 | 16 | 15 |
| Grocers | 30 | 28 | 21 | 16 |
| Shoemakers | 30 | 29 | 16 | 18 |
| Railwaymen | 1 | 2 | 9 | 8 |
| Labourers | 22 | 21 | 7 | 5 |

## The Ipswich election of 1857

The pollbook is in the Institute of Historical Research.

Result: J. C. Cobbold, Conservative 779
H. E. Adair, Liberal 759
J. C. Marshman, Liberal 738
H. J. Selwin, Conservative 707

| Selected categories | Adair | Marshman | Cobbold | Selwin |
|---|---|---|---|---|
| Clergymen | 2 | 2 | 3 | 3 |
| Organists | 1 | 1 | 1 | 1 |
| Sexton | 0 | 0 | 1 | 1 |

*The Ipswich election of 1857 (cont.)*

| Selected categories | Adair | Marshman | Cobbold | Selwin |
|---|---|---|---|---|
| R.C. priest | 1 | 0 | 0 | 0 |
| Dissenting ministers | 7 | 7 | 0 | 0 |
| Surgeons | 7 | 6 | 16 | 16 |
| Bankers | 3 | 3 | 1 | 1 |
| Ironfounders | 7 | 7 | 2 | 2 |
| Mariners | 16 | 15 | 22 | 19 |
| Shipwrights | 3 | 8 | 9 | 3 |
| Pilots | 0 | 0 | 4 | 4 |
| Railwaymen | 4 | 4 | 7 | 5 |
| Labourers | 15 | 15 | 6 | 6 |

## The Ipswich election of 1859

The pollbook is in the Institute of Historical Research.

Result: J. C. Cobbold, Conservative 915
H. E. Adair, Liberal 862
H. J. Selwin, Conservative 837
John King, Liberal 386

| Selected categories | Adair | King | Cobbold | Selwin |
|---|---|---|---|---|
| Dissenting ministers | 7 | 4 | 0 | 0 |
| R.C. priest | 1 | 0 | 0 | 0 |
| Organist | 0 | 0 | 1 | 1 |
| Sexton | 0 | 0 | 1 | 1 |
| Officers | 1 | 0 | 5 | 4 |
| Pilots | 0 | 0 | 4 | 4 |
| Mariners | 14 | 7 | 41 | 38 |
| Shipwrights | 4 | 1 | 14 | 13 |
| Brewers | 7 | 1 | 3 | 3 |
| Publicans | 39 | 13 | 78 | 76 |
| Gentlemen | 92 | 42 | 99 | 90 |
| Lawyers | 8 | 3 | 24 | 23 |
| Surgeons | 6 | 2 | 17 | 17 |
| Bankers | 3 | 0 | 4 | 4 |
| Ironfounders | 11 | 4 | 5 | 5 |
| Farmers | 13 | 7 | 26 | 24 |
| Grocers | 33 | 17 | 23 | 21 |
| Butchers | 20 | 11 | 15 | 15 |
| Shoemakers | 33 | 26 | 21 | 16 |
| Railway personnel* | 4 | 0 | 5 | 4 |
| Tailors | 29 | 18 | 12 | 10 |
| Labourers | 23 | 8 | 11 | 12 |
| Carpenters | 23 | 13 | 21 | 21 |
| Harbourmaster | 1 | 1 | 0 | 0 |

\* The stationmaster plumped for Adair.

There were two manufacturers of shoes who voted Liberal; none voted Tory. Probably some of the shoemakers listed above were their employees.

*The Ipswich election of 1859 (cont.)*

Analysis of the vote

| Plumps | | Splits | |
|---|---|---|---|
| Adair | 354 | Adair and King | 382 |
| Cobbold | 9 | Adair and Cobbold | 104 |
| Selwin | 14 | Adair and Selwin | 21 |
| King | 4 | Cobbold and Selwin | 802 |
| | | King and Cobbold | 0 |
| | | King and Selwin | 0 |

A prefatory letter by Adair contains this remark: '...and I gratefully acknowledge the active cooperation and assistance which I have received from the Non-Electors of this Borough.'

## The Ipswich election of 1865

The pollbook is in the Institute of Historical Research.

Result: H. E. Adair, Liberal        990
J. C. Cobbold, Conservative  913
West, Liberal                        905
Tidmas, Conservative         776

| Selected categories | West | Tidmas |
|---|---|---|
| Gentlemen | 86 | 81 |
| Bankers | 2 | 2 |
| Surgeons or physicians | 9 | 17 |
| Brewers | 11 | 5 |
| Publicans | 36 | 71 |
| Beersellers | 2 | 5 |
| Railwaymen | 2 | 4 |
| Grocers | 30 | 24 |
| Shoemakers | 31 | 16 |
| Dissenting clergy | 9 | 0 |
| Sexton | 0 | 1 |
| R.C. priest* | 0 | 1 |
| Fisherman | 1 | 0 |
| Pilot | 0 | 1 |
| Shipwrights | 6 | 4 |
| Sailmakers | 1 | 2 |
| Engineers | 13 | 4 |
| Machinists | 3 | 0 |
| Mariners | 9 | 24 |
| Boatbuilder | 1 | 0 |
| Shipowners | 3 | 1 |
| Saddlers | 6 | 4 |
| Shipbuilders | 1 | 1 |
| Ironfounders | 4 | 3 |
| Boilermaker | 1 | 0 |
| Foundrymen | 2 | 0 |
| Waterman | 0 | 1 |

\* The priest voted for both Tory candidates.

### The Ipswich election of 1868

The pollbook is in the Institute of Historical Research.

Result: H. E. Adair, Liberal      2,321
         West, Liberal      2,195
       J. C. Cobbold, Conservative      2,044

| Selected categories | Adair | Cobbold |
|---|---|---|
| Gentlemen | 118 | 100 |
| Bankers | 3 | 1 |
| Surgeons or physicians | 11 | 14 |
| Brewers | 6 | 6 |
| Publicans | 15 | 71 |
| Beersellers | 10 | 19 |
| Railwaymen | 32 | 31 |
| Bargeman | 0 | 1 |
| Labourers | 186 | 160 |
| Shoemakers | 134 | 37 |
| Turnkeys | 5 | 2 |
| Sweeps | 0 | 4 |
| Dissenting ministers | 9 | 0 |
| Anglican clergy | 0 | 14 |
| R.C. priest | 0 | 1 |
| Saddlers | 5 | 4 |
| Mariners | 32 | 140 |
| Shipwrights | 6 | 38 |
| Pilots | 0 | 8 |
| Pilot master | 0 | 1 |
| Ship carpenters | 0 | 2 |
| Sailmakers | 3 | 7 |
| Boilermakers | 12 | 0 |
| Mastmakers | 0 | 2 |
| Foundrymen | 10 | 1 |
| Fishermen | 2 | 4 |
| Ironfounders | 8 | 5 |
| Postmen | 5 | 7 |
| Lightermen | 0 | 2 |
| Exciseman | 0 | 1 |
| Dredgerman | 0 | 1 |
| Watermen | 0 | 5 |

### The Lancaster election of 1865

The pollbook is in Manchester Public Library. No clerical votes were recorded in the pollbook. Occupations were only stated for the freemen voters (about 1,000), not for the £10 householders (about 300).

Result: Fenwick, Liberal          713
        Schneider, Liberal        687
        Lawrence, Conservative  665

Freemen only:

| selected categories | Fenwick | Lawrence |
|---|---|---|
| Gentlemen | 17 | 25 |
| Surgeons | 1 | 2 |
| Lawyers | 4 | 10 |
| Farmers | 24 | 54 |
| Innkeepers | 2 | 3 |
| Railway employees* | 4 | 2 |
| Shoemakers | 20 | 11 |
| Weavers† | 7 | 1 |
| Woolcombers | 4 | 2 |
| Cotton spinners | 7 | 3 |
| Silk spinners | 6 | 2 |
| Silk piecers | 3 | 1 |
| Silk combers | 3 | 0 |
| Silk boiler | 1 | 0 |
| Silk dressers | 4 | 1 |

\* The stationmaster voted Tory.

† All engaged in textile occupations are listed in the table.

The most numerous classes not listed in the table were fishermen, mariners, husbandmen, labourers, and metal craftsmen.

| Plumps | | Splits | |
|---|---|---|---|
| Fenwick | 2 | Fenwick and Schneider | 670 |
| Schneider | 2 | Lawrence and Fenwick | 41 |
| Lawrence | 609 | Schneider and Lawrence | 15 |

Of these, the £10 householders voted thus:

Fenwick     252
Schneider   244
Lawrence    170

The freemen voted thus:

| | Town | Country |
|---|---|---|
| Fenwick | 308 | 153 |
| Schneider | 299 | 144 |
| Lawrence | 295 | 200 |

No. on Register  1,419
No. voted        1,339
Turnout          94 %

### The Leeds election of 1834

Result: Edward Baines, Liberal     1,951
       Sir J. Beckett, Conservative    1,917
       Joshua Bower, Liberal        24

The votes analysed are those polled in Leeds township proper, which included about three-quarters of the electorate. Only those voters with names beginning A to M inclusive were analysed: it was felt that this was a sufficient and typical sample. About 400 voters of unclassifiable or unstated occupation, fairly evenly divided between parties, are not listed.

### Leeds township

| I. Occupations unconnected with textiles | Liberal | Conservative |
|---|---|---|
| Brewers and maltsters | 6 | 3 |
| Publicans | 25 | 47 |
| Beersellers | 4 | 7 |
| Shopkeepers | 139 | 120 |
| Building crafts | 31 | 24 |
| Metal crafts | 43 | 24 |
| Minor crafts | 50 | 30 |
| Shoemakers | 11 | 6 |
| Tailors | 16 | 18 |
| Gentlemen | 21 | 36 |
| Military and Naval officers | 1 | 2 |
| Medical | 4 | 19 |
| Legal | 8 | 16 |
| Bankers | 1 | 4 |
| Schoolmasters | 9 | 8 |
| Printers | 9 | 0 |
| Farmers | 2 | 6 |
| Commercial professions | 34 | 40 |
| General merchants | 69 | 69 |
| Builders | 3 | 14 |
| Mustard manufacturer | 0 | 1 |
| Servants, labourers | 7 | 18 |
| Anglican clergy | 0 | 7 |
| Sexton | 0 | 1 |
| Comb manufacturer | 1 | 0 |
| Tobacco manufacturers | 4 | 0 |
| **II. Textile vote** | | |
| Callenderers* | 2 | 0 |
| Textile merchants | 30 | 12 |
| Woolstaplers | 15 | 15 |
| Dyers* | 24 | 19 |
| Cloth dressers* | 10 | 4 |
| Flax dressers* | 2 | 2 |
| Flax spinners* | 4 | 0 |
| Worsted spinner* | 1 | 0 |

\* Probably operatives.

*The Leeds election of 1834 (cont.)*

|  | Liberal | Conservative |
|---|---|---|
| **II. Textile votes *(cont.)*** | | |
| Woolsorters* | 3 | 0 |
| Cloth drawers* | 2 | 0 |
| Overlookers* | 5 | 3 |
| Stuff manufacturers | 5 | 2 |
| Cloth manufacturers | 8 | 8 |
| Cloth glosser* | 1 | 0 |
| Linen manufacturers | 1 | 1 |
| Woollen printer* | 1 | 0 |
| Carpet manufacturers | 0 | 2 |
| Stocking manufacturer | 0 | 1 |
| Buckram manufacturer | 0 | 1 |
| Worsted manufacturers | 1 | 1 |
| Cloth miller | 0 | 1 |
| Stuff dresser | 0 | 1 |
| Stuff printer | 0 | 1 |
| Flax manufacturers | 2 | 1 |
|  | 117 | 75 |

* Probably operatives.

The following table gives an exhaustive analysis of the votes polled for the Out-townships of Leeds (Hunslet, Holbeck, Beeston, Wortley, Armley, Farnley, Bramley, Headingley, Potternewton, and Chapel Allerton).

### Out-townships

| I. Occupations unconnected with textiles | Liberal | Conservative |
|---|---|---|
| Building and wood crafts | 20 | 28 |
| Metal crafts | 36 | 26 |
| Minor crafts | 20 | 17 |
| Shoemakers | 16 | 2 |
| Tailors | 8 | 1 |
| Anglican clergy | 0 | 7 |
| Dissenting minister | 1 | 0 |
| Methodist minister | 1 | 0 |
| Schoolmasters | 5 | 3 |
| Publicans | 19 | 47 |
| Beersellers | 10 | 11 |
| Brewers and maltsters | 18 | 18 |
| Gentlemen | 16 | 32 |
| Medical | 5 | 3 |
| Legal | 0 | 3 |
| Bankers | 1 | 1 |
| Official and commercial | 16 | 14 |
| Farmers | 15 | 91 |
| Servants, labourers | 15 | 23 |
| Miscellaneous | 47 | 38 |
| Shopkeepers | 82 | 48 |
| Merchants, wholesalers | 17 | 25 |
| Tobacco manufacturer | 0 | 1 |

*The Leeds election of 1834 (cont.)*

| II. Textile votes | Liberal | Conservative |
|---|---|---|
| Cloth manufacturer | 62 | 46 |
| Clothiers | 99 | 84 |
| Cloth makers | 4 | 2 |
| Woolsorters* | 1 | 2 |
| Dyers* | 4 | 3 |
| Textile merchants | 6 | 6 |
| Overlookers* | 5 | 1 |
| 'Manufacturers' | 21 | 37 |
| Slubbers* | 1 | 1 |
| Cloth dressers* | 0 | 2 |
| Cloth drawers* | 4 | 0 |
| Cloth millers* | 2 | 0 |
| Bleacher | 1 | 0 |
| Silk manufacturer | 1 | 0 |
| Flax manufacturer | 1 | 0 |
| Flax spinners* | 5 | 0 |
| Woolstapler | 3 | 0 |
| | 220 | 184 |

\* Probably operatives.

## The Leeds election of 1847

The pollbook is in the Bodleian Library. Occupations are not stated, but the type of property qualifying a voter is included.

| Result: | Wm. Beckett, Conservative | 2,529 |
|---|---|---|
| | J. G. Marshall, Whig | 2,172 |
| | Joseph Sturge, Radical | 1,978 |

| Selected categories of property | Sturge | Marshall | Beckett |
|---|---|---|---|
| Factory or Mill | 112 | 75 | 85 |
| Foundry, machine shop | 11 | 15 | 12 |
| Sawmill | 2 | 3 | 3 |
| Chemical works | 4 | 5 | 3 |
| Dyehouse | 11 | 20 | 22 |
| Quarry | 1 | 2 | 3 |
| Tanhouse | 0 | 1 | 1 |
| Coalpit | 0 | 1 | 1 |

Some types of commercial or productive property—warehouses, brewhouses, offices, maltkilns, and small workshops—are not included in the above table, though data were available. Nevertheless, this table is a sufficient and illuminating indication of the extent to which the Leeds business world supported Sturge's pacifist radicalism.

## The Leicester Borough election of 1832

The pollbook is in the Guildhall Library.

Result: Evans, Liberal                    1,663 (of whom 256 were non-resident)
        Wynn Ellis, Liberal               1,527 (of whom 226 were non-resident)
        Boughton Leigh, Conservative      1,266 (of whom 243 were non-resident)

| Resident voters: selected categories | Evans | Ellis | Leigh |
|---|---|---|---|
| Clergy | 0 | 0 | 2 |
| Dissenting ministers | 5 | 5 | 0 |
| Parish clerks | 1 | 0 | 2 |
| Engineers | 1 | 2 | 0 |
| Woolstaplers | 15 | 15 | 5 |
| Manufacturer | 0 | 0 | 1 |
| Shoemakers | 43 | 45 | 35 |
| Gentlemen | 43 | 28 | 71 |
| Framework knitters | 273 | 270 | 83 |

## The Leicester Borough election of 1847

The pollbook is in the Guildhall Library.

Result: Sir J. Walmesley, Liberal   1,657
        R. Gardner, Liberal         1,614
        Jas. Parker, Conservative   1,423

The non-resident freemen voters (who are omitted from the analysis) polled: for Walmesley 130, for Gardner 127, for Parker 239.

| Resident voters: selected categories | Walmesley | Gardner | Parker |
|---|---|---|---|
| Surgeons | 8 | 7 | 17 |
| Shoemakers | 62 | 62 | 44 |
| Framework knitters | 233 | 238 | 81 |
| Labourers | 17 | 17 | 30 |
| Butchers | 23 | 23 | 36 |
| Grocers | 66 | 63 | 31 |
| Clergymen | 0 | 0 | 5 |
| Dissenting ministers | 6 | 6 | 1 |
| Clerk to Leicester Union | 0 | 0 | 1 |
| Woolstaplers | 2 | 2 | 0 |
| Engineers | 7 | 7 | 0 |
| Policemen | 8 | 8 | 0 |
| Gentlemen | 61 | 64 | 112 |
| Ironfounders | 3 | 3 | 2 |
| Sexton | 1 | 0 | 1 |
| Manufacturers | 14 | 14 | 3 |
| Banker | 0 | 0 | 1 |
| Gaoler | 0 | 0 | 1 |
| R.C. priest | 1 | 1 | 0 |

## The Leicester election of 1859

The pollbook is in the Guildhall Library.

Result: John Biggs, Liberal — 1,584
J. W. Noble, Liberal — 1,496
W. U. Heygate, Conservative — 1,479
J. D. Harris, Liberal — 1,397

### Whole pollbook

| Selected categories | Biggs | Noble | Harris | Heygate |
|---|---|---|---|---|
| Anglican clergy | 2 | 2 | 6 | 9 |
| Ministers | 4 | 0 | 8 | 0 |
| Parish clerk | 0 | 0 | 0 | 1 |
| Methodist minister | 0 | 0 | 1 | 0 |
| Organist | 0 | 1 | 0 | 1 |
| Baptist minister | 0 | 0 | 1 | 1 |
| Saddlers | 1 | 2 | 2 | 4 |
| Ironfounders | 2 | 3 | 6 | 7 |
| Engineers | 9 | 6 | 7 | 4 |
| Bankers | 1 | 0 | 2 | 2 |
| Surgeons | 7 | 14 | 12 | 15 |
| Warp hands | 11 | 11 | 6 | 2 |
| Labourers | 8 | 17 | 28 | 41 |
| Shoe manufacturers | 6 | 6 | 2 | 2 |
| Framesmiths | 30 | 24 | 14 | 5 |
| Loomhands | 4 | 2 | 8 | 1 |
| Woolstaplers | 20 | 13 | 15 | 10 |
| Framework knitters | 205 | 201 | 56 | 63 |
| Manufacturers | 59 | 43 | 38 | 26 |
| Woolcombers | 21 | 17 | 8 | 5 |
| Spinners | 12 | 5 | 17 | 9 |
| Beersellers | 9 | 15 | 2 | 5 |

### Electors of first four wards only
(pages 1–33 only of pollbook)

| Selected categories | Biggs | Noble | Harris | Heygate |
|---|---|---|---|---|
| Gentlemen | 32 | 19 | 47 | 51 |
| Shoemakers | 33 | 31 | 12 | 13 |
| Hosiers | 17 | 15 | 24 | 21 |
| Grocers | 42 | 33 | 40 | 30 |
| Butchers | 21 | 30 | 10 | 31 |
| Victuallers | 53 | 72 | 3 | 51 |
| Warehousemen | 5 | 5 | 8 | 5 |

## The Leicester Borough by-election of 1861

Result: W. U. Heygate, Conservative — 1,596
J. D. Harris, Liberal — 1,033
P. A. Taylor, Liberal — 977

Those in the first table below were analysed only for pages 1–13, or the first four wards, of the pollbook, and may therefore be untypical, though there is no

*The Leicester Borough by-election of 1861 (cont.)*

special reason to think so. Those in the second table were analysed for the whole of the pollbook, including out-voters. The occupations of about 50 people were omitted by the pollbook.

| Selected categories | Harris | Taylor | Heygate |
|---|---|---|---|
| Gentlemen | 4 | 5 | 13 |
| Shoemakers | 11 | 18 | 6 |
| Victuallers | 2 | 29 | 28 |
| Framework knitters | 23 | 60 | 18 |
| Shoe manufacturers | 1 | 4 | 4 |

| Selected categories | Harris | Taylor | Heygate |
|---|---|---|---|
| Surgeons | 8 | 3 | 13 |
| Manufacturers | 55 | 23 | 22 |
| Labourers | 4 | 11 | 62* |
| Dissenting ministers | 14 | 1 | 2 |
| Engineers | 6 | 3 | 4 |
| Railwaymen | 0 | 0 | 1 |
| Clergymen | 1 | 0 | 6 |
| Parish clerk | 0 | 0 | 1 |
| Turnkeys | 0 | 0 | 2 |
| Ironfounders | 3 | 0 | 3 |

\* These labourers were mostly non-resident freemen voters from the villages

### The Leicestershire election of August 1830

The pollbook is in the Institute of Historical Research.

Result: G. A. L. Keck, Conservative     3,517 } sitting members
       Lord Robert Manners, Conservative   3,000 }
       Thomas Paget, Liberal            2,203

The last contested election had been in 1775.

| Selected categories | Paget | Keck | Manners |
|---|---|---|---|
| Physicians | 14 | 37 | 32 |
| Officers | 0 | 3 | 3 |
| Bankers | 1 | 5 | 5 |
| Dissenting ministers | 13 | 4 | 2 |
| Parish clerks | 0 | 4 | 4 |
| Anglican clergy | 8 | 147 | 143 |
| Worsted spinners | 15 | 10 | 4 |
| Woolcombers | 9 | 7 | 3 |
| Woolstaplers | 9 | 15 | 11 |
| Weavers | 8 | 12 | 12 |
| Lace manufacturers | 33 | 7 | 5 |
| Lace makers | 39 | 11 | 6 |
| Hosiers | 67 | 45 | 31 |
| Framework knitters | 245 | 143 | 87 |

### The Leicestershire (South) election of 1841

The pollbook is in the Guildhall Library. It does not give occupations of voters, but the names of clergy are indicated by the prefix 'Rev.'.

Result: H. Halford, Conservative 2,638
C. W. Packe, Conservative 2,622
T. Gisborne, Liberal 1,213
Col. E. H. Cheney, Liberal 1,196

|  | Gisborne | Cheney | Halford | Packe | Abstained |
|---|---|---|---|---|---|
| Clergy | 2 | 2 | 40 | 40 | 28 |

### The Leicestershire (South) election of 1867

The pollbook is in the Guildhall Library. It does not give occupations of voters.

Result: T. T. Paget, Liberal 2,302
A. Pell, Conservative 2,263

|  | Paget | Pell | Abstained |
|---|---|---|---|
| Clergy | 20 | 78 | 16 |

### The Lewes election of 1835

The pollbook is in the Library of the Society of Genealogists.

Result: Sir Charles R. Blunt, Liberal 511
Thomas R. Kemp, Liberal 382
Hon. Henry Fitzroy, Conservative 359

| Selected categories | Blunt | Kemp | Fitzroy |
|---|---|---|---|
| Gentlemen | 24 | 23 | 12 |
| Clergymen | 1 | 1 | 3 |
| Dissenting ministers | 4 | 4 | 0 |
| Surgeons | 5 | 3 | 4 |
| Lawyers | 3 | 3 | 4 |
| Bankers | 1 | 1 | 2 |
| Grocers | 13 | 8 | 7 |
| Publicans | 11 | 10 | 7 |
| Beersellers | 2 | 1 | 5 |
| Shoemakers | 26 | 24 | 11 |
| Painters | 2 | 1 | 4 |
| Turnkeys | 0 | 1 | 2 |
| Labourers | 24 | 4 | 26 |

## The Lewes by-election of 1837

The pollbook is in the Library of the Society of Genealogists.

Result: Hon. H. Fitzroy, Conservative    397
John Easthope, Liberal                   371

| Selected categories | Easthope | Fitzroy |
|---|---|---|
| Gentlemen | 24 | 22 |
| Clergymen | 0 | 4 |
| Dissenting ministers | 4 | 1 |
| Surgeons | 1 | 5 |
| Lawyers | 6 | 4 |
| Bankers | 1 | 2 |
| Millers | 3 | 2 |
| Grocers | 7 | 11 |
| Butchers | 11 | 12 |
| Publicans | 9 | 7 |
| Beersellers | 2 | 3 |
| Shoemakers | 27 | 18 |
| Tailors | 17 | 12 |
| Carpenters | 29 | 11 |
| Painters | 4 | 6 |
| Parish clerk | 0 | 1 |
| Bargemasters | 1 | 1 |
| Bargemen | 6 | 2 |
| Turnkeys | 0 | 3 |
| Labourers | 14 | 17 |

## The Lewes election of 1841

The pollbook is in the Guildhall Library.

Result: Summers Harford, Liberal         411
H. Elphinstone, Liberal                  409
Hon. Henry Fitzroy, Conservative 407
Viscount Cantilupe, Conservative 388

On petition Mr Harford was unseated.

| Selected categories | Harford | Elphinstone | Fitzroy | Cantilupe |
|---|---|---|---|---|
| Gentlemen | 21 | 21 | 24 | 24 |
| Lawyers | 5 | 5 | 5 | 5 |
| Surgeons | 2 | 2 | 5 | 5 |
| Bankers | 1 | 1 | 2 | 2 |
| Parish clerks | 0 | 1 | 2 | 1 |
| Farmers | 2 | 2 | 5 | 4 |
| Dissenting ministers | 2 | 2 | 1 | 1 |
| Innkeepers | 10 | 9 | 9 | 8 |
| Beersellers | 4 | 4 | 2 | 2 |
| Shoemakers | 29 | 26 | 24 | 18 |
| Carpenters | 31 | 33 | 11 | 11 |
| Butchers | 12 | 13 | 10 | 9 |

*The Lewes election of 1841 (cont.)*

| Selected categories | Harford | Elphinstone | Fitzroy | Cantilupe |
|---|---|---|---|---|
| Grocers | 8 | 8 | 11 | 11 |
| Turnkeys | 1 | 0 | 5 | 4 |
| Bargemasters | 1 | 0 | 2 | 2 |
| Bargemen | 5 | 5 | 1 | 1 |

### The Lincoln City election of 1835

The pollbook is in the Guildhall Library.

Result: Bulwer, Liberal       562
Sibthorp, Conservative   406
Phipps, Liberal          335

| Freemen only:* selected categories | Bulwer | Phipps | Sibthorp |
|---|---|---|---|
| Surgeons | 1 | 1 | 4 |
| Shoemakers | 13 | 9 | 20 |
| Butchers | 6 | 5 | 9 |
| Grocers | 8 | 7 | 6 |
| Clergymen | 2 | 1 | 5 |
| Farmers | 4 | 3 | 33 |
| Labourers | 9 | 6 | 38 |
| Watermen | 6 | 4 | 11 |
| Sheriff's officers | 1 | 1 | 2 |
| Aldermen | 3 | 3 | 7 |
| Mayor | 0 | 0 | 1 |

* The table excludes £10 householders, whose occupations were not stated.

### The Lincoln City election of 1841

The pollbook is in the Guildhall Library.

Result: Sibthorp, Conservative   541
Collett, Conservative    481
Bulwer, Liberal          443
Seely, Liberal           340

| Freemen only: selected categories | Bulwer | Sibthorp | Collett | Seely |
|---|---|---|---|---|
| Surgeons | 1 | 3 | 2 | 0 |
| Shoemakers | 17 | 22 | 24 | 11 |
| Butchers | 4 | 6 | 5 | 3 |
| Grocers | 7 | 6 | 4 | 6 |
| Clergy | 0 | 1 | 1 | 0 |
| Farmers | 11 | 23 | 17 | 5 |
| Labourers | 11 | 40 | 42 | 10 |
| Watermen | 5 | 7 | 7 | 5 |
| Sheriff's officer | 0 | 1 | 1 | 0 |

## The Lincoln City election of 1848

The pollbook is in the Guildhall Library.

Result: Thomas B. Hobhouse, Liberal    552
L. C. Humphrey, Conservative    550

Freemen only:

| selected categories | Hobhouse | Humphrey |
|---|---|---|
| Surgeons | 0 | 3 |
| Shoemakers | 16 | 18 |
| Butchers | 6 | 7 |
| Grocers | 1 | 5 |
| Farmers | 5 | 16 |
| Watermen | 11 | 5 |
| Town clerk | 1 | 0 |
| Labourers | 25 | 33 |

## The Lincoln City election of 1859

The pollbook is in the Bodleian Library.

Result: Sibthorp, Conservative    740
Heneage, Liberal    658
Palmer, Liberal    629

Freemen only:

| selected categories | Heneage | Palmer | Sibthorp |
|---|---|---|---|
| Shoemakers | 17 | 11 | 20 |
| Gentlemen | 7 | 2 | 7 |
| Grocers | 3 | 0 | 4 |
| Farmers | 17 | 2 | 15 |
| Labourers | 23 | 22 | 31 |
| Publicans | 4 | 1 | 3 |
| Lawyers | 5 | 0 | 7 |
| Stonemasons | 4 | 3 | 5 |
| Basketmakers | 0 | 3 | 0 |
| Ironmoulder | 0 | 1 | 0 |
| Tailors | 6 | 6 | 6 |
| Watermen | 5 | 5 | 4 |
| Butchers | 9 | 3 | 9 |
| Merchants | 6 | 3 | 6 |
| Surgeons | 3 | 0 | 4 |

### The Lincoln City election of 1862

The pollbook is in the Bodleian Library.

Result: J. B. Moore, Conservative   715
        J. H. Palmer, Liberal       690

| Freemen only: selected categories | Palmer | Moore |
|---|---|---|
| Shoemakers | 14 | 16 |
| Grocers | 0 | 7 |
| Farmers | 5 | 18 |
| Labourers | 27 | 43 |
| Publicans | 1 | 3 |
| Boilermakers | 5 | 0 |
| Stonemasons | 3 | 5 |
| Basketmakers | 5 | 0 |
| Ironmoulder | 1 | 0 |
| Tailors | 9 | 7 |
| Gentlemen | 3 | 8 |
| Watermen | 2 | 8 |
| Butchers | 7 | 8 |
| Lawyers | 0 | 7 |
| Merchants | 2 | 5 |
| Surgeons | 0 | 6 |
| Turnkey | 0 | 1 |

### The Lincoln City election of 1865

The pollbook is in the Bodleian Library.

Result: C. Seely, Liberal          878
        E. Heneage, Liberal        870
        J. B. Moore, Conservative  765

| Freemen only: selected categories | Seely | Heneage | Moore |
|---|---|---|---|
| Shoemakers | 14 | 14 | 18 |
| Grocers | 1 | 2 | 5 |
| Farmers | 9 | 12 | 12 |
| Lawyers | 0 | 0 | 6 |
| Labourers | 50 | 52 | 34 |
| Publicans | 3 | 3 | 4 |
| Basketmakers | 4 | 4 | 1 |
| Ironmoulders | 2 | 2 | 0 |
| Tailors | 8 | 9 | 8 |
| Gentlemen | 4 | 6 | 7 |
| Watermen | 6 | 6 | 6 |
| Butchers | 7 | 8 | 8 |
| Boilermakers | 3 | 3 | 0 |
| Stonemasons | 4 | 3 | 3 |
| Merchants | 7 | 7 | 4 |
| Surgeons | 1 | 3 | 6 |
| Turnkey | 0 | 0 | 1 |

### The Lincolnshire by-election of 1823

The pollbook is in Peterborough Public Library.

Result: Ingilby    3,816
        Thorold    1,575

Ingilby represented the Whig influence of the Yarborough family, and Thorold campaigned in the name of the independence of the freeholders. The following analysis by hundreds is instructive in showing the territorial character of electoral allegiance.

|  | Ingilby | Thorold |
|---|---|---|
| **Holland** | | |
| Skirbeck | 205 | 99 |
| Kirton | 165 | 54 |
| Elloe | 181 | 37 |
| **Kesteven** | | |
| Boothby Graffoe | 21 | 142 |
| Langoe* | 99 | 94 |
| Flaxwell | 34 | 73 |
| Aswardhurn | 14 | 83 |
| Winnibriggs | 3 | 68 |
| Soke of Grantham | 1 | 132 |
| Loveden | 5 | 226 |
| **Lindsey** | | |
| Manley | 611 | 22 |
| Yarborough | 431 | 6 |
| Bradley | 175 | 5 |
| Ludborough | 13 | 2 |
| Louth Eske | 220 | 31 |
| Walshcroft | 145 | 4 |
| Calceworth | 144 | 13 |
| Candleshoe | 164 | 4 |
| Wraggoe | 44 | 19 |
| Gartree | 85 | 38 |
| Horncastle | 151 | 37 |
| Hill | 60 | 1 |
| Bolingbroke | 139 | 13 |
| Aslacoe | ? | ? |
| Well | 48 | 27 |
| Lawres | 192 | 23 |
| Corringham | 268 | 62 |
| Aveland | 19 | 105 |
| Beltisloe | 7 | 47 |
| Ness | 22 | 49 |

Even when one takes a hundred which was apparently evenly divided, a further breakdown reveals that this even division arises mainly from a chance equality between groups of villages which themselves voted largely en bloc.

\* See following table.

*The Lincolnshire by-election of 1823 (cont.)*

Analysis of Langoe Hundred in Kesteven by villages

| | Ingilby | Thorold |
|---|---|---|
| Billinghay | 1 | 49 |
| Blankney | 3 | 0 |
| Dunston | 6 | 0 |
| Dogdike | 3 | 3 |
| Heighington | 23 | 0 |
| Kyme | 1 | 7 |
| Hanworth | 6 | 1 |
| Kirkby Green | 1 | 0 |
| Metheringham | 9 | 7 |
| Martin | 11 | 1 |
| Necton | 1 | 0 |
| Scopwick | 6 | 0 |
| Timberland | 4 | 7 |
| Walcot | 8 | 20 |
| Washingborough | 17 | 0 |

## The Lincolnshire (South) election of 1841

The pollbook is in the Guildhall Library. It does not state the occupations of voters.

Result: C. Turnor, Conservative 4,579
Sir John Trollope, Bt., Conservative 4,564
Henry Handley, Liberal 2,960

| | Handley | Turnor | Trollope |
|---|---|---|---|
| Clergy | 16 | 106 | 109 |

## The Lindsey election of 1835

The pollbook is in the Guildhall Library.

Result: Hon. C. A. W. Pelham, Liberal 4,489
T. G. Corbett, Conservative 4,450
Sir W. A. Ingilby, Bt., Liberal 3,984

| Selected categories | Pelham | Ingilby | Corbett |
|---|---|---|---|
| Parish clerks | 26 | 14 | 39 |
| Cordwainers | 73 | 87 | 57 |
| Clergymen | 75 | 15 | 148 |
| Ministers | 5 | 9 | 1 |
| Surgeons | 30 | 22 | 30 |
| Grocers | 46 | 46 | 35 |
| Merchants | 22 | 21 | 32 |
| Weavers | 15 | 17 | 19 |
| Engineers | 2 | 2 | 1 |
| Fishermen | 6 | 0 | 4 |
| R.C. priests | 2 | 1 | 0 |
| Shipbuilder | 0 | 1 | 0 |
| Machine maker | 1 | 1 | 0 |
| Gaolers | 2 | 0 | 2 |

*The Lindsey election of 1835 (cont.)*

The introduction to the pollbook states: '. . . in every town throughout the county, committees of tradesmen were formed to secure the return of Sir William Ingilby: to counteract this, the principal farmers in most parishes exerted themselves with an ardour worthy of the cause they espoused, and to the exertions of the agriculturists, and the agriculturists alone, is this glorious victory to be attributed.'

### The Lindsey election of 1852

Result: The Rt. Hon. R. A. Christopher, Conservative    5,585
        J. B. Stanhope, Conservative    5,577
        Sir M. Cholmeley, Liberal    4,777

For about one-third of the total number of electors in the pollbook, no particulars of occupations are stated. The voting recorded below therefore might not be typical of the whole constituency: though there is no special reason to suggest this. The figures for clergymen are however probably nearly comprehensive, being based on the prefix 'Rev.' appearing before the name.

| Selected categories | Stanhope | Cholmeley | Christopher |
|---|---|---|---|
| Pages 1–22 of pollbook | | | |
| Farmers | 217 | 165 | 250 |
| Millers | 3 | 7 | 7 |
| Brewers | 4 | 2 | 4 |
| Innkeepers | 8 | 11 | 12 |
| Clergymen | 11 | 1 | 13 |
| Parish clerks | 2 | 1 | 3 |
| Dissenting ministers | 0 | 2 | 0 |
| Surgeons | 4 | 2 | 4 |
| Lawyers | 5 | 6 | 6 |
| Grocers | 2 | 6 | 3 |
| Butchers | 11 | 8 | 13 |
| Tailors | 5 | 13 | 6 |
| Cordwainers | 3 | 9 | 8 |
| Mariners | 1 | 6 | 0 |
| Whole pollbook | | | |
| Clergymen | 133 | 60 | 170 |
| Parish clerks | 9 | 7 | 10 |
| Dissenting ministers | 0 | 3 | 0 |
| Surgeons | 15 | 17 | 19 |
| Lawyers | 27 | 19 | 29 |
| Millers | 29 | 40 | 35 |
| Brewers | 8 | 10 | 7 |
| Innkeepers | 64 | 59 | 65 |
| Grocers | 30 | 30 | 32 |
| Butchers | 30 | 32 | 37 |
| Tailors | 20 | 44 | 22 |
| Cordwainers | 41 | 70 | 41 |
| Mariners | 1 | 17 | 2 |

| Plumps | | Splits | |
|---|---|---|---|
| Christopher | 158 | Christopher and Stanhope | 4,578 |
| Stanhope | 115 | Christopher and Cholmeley | 850 |
| Cholmeley | 3,037 | Stanhope and Cholmeley | 882 |

## The Liverpool by-election of November 1830*

The pollbook is in the Institute of Historical Research. It gives (page 80) its own occupational analysis of voting which, slightly abridged, is as follows:

Result:† J. E. Denison, Tory   2,106
Wm. Ewart, Reformer 2,019

Out-voters: Ewart   345
Denison   367

|  | Ewart | Denison |
|---|---|---|
| Gentlemen, merchants, brokers | 241 | 382 |
| Accountants, bookkeepers | 79 | 67 |
| Printers, stationers, etc. | 24 | 24 |
| Shipwrights, boatbuilders | 297 | 249 |
| Sailmakers | 89 | 98 |
| Coopers | 164 | 170 |
| Mariners, pilots, riggers‡ | 67 | 104 |
| Ropers, flaxdressers, etc. | 129 | 148 |
| Blockmakers | 55 | 86 |
| Woodworkers | 228 | 139 |
| Painters, plumbers | 66 | 58 |
| Ironmongers, smiths | 59 | 62 |
| Masons, bricklayers | 128 | 115 |
| Cordwainers | 57 | 26 |
| Jewellers, watchmakers | 64 | 40 |
| Butchers, bakers | 33 | 44 |
| Tallow chandlers | 23 | 24 |
| Brushmakers, tobacconists | 34 | 34 |
| Barbers, tailors, drapers | 32 | 29 |
| Hatters, saddlers, pawnbrokers | 38 | 28 |
| Ironfounders, engineers | 47 | 24 |
| Curriers and tanners | 229§ | 7 |
| Braziers and tinmen | 37 | 28 |
| Potters, pipemakers | 16 | 12 |
| Labourers, servants | 36 | 23 |
| Druggists, silversmiths | 15 | 13 |
| Dyers, furriers | 17 | 13 |
| Teachers | 14 | 15 |
| Hosiers | 14 | 17 |
| Divers others | 94 | 113 |
|  | 2,019 | 2,106 |

* On the death of Mr Huskisson.
† Other authorities such as Bean and Dod give the result as Ewart, Whig, 2,215, Denison, Whig, 2,186.
‡ According to my own calculations from the pollbook, the pilots voted as follows:

Ewart   9
Denison   39

§ This figure is certainly wildly wrong.

## The Liverpool election of 1832

Result: Ewart, Liberal     4,931
Lord Sandon, Conservative     4,260
Thornely, Liberal     4,096
Sir H. Douglas, Conservative     3,249

The voting of the following occupations was only analysed as far as the bottom of page 44 of the pollbook (to the name 'Isaac, John Edmund'), and there abandoned as a sufficiently large and typical sample of the whole.

| | Ewart | Thornely | Sandon | Douglas |
|---|---|---|---|---|
| Gentlemen | 128 | 107 | 84 | 61 |
| Merchants | 151 | 118 | 175 | 135 |
| Grocers | 53 | 42 | 19 | 10 |

All the votes cast by the members of the occupations below have been analysed as follows:

| | Ewart | Thornely | Sandon | Douglas |
|---|---|---|---|---|
| **I. Manufacture** | | | | |
| Sugar refiners | 4 | 4 | 4 | 4 |
| Soap manufacturers | 6 | 6 | 4 | 4 |
| Glass manufacturers | 1 | 1 | 4 | 4 |
| Tobacco manufacturers | 7 | 5 | 4 | 3 |
| Ironfounders | 21 | 18 | 15 | 13 |
| Organbuilders | 2 | 1 | 1 | 3 |
| **II. Mercantile** | | | | |
| Bankers | 13 | 11 | 13 | 8 |
| Corn merchants | 20 | 20 | 9 | 6 |
| Cotton brokers | 18 | 17 | 13 | 11 |
| Timber merchants | 27 | 24 | 26 | 24 |
| **III. Professions** | | | | |
| Clergy and ministers* | 20 | 16 | 33 | 28 |
| Surgeons, physicians | 66 | 57 | 41 | 30 |
| Lawyers | 24 | 18 | 36 | 29 |
| Royal Navy | 3 | 3 | 9 | 6 |
| Architects | 7 | 7 | 9 | 8 |
| Organists | 0 | 0 | 2 | 2 |
| Sexton | 0 | 0 | 1 | 1 |
| **IV.** | | | | |
| Innkeepers | 316 | 269 | 118 | 63 |
| Tailors | 94 | 81 | 52 | 29 |
| Butchers | 58 | 48 | 47 | 29 |
| Farmers | 3 | 3 | 2 | 2 |
| **V. Marine** | | | | |
| Master mariners | 14 | 9 | 24 | 16 |
| Mariners | 57 | 51 | 71 | 59 |
| Sailmakers | 61 | 47 | 86 | 76 |
| Pilots | 11 | 6 | 34 | 23 |
| Shipwrights† | 61 | 39 | 320 | 287 |

* The Rev. Jabez Bunting, the 'Methodist Pope', plumped for Lord Sandon. The future radicals, William Rathbone and Robertson Gladstone, on this occasion each split their votes between Sandon and Ewart.

† This includes only shipwrights voting by virtue of a qualification as freemen. The very few shipwrights voting as £10 householders have been omitted.

*The Liverpool election of 1832 (cont.)*

## Summary

The pollbook itself contains a general summary of voting at this election, which is reproduced here as it stands. No detailed breakdown was given in the pollbook.

A. Gentry, clergy, merchants, bankers, brokers, medical and legal professions, wine merchants and wholesale dealers:

| | |
|---|---|
| Ewart, Liberal | 1,134 |
| Thornely, Liberal | 922 |
| Sandon, Conservative | 1,187 |
| Douglas, Conservative | 912 |

B. Tradesmen including innkeepers

| | |
|---|---|
| Ewart | 2,244 |
| Thornely | 1,859 |
| Sandon | 1,322 |
| Douglas | 945 |

C. Mechanics, shipwrights, coopers, sailmakers, etc.

| | |
|---|---|
| Ewart | 1,553 |
| Thornely | 1,315 |
| Sandon | 1,751 |
| Douglas | 1,392 |

## The Liverpool election of 1835

The pollbook is in the Institute of Historical Research.

| Result: | | |
|---|---|---|
| Lord Sandon, Conservative | 4,407 |
| Wm. Ewart, Liberal | 4,075 |
| Sir Howard Douglas, Bt., Conservative | 3,869 |
| James Morris, Liberal | 3,627 |

| Selected categories | Ewart | Morris | Sandon | Douglas |
|---|---|---|---|---|
| Anglican clergy | 4 | 5 | 30 | 27 |
| Dissenting ministers | 13 | 13 | 2 | 1 |
| Servants | 0 | 0 | 4 | 3 |
| Labourers* | 89 | 76 | 60 | 54 |
| Curriers | 7 | 6 | 6 | 5 |
| Bankers | 7 | 5 | 9 | 7 |
| Surgeons | 48 | 45 | 42 | 37 |
| Jewish Rabbi | 1 | 1 | 0 | 0 |
| Pilots | 6 | 1 | 33 | 28 |
| R.C. priests | 4 | 4 | 0 | 0 |
| Police | 0 | 0 | 3 | 3 |
| Sexton | 0 | 0 | 1 | 1 |

* Freemen labourers were markedly Tory, non-freemen labourers (£10 householders) markedly Liberal.

*The Liverpool election of 1835 (cont.)*

| Selected categories | Ewart | Morris | Sandon | Douglas |
|---|---|---|---|---|
| Borough officers | 0 | 0 | 2 | 2 |
| Turnkey | 1 | 0 | 1 | 0 |
| Freemen sailmakers | 37 | 28 | 93 | 89 |
| Non-freemen sailmakers (£10 householders) | 11 | 9 | 6 | 4 |
| Shipowners | 6 | 7 | 6 | 5 |
| Shipbuilders | 4 | 4 | 14 | 12 |
| Shipbrokers | 4 | 4 | 3 | 3 |
| Boatbuilders* | 3 | 2 | 18 | 17 |
| Merchants (freemen) | 46 | 45 | 123 | 118 |
| Merchants (non-freemen) | 242 | 236 | 336 | 293 |
| Shipwrights (freemen) | 29 | 20 | 326 | 325 |
| Shipwrights (non-freemen) | 7 | 8 | 23 | 20 |

\* All boatbuilders were freemen voters, not £10 householders.


## The Liverpool election of 1841

The pollbook is in the Institute of Historical Research.

Result: Viscount Sandon, Conservative        5,979
Cresswell Creswell, Conservative        5,792
Sir Joshua Walmsley, Liberal        4,647
Lord Palmerston, Liberal        4,431

| Selected categories | Walmsley | Palmerston | Sandon | Creswell |
|---|---|---|---|---|
| Anglican clergy | 5 | 5 | 42 | 42 |
| Surgeons | 61 | 59 | 73 | 67 |
| Dissenting ministers | 13 | 13 | 0 | 0 |
| Bankers | 7 | 8 | 11 | 11 |
| Officers | 2 | 2 | 6 | 6 |
| Policemen | 2 | 1 | 6 | 6 |
| Stevedores | 6 | 6 | 3 | 3 |
| Turnkeys | 0 | 0 | 2 | 2 |
| Sextons | 0 | 0 | 2 | 2 |
| Parish clerks | 0 | 0 | 2 | 2 |
| Pilots | 1 | 2 | 65 | 65 |
| Sailmakers | 27 | 25 | 85 | 82 |
| Shipowners | 6 | 6 | 13 | 13 |
| Shipbrokers | 8 | 7 | 13 | 11 |
| Shipbuilders | 4 | 4 | 18 | 18 |
| Shipwrights | 67 | 62 | 350 | 346 |

### An example of the non-industrial character of London extreme radicalism

The following analysis of the membership of the West End section of the International Workingmen's Association, the 'First International', is based on a manuscript of 29 March 1873 in the Jung Nachlass, item no. 165, in the possession of the Instituut voor Soziale Geschiedenis, Amsterdam, by whose courtesy it is used.

| | |
|---|---|
| Bootmakers | 6 |
| Painters | 5 |
| Portmanteau makers | 3 |
| Carriage wheelwright | 1 |
| Tailors | 5 |
| Railway official | 1 |
| Labourer | 1 |
| Furniture decorator | 1 |
| Plumber | 1 |
| Cooperative shopkeeper | 1 |
| Blacksmiths | 2 |
| Trunk maker | 1 |
| Unstated | 2 |

### Voting at Loughborough in the Leicestershire election of 1830*

Result: G. A. L. Keck, Tory 3,517⎫ sitting members
Lord R. Manners, Tory 3,000⎭
Thos. Paget, Whig 2,203

The last contested election was in 1775.
Taking the voters for Loughborough only:

| | |
|---|---|
| Keck | 102 |
| Manners | 72 |
| Paget | 139 |

| All voters: | Paget | Keck |  | | Paget | Keck |
|---|---|---|---|---|---|---|
| I. Respectables | | | | Maltsters | 0 | 2 |
| Banker | 0 | 1 | | Innkeepers | 0 | 3 |
| Nonconformist | 1 | 0 | | Carriage makers | 2 | 0 |
| clergy | | | | Millers | 3 | 0 |
| Teachers | 0 | 2 | | | 10 | 7 |
| Clerks | 0 | 4 | | III. Textiles | | |
| Surgeon | 0 | 1 | | Hosiers | 3 | 1 |
| Auctioneer | 1 | 0 | | Framework knitters | 2 | 0 |
| Gentlemen | 6 | 8 | | Lacemakers | 24 | 1 |
| Attorney | 0 | 1 | | Woolstaplers | 1 | 2 |
| Servants | 4 | 2 | | Dyers | 2 | 0 |
| | 12 | 19 | | | 32 | 4 |
| II. Business | | | | IV. | | |
| Timber merchant | 0 | 1 | | Yeomen | 4 | 5 |
| Brick maker | 1 | 1 | | Farmers | 6 | 18 |
| Builders | 4 | 0 | | | | |

* See p. 127 above also for the table on the Leicestershire election of 1830 generally.

*Voting at Loughborough in the Leicestershire election of 1830 (cont.)*

| | Paget | Keck | | Paget | Keck |
|---|---|---|---|---|---|
| V. Shopkeepers | | | Blacksmiths | 3 | 0 |
| Grocers | 6 | 2 | Roper | 0 | 1 |
| Bakers | 3 | 1 | Machinemakers | 6 | 0 |
| Wine merchant | 1 | 1 | Building and wood | 8 | 6 |
| Drapers | 4 | 1 | Cooper | 0 | 1 |
| Butcher | 1 | 1 | Nailmakers | 3 | 0 |
| Chandler | 1 | 0 | Brazier | 1 | 0 |
| Druggist | 0 | 1 | | 22 | 9 |
| | 16 | 7 | VII. | | |
| VI. Crafts | | | Labourers | 6 | 4 |
| Tailor | 1 | 1 | Miscellaneous | 3 | 4 |

## The Macclesfield election of 1835

The pollbook is in the British Museum. Occupations of voters are not stated directly, but the type of property owned by each elector is given.

Result: John Ryle, Conservative 464
John Brocklehurst, Liberal 424
Thos. Grimsditch, Conservative 342

| Type of property | Brocklehurst | Ryle | Grimsditch |
|---|---|---|---|
| Factory | 39 | 42 | 22 |
| Workshop | 7 | 7 | 2 |
| Dyehouse | 5 | 6 | 5 |
| Foundry | 2 | 2 | 0 |
| Public house | 41 | 56 | 57 |

## The Maidstone election of 1830

The pollbook is in the Library of the Society of Genealogists.

Result: A. W. Robarts, Whig 470 (227 plumps)
H. Winchester, Tory 387 (237 plumps)
P. Rawlings, Tory 156 (20 plumps)*
W. G. T. D. Tyssen, Whig 6

Alderman Winchester represented the high church, and Robarts the independent interest.

| Selected categories | Robarts | Winchester | Rawlings |
|---|---|---|---|
| Gentlemen | 27 | 21 | 2 |
| Papermakers | 44 | 33 | 7 |
| Cordwainers | 17 | 12 | 10 |
| Watermen | 53 | 15 | 34 |

Cross votes

Robarts and Winchester 126
Robarts and Rawlings 112

* According to Henry Stooks Smith, Rawlings had 195 votes.

## The Maidstone election of 1832

The pollbook is in the Institute of Historical Research.

Result: A. W. Robarts, Liberal   500
Barnett, Liberal   469
Lewis, Conservative   422

There was very little cross voting (or plumping on the Liberal side).

| Selected categories | Robarts | Lewis |
|---|---|---|
| Gentlemen | 35 | 29 |
| Physicians and surgeons | 2 | 6 |
| Military and Naval | 0 | 1 |
| Banker | 0 | 1 |
| Papermakers | 30 | 22 |
| Grocers | 28 | 6 |
| Tailors | 7 | 6 |
| Victuallers | 21 | 16 |
| Beersellers | 2 | 3 |
| Brewers | 4 | 2 |
| Dissenting ministers | 2 | 0 |
| Wesleyan minister | 1 | 0 |

## The Maidstone election of 1841

The pollbook is in the Institute of Historical Research.

Result: A. J. B. Beresford Hope, Conservative   765
George Dodd, Conservative   725
David Salomons, Liberal   418

| Selected categories | Salomons | Hope | Dodd |
|---|---|---|---|
| Clergymen | 0 | 1 | 1 |
| Sexton | 0 | 1 | 1 |
| Dissenting ministers | 3 | 0 | 0 |
| Turnkey | 0 | 1 | 0 |
| Policemen | 2 | 4 | 4 |
| Bankers | 0 | 2 | 2 |
| Surgeons | 3 | 7 | 7 |
| Victuallers | 10 | 22 | 19 |
| Beersellers | 2 | 4 | 4 |
| Farmers | 5 | 22 | 22 |
| Watermen | 19 | 24 | 23 |
| Mariners | 3 | 3 | 4 |
| Labourers | 15 | 55 | 50 |
| Shoemakers | 24 | 34 | 31 |
| Butchers | 14 | 18 | 17 |
| Grocers | 16 | 10 | 10 |
| Paper manufacturers | 0 | 2 | 2 |
| Papermakers | 31 | 58 | 51 |

## The Maidstone by-election of 1853*

The pollbook is in the Institute of Historical Research.

Result: Wm. Lee, Liberal                    748
      Chas. Wykeham Martin, Liberal    738

| Selected categories | Lee | Martin |
|---|---|---|
| Clergymen | 1 | 9 |
| Surgeons | 6 | 13 |
| Bankers | 0 | 3 |
| Dissenting ministers | 6 | 0 |
| Policemen | 1 | 7 |
| Turnkeys | 0 | 2 |
| Parish clerk | 0 | 1 |
| Officers | 0 | 3 |
| Watermen | 17 | 30 |
| Mariners | 4 | 2 |
| Labourers | 41 | 47 |
| Victuallers | 17 | 20 |
| Beersellers | 17 | 10 |
| Farmers | 8 | 25 |
| Grocers | 34 | 14 |
| Butchers | 12 | 20 |
| Shoemakers | 37 | 26 |
| Paper manufacturers | 2 | 6 |
| Papermakers | 47 | 24 |

\* No analysis of Maidstone voting is possible between 1841 and 1853, as the pollbook for 1852 does not give occupations, and there was no contest in 1847.

Result: 1847   Hope, Conservative ⎱ unopposed
             Dodd, Conservative ⎰

    1852   Whatman, Liberal          844
           Dodd, Conservative       708
           Lee, Liberal              580

## The Maidstone election of 1857

The pollbook is in the Institute of Historical Research.

Result: A. J. Beresford Hope, Conservative    801
      Capt. Edward Scott, Conservative      759
      Wm. Lee, Liberal                      689
      H. Mildmay, Liberal                   655

| Selected categories | Lee | Mildmay | Hope | Scott |
|---|---|---|---|---|
| Bankers | 0 | 0 | 3 | 3 |
| Lawyers | 2 | 2 | 5 | 6 |
| Surgeons | 8 | 8 | 6 | 7 |
| Officers | 1 | 1 | 3 | 3 |

*The Maidstone election of 1857 (cont.)*

| Selected categories | Lee | Mildmay | Hope | Scott |
|---|---|---|---|---|
| Clergymen | o | o | 2 | 2 |
| Paper manufacturers | 2 | 2 | 4 | 4 |
| Papermakers | 42 | 39 | 27 | 22 |
| Victuallers | 16 | 14 | 26 | 24 |
| Beersellers | 6 | 5 | 14 | 12 |
| Farmers | 9 | 9 | 25 | 24 |
| Shoemakers | 37 | 34 | 30 | 29 |
| Grocers | 37 | 39 | 10 | 13 |
| Butchers | 13 | 11 | 22 | 20 |
| Railwaymen | 2 | 2 | 4 | 4 |
| Labourers | 33 | 33 | 58 | 57 |
| Turnkeys | o | o | 2 | 2 |
| Mariners | 3 | 2 | 11 | 10 |
| Watermen | 13 | 11 | 18 | 17 |
| Dissenting ministers | 2 | 2 | o | o |

## The Maidstone election of 1859

The pollbook is in the Library of the Society of Genealogists.

Result: Wm. Lee, Liberal      776
Chas. Buxton, Liberal      776
John Wardlaw, Conservative      751
E. V. Harcourt, Conservative      749

| Selected categories | Lee | Buxton | Wardlaw | Harcourt |
|---|---|---|---|---|
| Gentlemen | 32 | 31 | 49 | 46 |
| Surgeons and physicians | 6 | 6 | 8 | 8 |
| Lawyers | 6 | 6 | 8 | 8 |
| Bankers | o | o | 5 | 5 |
| Anglican clergy | o | o | 2 | 2 |
| Dissenting ministers | 3 | 3 | o | o |
| Paper manufacturers | 4 | 4 | 2 | 2 |
| Brewers | 3 | 3 | 6 | 6 |
| Publicans | 17 | 16 | 26 | 25 |
| Beersellers | 7 | 7 | 17 | 17 |
| Papermakers | 51 | 51 | 22 | 22 |
| Shoemakers | 42 | 41 | 21 | 21 |
| Turnkeys | 1 | o | 7 | 10 |
| Mariners | 22 | 22 | 19 | 19 |

## The Maidstone election of 1865

The pollbook is in the Institute of Historical Research.

Result: Lee, Liberal              869
        Whatman, Liberal          867
        Betts, Conservative       838
        Wardlaw, Conservative     801

All but 60 out of 1,696 votes were straight party votes split between the two party candidates.

The table gives a comprehensive analysis of all votes cast for Lee and Betts:

|                                | Liberal | Con-servative |
|--------------------------------|---------|---------------|
| Gentlemen                      | 38      | 45            |
| Officers, doctors, lawyers     | 15      | 29            |
| Dissenting ministers           | 7       | 0             |
| Bankers                        | 0       | 4             |
|                                |         |               |
| Commercial professions*        | 38      | 48            |
| Builders, employers            | 14      | 11            |
| Merchants, wholesalers†        | 28      | 26            |
| Papermakers                    | 62      | 32            |
|                                |         |               |
| Brewers                        | 4       | 7             |
| Publicans                      | 22      | 33            |
| Beersellers                    | 14      | 21            |
| Shopkeepers                    | 164     | 144           |
|                                |         |               |
| Tailors                        | 37      | 20            |
| Shoemakers                     | 41      | 30            |
| Building and wood trades       | 126     | 79            |
| Metal trades                   | 47      | 65            |
|                                |         |               |
| Minor crafts                   | 72      | 50            |
| Labourers                      | 65      | 82            |
| Servants                       | 12      | 17            |
| Bargeowner                     | 1       | 0             |
|                                |         |               |
| Mariners                       | 17      | 22            |
| Prison employees               | 0       | 5             |
| Sexton                         | 0       | 1             |
| Organist                       | 0       | 1             |
|                                |         |               |
| Scripture-reader               | 0       | 1             |
| Miscellaneous                  | 42      | 58            |

\* Surveyors, clerks, agents, auctioneers, commercial travellers, house agents, accountants, brokers.
† Merchants: coal and corn dealers, millers, marine stores, timber, and general dealers.

## The Maidstone election of 1870

The pollbook is in the Institute of Historical Research.

Result: Sir John Lubbock, Liberal      1,504
Wm. F. White, Conservative      1,402

| Selected categories | Liberal | Con-servative |
|---|---|---|
| Gentlemen | 41 | 50 |
| Surgeons or physicians | 3 | 13 |
| Bankers | 0 | 3 |
| Schoolmasters | 4 | 5 |
| Brewers | 3 | 5 |
| Publicans | 19 | 25 |
| Beersellers | 5 | 19 |
| Railwaymen* | 40 | 9 |
| Mariners | 7 | 8 |
| Bargemen | 3 | 10 |
| Sweeps | 0 | 3 |
| Prison employees† | 0 | 22 |
| R.C. priest | 1 | 0 |
| Dissenting ministers | 7 | 0 |
| Anglican clergy | 0 | 10 |
| Sexton | 0 | 1 |
| Vestry clerk | 0 | 1 |

\* The Maidstone stationmaster voted Liberal.
† The Deputy Governor of Maidstone Jail voted Tory.


## The Manchester election of 1839

The pollbook for the Manchester by-election of 6 September 1839 is in Manchester Public Library. It is more or less alphabetical but it does not give occupations. There is, however, a Manchester Directory for 1840 which gives, *inter alia*, a list of Manchester clergymen, priests and ministers. The names given in the directory were checked against the pollbook with the following results:

Anglican clergy: Tory    11
             Liberal    1
             Abstained    36

Other clergy
Baptists: Liberal    2
         Tory    0
         Abstained    1
Independents: Liberal    3
            Tory    0
            Abstained    5
Unitarians: Liberal    3
           Tory    0
           Abstained    3

None of the dozen or so Methodist ministers, and none of the 11 Catholic priests, appear to have voted. The large number of non-voters was largely due

*The Manchester election of 1839 (cont.)*

to many clergy living outside the narrow boundaries of electoral Manchester, and especially in Salford.

The only Liberal Anglican was a curate. The Collegiate Church provided six Tory votes.

## The Newark election of 1830

The pollbook is in the Guildhall Library.

| Result: | Willoughby | 775 |
|---|---|---|
| | Sadler | 746 |
| | Wilde | 652 |

Willoughby and Sadler represented the interest of the Duke of Newcastle, while Mr Serjeant Wilde stood for the independence of the people.

Voters A–H inclusive only:

| selected categories | Willoughby | Sadler | Wilde |
|---|---|---|---|
| Labourers | 64 | 64 | 66 |
| Shoemakers | 12 | 12 | 18 |
| Watermen | 13 | 9 | 17 |
| Surgeons | 2 | 4 | 2 |
| Clergy | 1 | 1 | 0 |
| Dissenting minister | 0 | 0 | 1 |
| Gentlemen | 7 | 6 | 4 |
| Weavers | 1 | 1 | 10 |
| Parish clerk | 1 | 1 | 0 |
| Police | 1 | 1 | 0 |

## The Newport, Isle of Wight, election of 1852

The pollbook is in the British Museum.

| Result: | W. Biggs, Liberal | 310 |
|---|---|---|
| | W. Massey, Liberal | 306 |
| | W. H. C. Plowden, Conservative | 266 |
| | C. W. Martin, Conservative | 256 |

| Selected categories | Biggs | Massey | Plowden | Martin |
|---|---|---|---|---|
| Lacemakers | 35 | 35 | 1 | 1 |
| Ministers | 2 | 2 | 0 | 0 |
| Tailors | 24 | 24 | 11 | 11 |
| Grocers | 18 | 18 | 12 | 12 |
| Butchers | 14 | 15 | 5 | 5 |
| Gentlemen | 8 | 8 | 10 | 11 |
| Millers | 2 | 2 | 4 | 4 |
| Carpenters | 7 | 7 | 7 | 7 |
| Saddlers | 1 | 1 | 4 | 4 |
| Labourers | 5 | 5 | 10 | 10 |
| Mariners | 8 | 8 | 7 | 7 |
| Sailmakers | 1 | 1 | 2 | 2 |
| Servants | 0 | 0 | 4 | 4 |
| Town clerk | 0 | 0 | 1 | 1 |
| Relieving officer | 0 | 0 | 1 | 1 |
| Police inspector | 0 | 0 | 1 | 1 |
| Town sergeant | 0 | 0 | 1 | 1 |
| Lawyers | 3 | 3 | 6 | 5 |

### The Norfolk East election of 1841

The pollbook is in the Bodleian Library.

Result: Edmond Wodehouse, Conservative   3,498
H. N. Burroughes, Conservative   3,437
Sir W. Folkes, Bt., Liberal   1,379

This pollbook does not list occupations as such, but Anglican clergy are indicated by the abbreviation 'clk', and these voted as follows:

Burroughes   184
Wodehouse   183
Folkes   13
Abstained*   191

\* Many of these lived at a distance from Norfolk.

### The Northampton Borough election of 1831

The pollbook (74 pages) is in the Institute of Historical Research.

Result: Sir George Robinson, Liberal   1,570
Robert Vernon Smith, Liberal   1,279
Sir R. H. Gunning, Bt., Conservative   1,157
Jas. Lyon, Conservative   185

| Selected categories | Gunning | Lyon | Robinson | Smith |
|---|---|---|---|---|
| | Pages 1–28 of pollbook | | | |
| Shoemakers | 52 | 3 | 221 | 261 |
| | Whole pollbook | | | |
| Gentlemen | 78 | 16 | 54 | 36 |
| Lawyers | 8 | 3 | 1 | 1 |
| Surgeons | 10 | 2 | 4 | 2 |
| Bankers | 0 | 0 | 2 | 0 |
| Sextons | 4 | 1 | 1 | 0 |
| Parish clerks | 2 | 0 | 0 | 0 |
| R.C. priest | 0 | 0 | 1 | 1 |
| Dissenting ministers | 0 | 0 | 6 | 6 |
| Gaolers | 4 | 1 | 3 | 0 |
| Watermen | 13 | 0 | 4 | 2 |
| Butchers | 33 | 8 | 31 | 19 |
| Grocers | 10 | 3 | 15 | 13 |
| Publicans | 28 | 4 | 21 | 12 |

## The Northampton Borough election of 1852

The pollbook is in the Northamptonshire County Record Office.

Result: R. Vernon Smith, Liberal       858
       R. Currie, Liberal             824
       G. Ward Hunt, Conservative     746
       J. I. Lockhart, Chartist       109

Lockhart's votes were not analysed.

| Selected categories | Smith | Currie | Hunt |
|---|---|---|---|
| Engineers | 6 | 6 | 0 |
| Shoemakers | 191 | 202 | 75 |
| Shoe manufacturers | 63 | 64 | 12 |
| Iron founders | 1 | 1 | 3 |
| Foundrymen | 9 | 8 | 9 |
| Railway employees | 0 | 0 | 5 |
| Labourers | 14 | 9 | 44 |
| Merchants | 4 | 4 | 0 |
| Druggists | 4 | 3 | 10 |
| Publicans | 41 | 39 | 37 |
| Grocers | 11 | 12 | 11 |
| Butchers | 21 | 18 | 29 |
| Gentlemen | 25 | 23 | 13 |
| Servants | 1 | 1 | 3 |
| Solicitors | 5 | 4 | 15 |
| Surgeons | 6 | 6 | 10 |
| Bankers | 1 | 1 | 0 |
| Farmers | 1 | 1 | 5 |
| Dissenting ministers | 5 | 5 | 1 |
| Anglican clergy | 1 | 0 | 6 |
| Sweeps | 1 | 2 | 2 |
| Police | 2 | 1 | 1 |
| Clerk | 0 | 0 | 1 |
| Organbuilder | 0 | 0 | 1 |
| Rate collectors | 0 | 0 | 2 |
| Registrar | 0 | 0 | 1 |
| Postboys | 0 | 0 | 2 |
| Saddlers | 2 | 1 | 6 |
| Sextons | 0 | 0 | 2 |
| Relieving officer | 0 | 0 | 1 |
| Turnkey | 0 | 0 | 1 |
| Parish clerk | 0 | 0 | 1 |

Those abstaining included 2 Dissenting ministers, 4 Anglican clergy, and the Catholic bishop.

## The Northamptonshire election of 1831

The pollbook is in the Guildhall Library. The following analysis was printed by the compilers of the pollbook and is reproduced here unabridged.

Result: Althorp (A), Reformer    2,462  
Milton (M), Reformer    2,113  
Cartwright (C), Tory    1,995  
Knightley (K), Tory    1,401

Knightley said 'for his part he considered Parliamentary reform meant Parliamentary robbery'. Classification of Freeholders in respect to their rank and occupations, with the distribution of their votes to the several candidates:

| No. of each | Rank and occupation | Althorp | Milton | Cartwright | Knightley |
|---|---|---|---|---|---|
| 1 | Earl | 1 | 0 | 0 | 0 |
| 1 | Lord | 0 | 0 | 1 | 0 |
| 3 | Honorables | 1 | 1 | 2 | 2 |
| 6 | Baronets | 3 | 3 | 3 | 3 |
| 1 | General in the Army | 1 | 1 | 0 | 0 |
| 2 | Colonels ditto | 1 | 1 | 1 | 1 |
| 1 | Major, R.N. | 1 | 1 | 0 | 0 |
| 141 | Esquires | 54 | 43 | 92 | 80 |
| 374 | Gentlemen | 223 | 205 | 169 | 117 |
| 239 | Clergymen | 62 | 49 | 184 | 169 |
| 20 | Dissenting ministers | 19 | 20 | 0 | 0 |
| 42 | Attorneys at Law and Solicitors | 16 | 15 | 27 | 25 |
| 46 | Doctors in Medicine, Surgeons, etc. | 24 | 19 | 26 | 19 |
| 10 | Bankers | 7 | 6 | 4 | 2 |
| 9 | Merchants | 7 | 5 | 4 | 2 |
| 4 | Ironfounders | 4 | 4 | 0 | 0 |
| 14 | Ironmongers | 10 | 8 | 6 | 2 |
| 59 | Drapers | 45 | 41 | 17 | 12 |
| 78 | Grocers | 60 | 52 | 24 | 15 |
| 2 | Tea dealers | 2 | 2 | 0 | 0 |
| 3 | Tallow chandlers | 3 | 3 | 0 | 0 |
| 1 | Cheesemonger | 1 | 1 | 0 | 0 |
| 8 | Druggists | 5 | 4 | 4 | 3 |
| 23 | Boot & Shoe manufacturers | 23 | 21 | 1 | 0 |
| 3 | Tanners | 2 | 3 | 0 | 0 |
| 14 | Curriers | 13 | 12 | 2 | 1 |
| 4 | Leather Factors, etc. | 4 | 3 | 1 | 0 |
| 5 | Feltmongers | 5 | 3 | 2 | 0 |
| 7 | Woolstaplers | 5 | 6 | 1 | 0 |
| 4 | Ribbon and Silk Manufacturers | 4 | 4 | 0 | 0 |
| 5 | Hosiers | 3 | 3 | 2 | 2 |
| 1 | Carpet Manufacturer | 1 | 1 | 0 | 0 |

*The Northamptonshire election of 1831 (cont.)*

| No. of each | Rank and occupation | Althorp | Milton | Cartwright | Knightley |
|---|---|---|---|---|---|
| 5 | Land Surveyors | 2 | 2 | 3 | 3 |
| 7 | Printers | 3 | 3 | 4 | 4 |
| 8 | Booksellers and Stationers | 6 | 4 | 4 | 2 |
| 11 | Common Brewers | 5 | 4 | 7 | 6 |
| 12 | Coal Merchants | 8 | 5 | 7 | 4 |
| 1 | Cloth Worker | 1 | 1 | 0 | 0 |
| 3 | Horse Dealers | 1 | 1 | 1 | 1 |
| 3 | Coach Builders | 1 | 0 | 3 | 2 |
| 6 | Lace Merchants | 5 | 4 | 1 | 1 |
| 14 | Timber Merchants | 10 | 6 | 8 | 4 |
| 11 | Builders | 7 | 8 | 3 | 3 |
| 126 | Carpenters | 85 | 75 | 51 | 28 |
| 49 | Bricklayers and Masons | 30 | 22 | 23 | 13 |
| 22 | Plumbers, Glaziers & Painters | 14 | 11 | 11 | 5 |
| 51 | Smiths | 38 | 27 | 24 | 9 |
| 18 | Slaters & Plasterers | 6 | 4 | 14 | 9 |
| 7 | Brickmakers | 5 | 6 | 1 | 1 |
| 1 | Lime-burner | 1 | 1 | 0 | 0 |
| 7 | Cabinetmakers | 5 | 4 | 2 | 2 |
| 5 | Upholsterers | 3 | 1 | 4 | 2 |
| 15 | Wine and Spirit Merchants | 10 | 8 | 7 | 5 |
| 140 | Innholders, Victuallers, etc. | 88 | 79 | 58 | 37 |
| 39 | Maltsters | 28 | 17 | 21 | 9 |
| 117 | Butchers | 75 | 58 | 59 | 34 |
| 108 | Bakers | 67 | 60 | 46 | 36 |
| 5 | Corn Dealers | 3 | 2 | 3 | 1 |
| 58 | Millers | 45 | 35 | 20 | 11 |
| 2 | Mealmen | 1 | 2 | 0 | 1 |
| 1 | Corn Meter | 1 | 1 | 0 | 0 |
| 3 | Millwrights | 3 | 2 | 1 | 0 |
| 1,588 | Agriculturalists | 920 | 772 | 779 | 536 |
| 10 | Auctioneers | 9 | 9 | 1 | 1 |
| 67 | Nurserymen and Gardeners | 42 | 43 | 26 | 19 |
| 2 | Seedsmen | 1 | 1 | 1 | 1 |
| 9 | Saddlers | 5 | 4 | 4 | 4 |
| 6 | Hatters | 5 | 4 | 2 | 1 |
| 14 | Collar & Harness Makers | 9 | 8 | 6 | 5 |
| 15 | Hairdressers and Perfumers | 12 | 8 | 6 | 4 |
| 40 | Tailors | 25 | 26 | 12 | 12 |
| 2 | Glovers and Breeches Makers | 1 | 1 | 1 | 1 |

*The Northamptonshire election of 1831 (cont.)*

| No. of each | Rank and occupation | Althorp | Milton | Cartwright | Knightley |
|---|---|---|---|---|---|
| 7 | Watchmakers | 7 | 6 | 1 | 0 |
| 4 | Confectioners | 4 | 3 | 0 | 1 |
| 40 | Wheelwrights | 27 | 21 | 19 | 11 |
| 16 | Coopers | 12 | 11 | 5 | 3 |
| 3 | Turners & Chairmakers | 3 | 3 | 0 | 0 |
| 5 | Basket & Mat Makers | 4 | 3 | 2 | 1 |
| 5 | Braziers & Tin-plate Workers | 4 | 3 | 2 | 1 |
| 4 | Fishmongers | 3 | 2 | 2 | 1 |
| 8 | Veterinary Surgeons | 5 | 5 | 3 | 3 |
| 1 | Paper Maker | 0 | 1 | 0 | 0 |
| 1 | Banker's Clerk | 1 | 1 | 0 | 0 |
| 1 | Artist | 1 | 1 | 0 | 0 |
| 2 | Pawnbrokers | 2 | 2 | 0 | 0 |
| 2 | Dyers | 2 | 2 | 0 | 0 |
| 114 | Shoemakers | 89 | 88 | 28 | 14 |
| 16 | Weavers | 13 | 12 | 1 | 1 |
| 2 | Woolcombers | 1 | 2 | 0 | 0 |
| 5 | Hawkers | 2 | 4 | 2 | 0 |
| 20 | Shopkeepers, etc. | 16 | 12 | 8 | 4 |
| 2 | Flax Dressers, etc. | 2 | 2 | 0 | 0 |
| 2 | Brush and Sieve Makers | 2 | 2 | 0 | 0 |
| 1 | Straw Manufacturer | 1 | 1 | 0 | 0 |
| 1 | Gunmaker | 1 | 1 | 0 | 0 |
| 1 | Whip Manufacturer | 1 | 1 | 0 | 0 |
| 1 | Saddle-tree Maker | 1 | 1 | 0 | 0 |
| 1 | Parchment Maker | 0 | 1 | 0 | 1 |
| 1 | Pattern Maker | 1 | 1 | 0 | 0 |
| 1 | Pipe maker | 1 | 0 | 1 | 0 |
| 1 | Tawer | 0 | 0 | 1 | 1 |
| 5 | Sawyers | 2 | 1 | 4 | 2 |
| 11 | Pig Jobbers | 3 | 6 | 7 | 5 |
| 14 | Common Carriers | 9 | 9 | 4 | 4 |
| 1 | Gaoler | 1 | 0 | 1 | 0 |
| 1 | Sheriff's Officer | 1 | 0 | 1 | 0 |
| 1 | Attorney's Clerk | 0 | 0 | 1 | 0 |
| 4 | Toll Collectors & Road Surveyors | 3 | 3 | 1 | 1 |
| 65 | Schoolmasters | 21 | 13 | 53 | 31 |
| 1 | Sailor | 1 | 1 | 0 | 0 |
| 1 | Ship Caulker | 1 | 1 | 0 | 0 |
| 1 | Coachman | 0 | 0 | 1 | 0 |
| 17 | Gamekeepers and Servants | 8 | 7 | 9 | 9 |
| 1 | Overseer | 0 | 0 | 1 | 1 |
| 31 | Parish Clerks | 9 | 11 | 19 | 13 |
| 21 | Beedsmen or Inmates of Almshouses | 1 | 0 | 20 | 21 |

*The Northamptonshire election of 1831 (cont.)*

The votes of a few of the most prominent classes

| | No. | Single votes | | | | Double votes | | | | | | Summary | | | |
|---|---|---|---|---|---|---|---|---|---|---|---|---|---|---|---|
| | | A | M | C | K | A and M | A and C | A and K | M and C | M and K | C and K | A | M | C | K |
| **The magistracy** | | | | | | | | | | | | | | | |
| Laymen | 27 | 1 | — | — | — | 4 | 3 | — | — | — | 19⎫ | 9 | 4 | 42 | 38 |
| Clergy | 20 | — | — | — | — | — | 1 | — | — | — | 19⎭ | | | | |
| The clergy | 239 | 3 | 2 | 6 | 3 | 46 | 13 | — | — | 1 | 165 | 62 | 49 | 184 | 169 |
| Solicitors etc. | 42 | — | — | 1 | — | 15 | 1 | — | — | — | 25 | 16 | 15 | 27 | 25 |
| **Medical practitioners** | | | | | | | | | | | | | | | |
| M.D.'s | 10 | — | — | — | — | 4 | — | — | — | — | 6⎫ | 24 | 19 | 26 | 19 |
| Surgeons, etc. | 36 | — | 1 | 3 | — | 14 | 5 | 1 | — | — | 12⎭ | | | | |
| Agriculturalists, described as graziers, farmers and yeomen | 1,588 | 39 | 32 | 88 | 10 | 714 | 164 | 3 | 15 | 11 | 512 | 920 | 772 | 779 | 536 |
| Schoolmasters | 65 | — | 2 | 10 | — | 10 | 11 | — | 1 | — | 31 | 21 | 13 | 53 | 31 |
| Parish clerks | 31 | 1 | 4 | 5 | — | 7 | 1 | — | — | — | 13 | 9 | 11 | 19 | 13 |

## The Norwich election of 1830 (29–30 July)

The pollbook is in Manchester University Library. The pollbook used by Mr Brecknell is in Norwich City Library.

| Result: | Grant, Whig | 2,279 |
| | Gurney, Whig | 2,263* |
| | Peel, Tory | 1,912 |
| | Ogle, Tory | 1,762 |
| Splits: | Gurney and Grant | 2,231 |
| | Peel and Ogle | 1,756 |

According to calculations made and kindly shown to me by Mr N. P. Brecknell, these groups voted as follows:

| | For Gurney and Grant | For Peel and Ogle |
|---|---|---|
| Cordwainers | 125 | 88 |
| Manufacturers (textile) | 50 | 22 |
| Textile workers (silk and worsted weavers and wool combers) | 310 | 137 |
| 'Freeholders' (various social positions and occupations) | 362 | 276 |

In 1830 there were 4,202 freemen voters.

According to my own calculations, selected categories of 'in-voters' (residents) and 'out-voters' voted as follows:

In-voters

| Selected categories | Gurney | Grant | Peel | Ogle |
|---|---|---|---|---|
| Gentlemen | 112 | 115 | 124 | 122 |
| Bankers | 2 | 2 | 1 | 1 |
| Surgeons | 6 | 6 | 11 | 11 |
| Farmers | 3 | 3 | 2 | 2 |
| Lawyers | 8 | 10 | 33 | 32 |
| Merchants | 23 | 23 | 11 | 10 |
| Aldermen and Mayor | 7 | 7 | 11 | 11 |
| Architects | 0 | 0 | 2 | 2 |
| Servants, gardeners, etc. | 31 | 31 | 39 | 35 |
| Dissenting ministers | 1 | 2 | 0 | 0 |
| Brewers | 8 | 7 | 6 | 5 |
| Publicans | 34 | 33 | 35 | 32 |
| Tailors | 56 | 54 | 47 | 43 |
| Printers | 7 | 8 | 14 | 14 |
| Butchers | 20 | 20 | 14 | 14 |
| Grocers | 44 | 44 | 25 | 24 |
| Watermen | 29 | 26 | 19 | 18 |
| Labourers | 10 | 7 | 23 | 21 |
| Out-voters | | | | |
| Gentlemen | 87 | 85 | 72 | 68 |
| Farmers | 71 | 71 | 33 | 32 |
| Merchants | 14 | 15 | 7 | 7 |
| Officers | 0 | 0 | 11 | 10 |
| Lawyers | 7 | 4 | 14 | 10 |
| Labourers | 9 | 9 | 5 | 4 |

None of the subsequent pollbooks for Norwich elections stated voters' occupations.

* Henry Stooks Smith gives Gurney 2,363 votes.

### The Nottingham Borough election of 1852

The pollbook is in the Guildhall Library.

Result: Rt. Hon. Edward Strutt, Liberal     1,960
         John Walter, Conservative     1,863
         Charles Sturgeon, Chartist       512

| Selected categories | Sturgeon | Strutt | Walter |
|---|---|---|---|
| Lace manufacturers | 4 | 114 | 52 |
| Labourers | 12 | 9 | 29 |
| Surgeons | 0 | 12 | 13 |
| Merchants | 1 | 7 | 8 |
| Police | 0 | 3 | 1 |
| Ironfounders | 0 | 5 | 1 |
| Postmaster | 0 | 0 | 1 |
| Ministers | 0 | 5 | 2 |
| Railwaymen | 0 | 3 | 1 |
| Bankers | 0 | 3 | 4 |
| Coalmaster | 0 | 1 | 0 |
| Clergy | 0 | 1 | 1 |

### The Nottinghamshire (South) election of 1846

The pollbook is in the Guildhall Library. It does not state the occupations of voters. The by-election was caused by the acceptance of office by the Earl of Lincoln; the issue was Free Trade in corn, raised by the 'Nottinghamshire Agricultural Protection Society', who brought forward T. B. Hildyard of Flintham Hall, Notts.

Result: T. B. Hildyard, Conservative     1,736
         Lord Lincoln, Peelite       1,049

| | Lincoln | Hildyard |
|---|---|---|
| Clergy | 21 | 29 |

### The Oldham election of 1832

The pollbook is in Oldham Public Library.

The following table gives an analysis of the small Tory and Whig minority in the first election ever held at Oldham, 1832. The popular party (those voting for the successful candidates Fielden and Cobbett) have not been analysed.

| | Bright (Whig) | Burge (Tory) |
|---|---|---|
| Gentlemen | 11 | 8 |
| Surgeons | 2 | 0 |
| Solicitors | 3 | 0 |
| Clergymen | 1 | 3 |
| Auctioneers, surveyors, etc. | 4 | 4 |
| Farmers | 16 | 12 |
| Innkeepers | 1 | 1 |
| Clerks | 5 | 3 |
| Butchers | 4 | 2 |
| Other shopkeepers | 12 | 8 |
| Building and metal craftsmen | 10 | 9 |

*The Oldham election of 1832 (cont.)*

|  | Bright (Whig) | Burge (Tory) |
|---|---|---|
| Corn, timber, coal and waste dealers | 9 | 2 |
| Hat manufacturers | 16 | 2 |
| Cotton manufacturers | 6 | 2 |
| Machine makers | 3 | 0 |
| Cotton spinners | 28 | 12 |
| Other operatives | 4 | 2 |
| Coal master | 0 | 1 |
| Colliers | 0 | 2 |
| Miscellaneous | 15 | 13 |

### The Oldham election of 1847

Oldham Public Library has pollbooks giving occupations for 1832, 1852, 1865 and for the 1852 by-election. The 1847 pollbook, though not giving occupations, contains these remarks in its preface:

'We the Committee of Working Men beg to call the especial attention of the Factory Workers and the Public of Oldham to this Fact, that nearly all the Mill Owners and Manufacturers (about 200) in the Borough voted against Mr Fielden, a significant proof as to whether it was "Dictation" or the Ten Hours Bill which has called forth their vengeance.

The attention of the Industrious Classes and Public of this Borough is also drawn to the conduct of the Religious, Dissenting, and Nonconforming part of the Electors, in splitting their votes between Fox and Duncuft, one of whom, as a Churchman...' [etc.]

There follows a list of employers who voted against Fielden. Of these, some 98, marked with an asterisk, were subscribers to the Anti-Corn Law League.

### The Oldham election of July 1852

The pollbook is in Oldham Public Library.

Result: Cobbett, Conservative 957
Duncuft, Conservative 868
Fox, Liberal 777

| Selected categories* | Duncuft and Cobbett | Cobbett and Fox | Duncuft and Fox | Fox | Cobbett | Duncuft |
|---|---|---|---|---|---|---|
| Agents and foremen | 5 | 0 | 6 | 41 | 6 | 4 |
| Cotton waste dealers | 9 | 0 | 2 | 30 | 0 | 0 |
| Spinners and manu-facturers | 40 | 9 | 35 | 187 | 13 | 30 |
| Farmers | 141 | 26 | 12 | 15 | 7 | 3 |
| Beersellers | 89 | 20 | 6 | 13 | 16 | 1 |
| Innkeepers | 83 | 20 | 2 | 13 | 10 | 7 |
| Shopkeepers | 172 | 35 | 51 | 149 | 28 | 14 |
| Clergy, gentry, pro-fessional | 88 | 0 | 0 | 63 | 0 | 18 |

* About 100 votes are not listed in the table as the occupation of those giving them was either not stated in the pollbook, or it fell outside the main categories.

## The Oldham by-election of 1852

The pollbook is in Oldham Public Library.

Result: Fox, Liberal        895
Heald, Conservative 783

| All voters | Fox | Heald |
|---|---|---|
| Gentry, clergy, professional | 79 | 99 |
| Innkeepers | 42 | 86 |
| Beersellers | 32 | 109 |
| Farmers | 70 | 174 |
| Cotton spinners, manufacturers, and other employers | 214 | 75 |
| Grocers | 96 | 87 |
| Tailors and drapers | 44 | 11 |
| Butchers | 9 | 28 |
| Other shopkeepers | 116 | 62 |
| Shoemakers, cloggers | 22 | 13 |
| Unclassified and miscellaneous | 69 | 53 |

## The Oldham election of 1865

The pollbook is in Oldham Public Library.

Result: Hibbert, Liberal        1,105
Platt, Liberal            1,076
Cobbett, Conservative    898
Spinks, Conservative     845

Of these:        For Cobbett and Spinks      800
For Hibbert and Platt      1,031

Only these latter 'straight party votes' are analysed below.*

| Selected categories | Liberal | Conservative |
|---|---|---|
| I. Gentlemen | 7 | 34 |
| Anglican clergy | 0 | 8 |
| Dissenting ministers | 3 | 0 |
| Solicitors | 4 | 7 |
| Surgeons | 5 | 5 |
| R.C. priest | 1 | 0 |
| Auctioneers | 3 | 0 |
| Architects | 4 | 1 |
| Schoolmasters | 4 | 2 |
| Surveyors | 0 | 2 |
| Organist | 0 | 1 |
| Governor of workhouse | 0 | 1 |
| II. Innkeepers | 41 | 80 |
| Beersellers | 30 | 74 |
| Brewer | 0 | 1 |
| Farmers | 38 | 111 |

* A multitude of minor occupations and many voters whose occupations were not given are not listed.

*The Oldham election of 1865 (cont.)*

| Selected categories | Liberal | Conservative |
|---|---|---|
| III. Colliery owner | 3 | 2 |
| Collier | 1 | 0 |
| Colliery manager | 0 | 1 |
| Colliery overlooker | 0 | 1 |
| IV. Grocers | 34 | 46 |
| Butchers | 12 | 20 |
| Pawnbrokers | 4 | 3 |
| Druggist | 9 | 5 |
| Other shopkeepers | 76 | 40 |
| V. Engine-driver | 3 | 1 |
| Stationmaster | 1 | 0 |
| VI. Cotton spinners | 156 | 44 |
| Cotton manufacturers | 1 | 7 |
| Cotton waste dealers | 34 | 13 |
| Managers | 12 | 3 |
| VII. Clerks | 15 | 4 |
| Mechanics | 35 | 4 |
| Shoemakers, cloggers | 19 | 9 |
| Tailors | 8 | 2 |
| Ironfounders | 6 | 1 |
| Timber dealers | 5 | 0 |

## The Oxford City election of 1835

The pollbook is in the Bodleian Library.

Result: W. H. Hughes, Conservative    1,394
D. Maclean, Conservative    1,217
T. Stonor, Liberal    1,022

| Selected categories | Stonor | Hughes | Maclean |
|---|---|---|---|
| Servants | 8 | 28 | 30 |
| Policemen | 3 | 4 | 4 |
| Surgeons | 0 | 1 | 3 |
| Dissenting ministers | 1 | 1 | 1 |
| Governor of gaol | 0 | 1 | 1 |
| R.C. priest | 1 | 1 | 0 |
| College servants | 8 | 120 | 153 |
| Doctors of Divinity | 0 | 0 | 3 |
| Doctors of Law | 0 | 0 | 1 |
| Bedels | 0 | 2 | 4 |
| Professors | 1 | 1 | 4 |
| Manciples | 0 | 1 | 2 |
| Parish clerks | 1 | 3 | 5 |
| Organists | 0 | 1 | 2 |
| Anglican clergy | 0 | 5 | 11 |
| University Marshal | 0 | 0 | 1 |

## The Oxford City election of 1841

The pollbook is in the Bodleian Library.

Result: Langston, Liberal          1,349
        Maclean, Conservative      1,238
        Malcolm, Conservative      1,031

Freemen:

| selected categories | Langston | Maclean | Malcolm |
|---|---|---|---|
| Carpenters | 48 | 17 | 9 |
| Tailors | 103 | 76 | 59 |
| Butchers | 25 | 21 | 13 |
| Gentlemen | 26 | 36 | 32 |
| Victuallers | 12 | 3 | 3 |
| Wine merchants | 5 | 5 | 5 |
| Shoemakers | 67 | 50 | 40 |
| Labourers | 21 | 16 | 12 |
| Servants | 4 | 9 | 9 |
| Lawyers | 4 | 8 | 9 |
| Saddlers | 7 | 5 | 4 |
| Farmers | 6 | 15 | 17 |
| Grocers | 9 | 13 | 12 |
| College servants | 0 | 12 | 11 |
| Surgeons | 0 | 4 | 4 |
| Bankers | 0 | 4 | 4 |

£10 Householders:

| selected categories | Langston | Maclean | Malcolm |
|---|---|---|---|
| Labourers | 17 | 13 | 7 |
| Butchers | 18 | 8 | 6 |
| Tailors | 50 | 23 | 17 |
| Servants | 15 | 71 | 69 |
| College servants | 7 | 68 | 67 |
| Victuallers | 45 | 34 | 26 |
| Lawyers | 4 | 5 | 3 |
| Shoemakers | 35 | 19 | 14 |
| Grocers | 15 | 7 | 5 |
| Carpenters | 50 | 24 | 15 |
| Saddlers | 4 | 2 | 0 |
| Gentlemen | 29 | 28 | 23 |
| Surgeons | 2 | 10 | 8 |
| Police | 1 | 5 | 4 |
| Dissenting ministers | 2 | 1 | 1 |
| Farmers | 0 | 2 | 2 |
| Banker | 1 | 0 | 0 |
| Organists | 0 | 3 | 3 |

## The Peterborough elections of 1852

From the report on the Peterborough election, *Parl. Papers* 1852–3, XVII, 623.

In 1852 Peterborough had 532 electors, nearly half of whom were tenants of Earl Fitzwilliam. 432 out of 532 were £10 householders. Of the £10 householders who were tenants of the Earl, there voted as follows:

| July 1852 | Fitzwilliam (Liberal) | Watson (Liberal) | Clifton (Conservative) |
|---|---|---|---|
| Plumps | 2 | 4 | 20 |
| Splits | 113 | 113 | — |
| Splits | 12 | — | 12 |
| Splits | — | 2 | 2 |
| | 127 | 119 | 34 |

December 1852*

| | |
|---|---|
| Sir G. C. Lewis (Liberal) | 110 |
| Whalley (Independent, against Fitzwilliam) | 38 |

The point brought out here is that, even when there was no great issue at stake, and even when aristocratic influence was supported, as in this case, by disguised evictions and loss of custom, a sizeable minority of urban tenants would vote against what they thought were the wishes of their landlords.

* McCalmont gives the overall result as Lewis 218, Whalley 233.

## The Preston election of 8 December 1830

The pollbook, which is in Manchester Public Library, takes the form of a single alphabetical list of 7,122 voters. Only those whose names began with A and B are analysed below.

| | | |
|---|---|---|
| Result: Henry Hunt | 3,730 | |
| Rt. Hon. E. G. Stanley | 3,392 | |

| Voters A and B only | Stanley | Hunt |
|---|---|---|
| I. The upper crust | | |
| Gentlemen | 27 | 1 |
| Lawyers | 5 | 0 |
| Surgeons | 3 | 0 |
| II. Business and dependants | | |
| Innkeepers | 10 | 0 |
| Schoolmasters | 9 | 0 |
| Commercial and clerical | 15 | 6 |
| Sexton | 1 | 0 |
| Yeoman | 0 | 1 |
| Builders | 2 | 0 |
| Cheese, flour, corn dealers | 6 | 0 |
| Timber merchant | 1 | 0 |
| Millers | 5 | 5 |
| Coal dealers | 3 | 3 |
| Brewers | 2 | 7 |
| Others* | 2 | 3 |

* Coachmaker, pipemaker, blacking maker, malt crusher.

*The Preston election of 8 December 1830 (cont.)*

| Voters A and B only | Stanley | Hunt |
|---|---|---|
| III. Retailers | | |
| Butchers | 4 | 0 |
| Booksellers | 0 | 2 |
| Other shopkeepers | 42 | 13 |
| IV. Unskilled, servants, etc. | | |
| Miscellaneous* | 16 | 9 |
| Servants, etc.† | 22 | 1 |
| Lamplighters | 3 | 0 |
| Constables | 2 | 0 |
| Boatmen | 3 | 0 |
| Porters | 3 | 1 |
| Rag gatherers | 1 | 5 |
| Carters | 17 | 3 |
| Labourers | 32 | 35 |
| V. Textiles | | |
| Flax dressers | 2 | 2 |
| Warehousemen | 9 | 0 |
| Overlookers | 3 | 2 |
| Engine tenders | 6 | 0 |
| Cotton manufacturers | 3 | 0 |
| Calico printer | 1 | 1 |
| Sizers | 3 | 2 |
| Dressers | 6 | 1 |
| Carders | 6 | 3 |
| Warpers | 19 | 8 |
| Spinners | 24 | 56 |
| Weavers | 28 | 172 |
| Other operatives‡ | 5 | 9 |
| Mechanics | 16 | 36 |
| Reed, roller, shuttle, spindle makers | 1 | 6 |
| VI. Craftsmen | | |
| Shoemakers, cloggers | 15 | 25 |
| Tailors | 4 | 14 |
| Sawyers | 5 | 8 |
| Smith, blacksmith | 4 | 8 |
| Tin, brass, tinplate, silver; watch-makers and gunsmiths | 12 | 3 |
| Moulder, ironfounder | 4 | 6 |
| Bricklayer, plasterer, mason, painter, slater | 10 | 6 |
| Printers | 6 | 2 |
| Grinder, screwmaker, nailor, foundryman, filecutter | 2 | 8 |
| Chair, brush, basket, and cabinet-maker, turner, upholsterer | 10 | 11 |

* Sweep, town crier, hawker, farrier, horsebreaker, discharger, waterman, bailiff, postboy, turnkey, watchman, horsekeeper, jobber, horsetender, scavenger, pavior, husbandman.
† Servants, coachmen, gardeners, grooms, ostlers, waiters.
‡ Rover, drawer-in, twister, stripper, stretcher.

*The Preston election of 8 December 1830 (cont.)*

VI.   Craftsmen (*cont.*)

|  | Stanley | Hunt |
|---|---|---|
| Joiners, carpenters | 18 | 22 |
| Saddlers | 4 | 1 |
| Plumbers | 4 | 0 |
| Tanner, currier, skinner | 4 | 5 |
| Potter | 0 | 2 |
| Others* | 6 | 2 |

\* Umbrella and staymaker, bookbinder, cooper, roper.

### The Preston election of 1841

The pollbook is in Manchester Public Library.

| Result: | | |
|---|---|---|
| Sir Hesketh Fleetwood, Liberal | 1,655 |
| Sir George Strickland, Liberal | 1,629 |
| R. Townley Parker, Conservative | 1,270 |
| Charles Swainson, Conservative | 1,255 |

Selected categories only:

| | Fleetwood | Strickland | Parker | Swainson |
|---|---|---|---|---|
| I. Respectables and dependants | | | | |
| Gentlemen | 24 | 22 | 40 | 40 |
| Surgeons | 5 | 4 | 11 | 10 |
| Attorneys | 13 | 13 | 41 | 41 |
| Anglican clergy | 0 | 0 | 4 | 4 |
| Parish clerk | 0 | 0 | 1 | 1 |
| Bankers | 3 | 3 | 6 | 6 |
| Manufacturers | 10 | 10 | 11 | 11 |
| Turnkeys | 0 | 0 | 2 | 2 |
| Constable | 0 | 0 | 1 | 1 |
| Ministers | 3 | 4 | 0 | 0 |
| Auctioneers | 3 | 2 | 4 | 3 |
| II. Trade | | | | |
| Innkeepers | 27 | 27 | 26 | 26 |
| Beersellers | 6 | 6 | 0 | 0 |
| Butchers | 14 | 15 | 20 | 21 |
| Farmers | 2 | 1 | 7 | 7 |
| III. Labour | | | | |
| Tailors | 40 | 37 | 22 | 21 |
| Shoemakers | 83 | 81 | 30 | 30 |
| Cloggers | 13 | 13 | 0 | 0 |
| Overlookers | 25 | 25 | 36 | 35 |
| Spinners | 112 | 112 | 89 | 89 |
| Weavers | 261 | 260 | 90 | 93 |

### The Preston election of 1852

This analysis is based on a pollbook in Manchester Public Library. A note at the end explains, 'When the Elector is registered through a £10 Qualification, his Profession or Business is not given.' As most electors were qualified as £10 householders, the analysis below creates no presumption as to the general

*The Preston election of 1852 (cont.)*

voting pattern except for occupations like weavers and spinners who were un-likely to be qualified except as freemen.

|  |  |
|---|---|
| Result: Robert Townley Parker, Conservative | 1,335 |
| Sir George Strickland, Bt., Radical | 1,253 |
| C. P. Grenfell, Whig | 1,127 |
| James German, Radical | 692 |

Freemen voters only:

| selected categories | Strickland | German | Grenfell | Parker |
|---|---|---|---|---|
| Manufacturers | 2 | 1 | 0 | 1 |
| Overlookers | 18 | 5 | 13 | 12 |
| Weavers | 137 | 64 | 90 | 44 |
| Spinners | 45 | 18 | 30 | 36 |
| Innkeepers | 3 | 0 | 2 | 5 |
| Brewers | 3 | 3 | 0 | 0 |
| Beersellers | 2 | 1 | 1 | 0 |
| Butchers | 5 | 6 | 7 | 10 |
| Shoemakers | 38 | 21 | 22 | 24 |
| Tailors | 15 | 12 | 8 | 8 |
| Gentlemen | 2 | 1 | 2 | 2 |
| Banker | 0 | 0 | 0 | 1 |
| Anglican clergy | 0 | 0 | 1 | 1 |
| Minister | 1 | 0 | 1 | 0 |
| Medical, legal, auctioneer | 0 | 0 | 0 | 3 |

| Parker's vote | | Strickland's vote | | Grenfell's vote | |
|---|---|---|---|---|---|
| Plumps | 358 | Plumps | 364 | Plumps | 75 |
| and Strickland | 101 | and Grenfell | 396 | and Parker | 621 |
| and Grenfell | 621 | and German | 392 | and Strickland | 396 |
| and German | 255 | and Parker | 101 | and German | 35 |

| German's vote | |
|---|---|
| Plumps | 10 |
| and Strickland | 392 |
| and Parker | 255 |
| and Grenfell | 35 |

The religious atmosphere of this election is shown in the following quotation from a contemporary broadsheet bound together with the 1852 pollbook:

### Popery—No Never
(Tune: 'Hearts of Oak')

*verse 2*    The vile priests of Rome would enslave us we know,
A wily, a base, an insidious foe:
They would make Britain's sons their base ignorant slaves,
As they have in each Land that their tyranny braves.
     Church and Queen is our cause,
     Firm and staunch are our men,
     Then PARKER FOR EVER
     Popery—no never.
     We'll vote, as did our Fathers vote,
     Again and again.

*The Preston election of 1852 (cont.)*

verse 3   The women of England so dear to these isles,
Shall mark all our acts, and reward with their smiles.
As they see us defending the land of their birth,
Old Protestant England—the pride of the Earth.
Church and Queen is our cause,
Firm and staunch are our men,
Then Grenfell FOR EVER
Popery—no never. . . [etc.]

### The Reading election of 1837

The pollbook is in the Guildhall Library.

Result: Talford, Liberal          468
Palmer, Liberal           457
Russell, Conservative      448

| Selected categories | Talford | Palmer | Russell |
|---|---|---|---|
| Surgeons | 5 | 5 | 7 |
| Clergy | 0 | 0 | 7 |
| Shoemakers | 6 | 6 | 3 |
| Dissenting ministers | 4 | 4 | 0 |
| Organist | 1 | 1 | 0 |
| Mayor | 1 | 1 | 0 |
| Parish clerk | 0 | 0 | 1 |
| Chymists | 2 | 2 | 3 |
| Biscuit maker | 1 | 0 | 0 |
| R.C. priest | 1 | 1 | 0 |
| Police | 1 | 1 | 0 |
| Manufacturer | 1 | 1 | 0 |

### The Reading election of 1841

The pollbook is in the Guildhall Library.

Result: Charles Russell, Conservative      576
Viscount Chelsea, Conservative      564
Thomas Mills, Liberal           409
Wm. Tooke, Liberal            396

| Selected categories | Mills | Tooke | Russell | Chelsea |
|---|---|---|---|---|
| Surgeons | 3 | 3 | 12 | 11 |
| Butchers | 6 | 6 | 6 | 6 |
| Grocers | 23 | 23 | 20 | 19 |
| Shoemakers | 26 | 25 | 16 | 15 |
| Labourers | 3 | 3 | 1 | 1 |
| Clergy | 0 | 0 | 10 | 10 |
| Parish clerk | 0 | 0 | 1 | 1 |
| Railwayman | 0 | 0 | 1 | 1 |
| Police | 0 | 0 | 1 | 1 |
| Farmers | 3 | 2 | 2 | 2 |
| Dissenting ministers | 2 | 2 | 1 | 1 |
| Engineers | 1 | 1 | 1 | 1 |
| Biscuit baker | 1 | 1 | 0 | 0 |
| Umbrella makers | 3 | 3 | 0 | 0 |

## The Rochdale election of 1841

The pollbook is in Rochdale Public Library.

Result:* W. S. Crawford, Radical    399
Fenton, Conservative    335

| | Radical | Con-servative | | Radical | Con-servative |
|---|---|---|---|---|---|
| **I. Drink interest** | | | Butchers | 14 | 11 |
| Beersellers | 28 | 24 | Clockmakers | 2 | 2 |
| Publicans | 14 | 31 | Cloggers | 4 | 2 |
| Others | 5 | 4 | Confectioners | 0 | 3 |
| | 47 | 59 | Curriers | 5 | 2 |
| | | | Drapers | 21 | 4 |
| **II. Textile interest** | | | Druggists | 4 | 4 |
| Weavers | 24 | 9 | Earthenware | 1 | 0 |
| Woolsorters | 3 | 5 | Fishmonger | 0 | 1 |
| Woolstaplers | 16 | 5 | Greengrocers | 3 | 0 |
| Machinery makers | 7 | 3 | Grocers | 58 | 22 |
| | | | Hatters | 7 | 2 |
| Overlookers | 1 | 5 | Ironmongers | 1 | 2 |
| Shoddy dealers | 0 | 6 | Pawnbrokers | 3 | 3 |
| Dyers | 5 | 1 | Saddlers | 2 | 1 |
| Cotton masters | 19 | 13 | Tailors | 9 | 6 |
| Cotton sheet makers | 1 | 1 | Tallow sellers | 1 | 1 |
| | | | Tripe seller | 0 | 1 |
| Fustian dresser | 0 | 1 | Watermen | 2 | 0 |
| Manufacturers | 26 | 16 | | 154 | 73 |
| | 102 | 65 | **V. Respectables and dependants** | | |
| **III. Craftsmen** | | | Agents | 4 | 3 |
| Blacksmiths | 3 | 3 | Auctioneers | 1 | 3 |
| Blacking maker | 1 | 0 | Bailiffs | 0 | 7 |
| Bricklayers | 2 | 1 | Bankers | 0 | 4 |
| Brush maker | 0 | 1 | Brokers | 1 | 4 |
| Coachmaker | 1 | 0 | Carriers | 3 | 2 |
| Engineers | 3 | 1 | Cheese factor | 1 | 0 |
| File cutters | 0 | 1 | Clerks | 5 | 8 |
| Ironfounders | 6 | 5 | Commercial traveller | 1 | 0 |
| Machine makers | 9 | 1 | Corn and malt | 6 | 2 |
| Masons | 0 | 3 | Farmers | 1 | 5 |
| Nail maker | 1 | 1 | Gardeners | 1 | 3 |
| Plumbers | 3 | 4 | Gentlemen | 6 | 22 |
| Printers | 3 | 2 | Ministers | 1 | 2 |
| Ropers | 2 | 2 | Organists, sextons | 0 | 4 |
| Tinplate makers | 5 | 2 | Schoolmasters | 5 | 3 |
| Wheelwrights | 3 | 1 | Solicitors | 5 | 14 |
| Whitesmiths | 2 | 0 | Surgeons | 4 | 4 |
| | 44 | 28 | Surveyor | 0 | 1 |
| **IV. Retailers** | | | Servants, etc. | 2 | 8 |
| Barbers | 6 | 3 | | 47 | 99 |
| Shoemakers | 11 | 3 | | | |

* McCalmont's figure of 338 for Fenton and 339 for Crawford does not accord with the pollbook or with Bean.

11-3

### The Rochdale election of 1857

The pollbook is in the Rochdale Public Library.

Result: Ramsay, Conservative  529
Miall, Liberal  487

| | Liberal | Con-servative | | Liberal | Con-servative |
|---|---|---|---|---|---|
| **I. Drink** | | | Warehousemen | 4 | 2 |
| Beersellers | 16 | 63 | Waste dealers | 6 | 11 |
| Publicans | 10 | 46 | Dentists | 2 | 0 |
| Wine dealers | 1 | 5 | Flannel dealers | 2 | 1 |
| Spirits dealer | 0 | 1 | Wool staplers | 13 | 6 |
| Maltster | 0 | 1 | | 87 | 98 |
| Hop merchant | 0 | 1 | | | |
| Brewer | 0 | 1 | **V. Craftsmen** | | |
| Cooper | 1 | 0 | Blacksmiths | 3 | 3 |
| | 28 | 118 | Boilermakers | 3 | 1 |
| **II. Capital** | | | Shoemakers | 13 | 5 |
| Bankers | 0 | 3 | Brass, iron founders | 6 | 5 |
| Woollen manu-facturers | 18 | 22 | Bricksetters | 3 | 1 |
| Corn millers | 1 | 2 | Brushmakers | 1 | 2 |
| Cotton spinners | 12 | 26 | Cabinet makers | 8 | 3 |
| Dyers | 3 | 1 | Coachbuilders | 6 | 9 |
| | 34 | 54 | Cardmakers | 2 | 0 |
| **III. Retailers** | | | Cloggers | 4 | 9 |
| Confectioners | 2 | 2 | Machine makers | 11 | 4 |
| Drapers | 35 | 8 | Mechanics | 5 | 1 |
| Druggists | 3 | 7 | Painters | 5 | 3 |
| Earthenware | 1 | 1 | Plumbers | 1 | 5 |
| Greengrocers | 4 | 0 | Reed makers | 4 | 2 |
| Grocers | 71 | 37 | Ropers | 1 | 1 |
| Hairdressers | 7 | 7 | Saddlers | 0 | 3 |
| Hatters | 5 | 1 | Shuttle makers | 3 | 0 |
| Ironmongers | 4 | 1 | Spindle makers | 0 | 2 |
| Pawnbrokers | 4 | 1 | Stone masons | 0 | 3 |
| Smallware | 7 | 4 | Tailors | 11 | 6 |
| Tallow sellers | 0 | 2 | Tinners | 2 | 3 |
| Bakers | 1 | 1 | Watch makers | 3 | 2 |
| Booksellers | 7 | 5 | Weavers | 3 | 5 |
| Butchers | 16 | 25 | Wool sorters | 8 | 2 |
| | 167 | 102 | Curriers | 4 | 1 |
| **IV. Respectables, merchants** | | | Engineers | 9 | 7 |
| Agents | 29 | 31 | Doffing Plate makers | 3 | 0 |
| Attorneys | 2 | 13 | Joiners | 11 | 7 |
| Auctioneers | 2 | 2 | | 133 | 95 |
| Brokers | 1 | 2 | | | |
| Cheese factors | 2 | 2 | **VI. Others** | | |
| Managers | 6 | 6 | Labourers | 3 | 2 |
| Ministers | 13 | 5 | Farmers | 0 | 4 |
| Schoolmasters | 2 | 4 | Gardeners | 0 | 3 |
| Surgeons | 2 | 11 | Carriers | 1 | 4 |
| Surveyors | 1 | 2 | Miscellaneous | 33 | 49 |
| | | | | 37 | 62 |

## The Rochester election of August 1830

The pollbook is in the Institute of Historical Research.

| | | |
|---|---|---|
| Result: Ralph Bernal, Whig | 429 | |
| Viscount Villiers, Tory | 417 | |
| John Mills, Tory | 339 | |

| Selected categories | Bernal | Villiers | Mills |
|---|---|---|---|
| Gentlemen | 52 | 56 | 22 |
| Officers | 3 | 3 | 0 |
| Surgeons | 7 | 8 | 2 |
| Solicitors | 3 | 6 | 2 |
| Farmers | 4 | 4 | 2 |
| Victuallers | 16 | 11 | 12 |
| Grocers | 5 | 6 | 9 |
| Chemists | 4 | 1 | 0 |
| Tailors | 15 | 7 | 14 |
| Cordwainers | 17 | 12 | 27 |
| Labourers | 7 | 9 | 10 |
| Shipwrights | 17 | 18 | 30 |
| Pilots | 3 | 3 | 1 |
| Mariners | 23 | 30 | 15 |
| Dredgermen | 26 | 22 | 39 |
| Cabinetmakers | 10 | 8 | 6 |

| Plumps | | Splits | |
|---|---|---|---|
| Bernal | 84 | Bernal and Villiers | 305 |
| Villiers | 50 | Bernal and Mills | 40 |
| Mills | 237 | Villiers and Mills | 62 |

Residences of voters at this election

| | |
|---|---|
| Rochester | 283 |
| Strood | 45 |
| Gillingham | 22 |
| Chatham | 67 |
| Rest of Kent | 161 |
| London | 178 |
| Rest of England | 23 |

## The Rochester election of 1835

The pollbook is in the Guildhall Library.

| | | |
|---|---|---|
| Result: Ralph Bernal, Liberal | 502 | |
| T. T. Hodges, Liberal | 443 | |
| Lord Chas. Wellesley, Conservative | 442 | |

| Selected categories | Bernal | Hodges | Wellesley |
|---|---|---|---|
| Shoemakers | 25 | 23 | 29 |
| Tailors | 15 | 13 | 15 |
| Fishermen | 16 | 13 | 14 |
| Dredgermen | 27 | 25 | 21 |
| Mariners | 18 | 15 | 11 |
| Saddlers | 6 | 6 | 2 |

*The Rochester election of 1835 (cont.)*

| Selected categories | Bernal | Hodges | Wellesley |
|---|---|---|---|
| Butchers | 20 | 19 | 11 |
| Grocers | 20 | 18 | 12 |
| Labourers | 6 | 3 | 7 |
| Surgeons | 7 | 6 | 3 |
| Victuallers | 38 | 33 | 19 |
| Gentlemen | 54 | 49 | 49 |
| Shipwrights | 2 | 4 | 22 |
| Pilots | 2 | 1 | 1 |
| Mayor | 0 | 0 | 1 |
| Serjeant at mace | 0 | 0 | 1 |
| Organist | 0 | 0 | 1 |
| Shipbuilders | 1 | 1 | 0 |
| Anglican clergy | 3 | 2 | 13 |
| Common councilmen | 2 | 2 | 5 |
| Aldermen | 3 | 3 | 5 |
| Verger | 0 | 0 | 1 |
| Farmers | 7 | 6 | 10 |
| Gaoler | 0 | 0 | 1 |
| Bankers | 2 | 2 | 0 |
| Police | 0 | 0 | 1 |
| Officers | 0 | 0 | 5 |
| Town clerk | 0 | 0 | 1 |
| Barge owner | 1 | 1 | 0 |

### The Rochester election of 1852

The pollbook is in the Guildhall Library.

Result: Villiers, Conservative 599
Maddock, Conservative 594
Bernal, Liberal 515
Twisden Hodges, Liberal 509

| Selected categories | Bernal | Hodges | Villiers | Maddock |
|---|---|---|---|---|
| Officers | 3 | 2 | 5 | 5 |
| Town Crier | 0 | 0 | 1 | 1 |
| Police | 0 | 0 | 9 | 9 |
| Farmers | 1 | 1 | 11 | 11 |
| Verger | 0 | 0 | 1 | 1 |
| Dredgermen | 6 | 7 | 14 | 15 |
| Bargemen | 6 | 6 | 3 | 3 |
| Pilots | 1 | 0 | 1 | 1 |
| Ship owners | 2 | 2 | 0 | 0 |
| Relieving officer | 1 | 1 | 0 | 0 |
| Parish clerks | 0 | 0 | 2 | 2 |
| Watermen | 1 | 1 | 3 | 3 |
| Sailmakers | 3 | 4 | 5 | 6 |
| Inspector of weights | 0 | 0 | 1 | 1 |
| Organist | 0 | 0 | 1 | 1 |
| Dissenting minister | 1 | 1 | 0 | 0 |

*The Rochester election of 1852 (cont.)*

| Selected categories | Bernal | Hodges | Villiers | Maddock |
|---|---|---|---|---|
| Shipwrights | 6 | 5 | 11 | 11 |
| Shipbuilder | 1 | 1 | 0 | 0 |
| Clergy | 1 | 1 | 3 | 3 |
| Surgeons | 4 | 4 | 5 | 6 |
| Shoemakers | 28 | 28 | 23 | 23 |
| Tailors | 10 | 10 | 10 | 10 |
| Fishermen | 11 | 9 | 16 | 14 |
| Mariners | 32 | 31 | 45 | 44 |
| Butchers | 11 | 11 | 17 | 17 |
| Grocers | 22 | 22 | 12 | 12 |
| Labourers | 18 | 18 | 17 | 17 |
| Victuallers | 25 | 25 | 17 | 17 |
| Gentlemen | 42 | 42 | 43 | 43 |

## The Rochester election of 1856

The pollbook is in the Guildhall Library.

Result: Wykeham Martin, Liberal   560
Henry Bodkin, Conservative   499

| Selected categories | Martin | Bodkin |
|---|---|---|
| Macebearers | 0 | 2 |
| Bankers | 0 | 2 |
| Relieving officers | 1 | 1 |
| Railwaymen | 2 | 1 |
| Parish clerk | 1 | 0 |
| Engineers | 4 | 0 |
| Officers | 1 | 4 |
| Pilot | 0 | 1 |
| Farmers | 5 | 11 |
| Police | 0 | 14 |
| Bargemen | 14 | 5 |
| Organist | 0 | 1 |
| Dredgermen | 9 | 10 |
| Inspector of weights | 0 | 1 |
| Town crier | 0 | 1 |
| Shipwrights | 6 | 13 |
| Clergy | 1 | 2 |
| Saddlers | 1 | 3 |
| Fishermen | 4 | 9 |
| Shoemakers | 29 | 17 |
| Tailors | 10 | 10 |
| Mariners | 35 | 23 |
| Butchers | 14 | 13 |
| Grocers | 19 | 9 |
| Labourers | 19 | 23 |
| Surgeons | 10 | 4 |
| Gentlemen | 47 | 32 |
| Shipowners | 2 | 0 |

## The Rochester election of 1859

The pollbook is in the Guildhall Library.

Result: Wykeham Martin, Liberal 665
Kinglake, Liberal 662
Money, Conservative 505
Mitchell, Conservative 492

| Selected categories | Martin | Kinglake | Money | Mitchell |
|---|---|---|---|---|
| Shoemakers | 23 | 22 | 18 | 17 |
| Fishermen | 1 | 1 | 3 | 3 |
| Mariners | 33 | 31 | 21 | 21 |
| Clergy | 2 | 2 | 7 | 7 |
| Dissenting ministers | 2 | 2 | 0 | 0 |
| Parish clerk | 0 | 0 | 1 | 1 |
| Organist | 0 | 0 | 1 | 1 |
| Labourers | 16 | 16 | 18 | 18 |
| Surgeons | 9 | 9 | 9 | 9 |
| Railwaymen | 2 | 2 | 1 | 1 |
| Officers | 1 | 1 | 1 | 1 |
| Shipowners | 4 | 4 | 0 | 0 |
| Shipwrights | 7 | 7 | 13 | 13 |
| Pilots | 1 | 1 | 1 | 1 |
| Dredgermen | 22 | 21 | 23 | 22 |
| Farmers | 2 | 2 | 11 | 15 |
| Barge builder | 1 | 1 | 0 | 0 |
| Barge owners | 2 | 2 | 1 | 1 |
| Bargemen | 20 | 16 | 0 | 0 |
| Sanitary inspector | 0 | 0 | 1 | 1 |
| Macebearers | 0 | 0 | 2 | 2 |
| Relieving officer | 1 | 1 | 0 | 0 |
| Engineers | 3 | 3 | 2 | 2 |
| Vergers | 0 | 0 | 2 | 2 |
| Town crier | 0 | 0 | 1 | 1 |
| Police | 0 | 0 | 2 | 2 |

## The Rochester election of 1865

The pollbook is in the Guildhall Library.

Result: Wykeham Martin, Liberal 855
Kinglake, Liberal 792
Smee, Conservative 414

| Selected categories | Martin | Kinglake | Smee |
|---|---|---|---|
| Shoemakers | 19 | 17 | 11 |
| Fishermen | 4 | 3 | 5 |
| Mariners | 39 | 38 | 17 |
| Clergy | 2 | 2 | 3 |
| Dissenting ministers | 1 | 1 | 0 |
| Parish clerks | 1 | 1 | 1 |

*The Rochester election of 1865 (cont.)*

| Selected categories | Martin | Kinglake | Smee |
|---|---|---|---|
| Labourers | 23 | 18 | 16 |
| Surgeons | 8 | 7 | 1 |
| Railwaymen | 13 | 13 | 1 |
| Officers | 3 | 3 | 1 |
| Shipwrights | 7 | 6 | 7 |
| Ship owner | 1 | 1 | 0 |
| Dredgermen | 15 | 13 | 3 |
| Farmers | 1 | 1 | 9 |
| Barge owners | 2 | 2 | 0 |
| Bargemen | 7 | 4 | 8 |
| Bargemasters | 21 | 21 | 7 |
| Engineers | 9 | 9 | 1 |
| Verger | 0 | 0 | 1 |
| Macebearer | 1 | 1 | 0 |

## The Rochester election of 1868

The pollbook is in the Institute of Historical Research.

Result: P. W. Martin, Liberal     1,458
J. A. Kinglake, Liberal     1,305
A. Smee, Conservative     703

| Selected categories | Martin | Smee |
|---|---|---|
| Anglican clergy | 0 | 4 |
| Vergers | 0 | 3 |
| Organist | 0 | 1 |
| Presbyterian minister | 1 | 0 |
| Publicans | 33 | 17 |
| Brewers | 2 | 2 |
| Beersellers | 11 | 8 |
| Labourers | 180 | 116 |
| Shoemakers | 25 | 12 |
| Surgeons | 5 | 4 |
| Gentlemen | 59 | 21 |
| Pensioners | 6 | 8 |
| Engineers | 6 | 0 |
| Postmen | 8 | 1 |
| Saddlers | 2 | 0 |
| Postmaster | 0 | 1 |
| Turnkeys | 9 | 5 |
| Customs | 4 | 1 |
| Coastguard | 2 | 0 |
| Wharfingers | 5 | 1 |
| Master mariners | 14 | 0 |
| Mariners | 40 | 21 |
| Sailmakers | 12 | 8 |
| Fishermen | 24 | 14 |

*The Rochester election of 1868 (cont.)*

| Selected categories | Martin | Smee |
|---|---|---|
| Shipwrights | 27 | 19 |
| Watermen | 10 | 6 |
| Dredgermen | 9 | 3 |
| Coalwhippers | 1 | 5 |
| Bargemasters and owners | 41 | 2 |
| Bargebuilder | 1 | 0 |
| Bargemen | 7 | 36 |

### The Rutland election of 1841

The pollbook is in Cambridge University Library.

Result: G. J. Heathcote, Liberal     767
Hon. W. H. Dawnay, Conservative     676
Hon. C. G. Noel, Liberal     664

| | Noel | Heathcote | Dawnay | Abstained |
|---|---|---|---|---|
| Clergymen | 9 | 19 | 39 | 8 |

### The Sandwich election of May 1831

The pollbook is in the Institute of Historical Research.

Result: Joseph Marryat, Whig     498
Sir E. T. Troubridge, Whig     397
S. G. Price, Tory     297

| Selected categories | Marryat | Troubridge | Price |
|---|---|---|---|
| Gentlemen | 43 | 36 | 30 |
| Officers | 4 | 15 | 4 |
| Surgeons | 1 | 3 | 1 |
| Sextons | 2 | 1 | 1 |
| Pilots | 3 | 1 | 2 |
| Innkeepers | 10 | 6 | 6 |
| Butchers | 7 | 5 | 4 |
| Grocers | 11 | 9 | 6 |
| Carpenters | 29 | 26 | 11 |
| Cabinetmakers | 15 | 10 | 7 |
| Labourers | 56 | 23 | 39 |
| Mariners | 36 | 35 | 12 |
| Tailors | 17 | 13 | 9 |
| Shoemakers | 24 | 15 | 13 |
| Weavers | 4 | 4 | 1 |
| Farmers | 16 | 17 | 2 |

| Plumps | | Splits | |
|---|---|---|---|
| Marryat | 20 | Marryat and Price | 156 |
| Troubridge | 61 | Price and Troubridge | 14 |
| Price | 127 | Troubridge and Marryat | 322 |

## The Sandwich election of 1852

The pollbook is in the Guildhall Library.

Result: Pelham Clinton, Peelite  460
French, Liberal  257

| Selected categories | French | Clinton |
|---|---|---|
| Pilots | 1 | 45 |
| Officers | 5 | 6 |
| Clergy | 0 | 5 |
| Surgeons | 3 | 5 |
| Mariners | 4 | 24 |
| Butchers | 2 | 15 |
| Grocers | 13 | 9 |
| Dissenting ministers | 4 | 0 |
| Shoemakers | 9 | 14 |
| Labourers | 2 | 21 |
| Master of the hospital | 0 | 1 |

## The Sandwich election of 1859

The pollbook is in the Guildhall Library.

Result: Hugessen, Liberal  497
Paget, Liberal  458
Fergusson, Conservative  404
Lewis, Conservative  328

| Selected categories | Hugessen | Paget | Fergusson | Lewis |
|---|---|---|---|---|
| Pilots | 26 | 24 | 11 | 7 |
| Officers | 5 | 6 | 6 | 6 |
| Clergy | 0 | 0 | 5 | 5 |
| Surgeons | 7 | 6 | 5 | 4 |
| Mariners | 14 | 15 | 11 | 11 |
| Butchers | 10 | 11 | 14 | 9 |
| Grocers | 21 | 21 | 8 | 8 |
| Dissenting ministers | 5 | 6 | 1 | 1 |
| Shoemakers | 10 | 10 | 6 | 6 |
| Labourers | 14 | 11 | 19 | 17 |
| Hospitalians | 6 | 7 | 1 | 0 |
| Farmers | 8 | 10 | 7 | 6 |
| Engineer | 0 | 0 | 1 | 1 |
| Railwayman | 1 | 0 | 1 | 0 |
| Fishermen | 0 | 0 | 2 | 2 |
| Gasworkers | 2 | 2 | 1 | 1 |

## The Sandwich, Deal, and Walmer election of 1868

The pollbook is in the Guildhall Library.

Result: E. H. Knatchbull-Hugessen, Liberal    933
H. A. Brassey, Liberal    923
Henry Worms, Conservative    710

| Selected categories | Hugessen | Brassey | Worms |
|---|---|---|---|
| Officers | 2 | 0 | 5 |
| Coastguards | 6 | 6 | 13 |
| Clergymen | 4 | 1 | 11 |
| Dissenting ministers | 4 | 4 | 0 |
| Sexton | 1 | 1 | 0 |
| R.C. priest | 1 | 1 | 0 |
| Brewers | 6 | 6 | 1 |
| Railwaymen | 7 | 5 | 3 |
| Surgeons | 7 | 7 | 3 |
| Lawyers | 2 | 1 | 3 |
| Farmers | 16 | 17 | 10 |
| Hospitalians | 12 | 11 | 1 |
| Butchers | 10 | 11 | 21 |
| Grocers | 22 | 22 | 12 |
| Victuallers | 46 | 45 | 48 |
| Beersellers | 2 | 2 | 4 |
| Shoemakers | 35 | 31 | 15 |
| Carpenters | 33 | 32 | 21 |
| Mariners | 134 | 133 | 60 |
| Labourers | 119 | 128 | 102 |
| Sweeps | 5 | 5 | 0 |
| Gentlemen | 72 | 68 | 53 |
| Pilots | 34 | 33 | 20 |
| Harbour master | 0 | 0 | 1 |

## The Scottish Universities election of 1868

G. W. T. Omond, in his book *The Lord Advocates of Scotland 1834–1880*, printed on page 245 an analysis of the voting of the ministers and clergy of the various denominations in the Scottish Universities election of 1868, when Playfair and Moncreiff were elected.

| | Liberal | Tory |
|---|---|---|
| Established Church | 67 | 1,221 |
| Free Church | 607 | 33 |
| United Presbyterian | 474 | 1 |
| Episcopalians | 4 | 78 |
| Not classified | 360 | 35 |
| | 1,512 | 1,368 |

If correct, these results are striking: but unfortunately no source is stated. Omond adds that a majority of the doctors in the constituency voted Liberal, and a majority of the lawyers were Tory.

## The Shrewsbury election of August 1830

The pollbook is in the Institute of Historical Research.

Result: Richard Jenkins, Tory   754
R. A. Slaney, Whig   563
Panton Corbett, Tory   446

| Selected categories | Slaney | Jenkins | Corbett |
|---|---|---|---|
| Parish clerks | 0 | 2 | 2 |
| Organist | 0 | 1 | 0 |
| Gentlemen | 12 | 25 | 24 |
| Bankers | 2 | 2 | 5 |
| Surgeons | 3 | 6 | 7 |
| Lawyers | 0 | 7 | 8 |
| Farmers | 2 | 1 | 1 |
| Innkeepers | 8 | 12 | 6 |
| Butchers | 35 | 60 | 31 |
| Grocers | 12 | 14 | 15 |
| Shoemakers | 112 | 100 | 28 |
| Weavers | 9 | 5 | 2 |
| Labourers | 28 | 32 | 13 |

| Splits | | Plumps | |
|---|---|---|---|
| Jenkins and Slaney | 362 | Slaney | 131 |
| Jenkins and Corbett | 357 | Jenkins | 35 |
| Slaney and Corbett | 70 | Corbett | 70 |

## The Shrewsbury election of 1837

The pollbook is in the Institute of Historical Research.

Result: Jenkins, Conservative   700
Slaney, Liberal   697
Pelham, Conservative   655
Dashwood, Liberal   537

| Selected categories | Slaney | Dashwood | Jenkins | Pelham |
|---|---|---|---|---|
| Gentlemen | 26 | 18 | 49 | 46 |
| Dissenting ministers | 3 | 3 | 0 | 0 |
| Parish clerks | 0 | 0 | 2 | 2 |
| Organist | 0 | 0 | 1 | 1 |
| Policeman | 1 | 1 | 0 | 0 |
| Gaoler | 1 | 1 | 0 | 0 |
| Bankers | 1 | 0 | 4 | 4 |
| Surgeons | 3 | 1 | 10 | 12 |
| Lawyers | 6 | 5 | 19 | 21 |
| Farmers | 4 | 2 | 4 | 4 |
| Publicans | 39 | 27 | 25 | 26 |
| Beersellers | 6 | 6 | 5 | 5 |

*The Shrewsbury election of 1837 (cont.)*

| Selected categories | Slaney | Dashwood | Jenkins | Pelham |
|---|---|---|---|---|
| Grocers | 19 | 15 | 18 | 17 |
| Butchers | 27 | 20 | 28 | 26 |
| Shoemakers | 64 | 62 | 40 | 39 |
| Carpenters | 16 | 15 | 23 | 21 |
| Tailors | 37 | 29 | 37 | 31 |
| Weavers | 6 | 6 | 2 | 2 |
| Curriers | 6 | 6 | 4 | 4 |
| Labourers | 19 | 17 | 16 | 15 |

Splits

Jenkins and Pelham   604
Slaney and Dashwood  536

### The Shrewsbury election of 1847

Result: E. H. Baldock, Peelite   767
R. A. Slaney, Liberal   743
G. Tomline, Liberal   740

| Selected categories | Tomline | Slaney | Baldock |
|---|---|---|---|
| Gentlemen | 28 | 51 | 42 |
| Surgeons | 7 | 6 | 8 |
| Solicitors | 24 | 10 | 22 |
| Bankers | 3 | 1 | 3 |
| Architects | 2 | 0 | 2 |
| Headmaster* | 0 | 1 | 0 |
| Brewers | 1 | 4 | 3 |
| Innkeepers | 35 | 31 | 31 |
| Beersellers | 8 | 7 | 7 |
| Grocers | 8 | 20 | 12 |
| Butchers | 37 | 21 | 35 |
| Organists | 2 | 1 | 3 |
| Vestry clerks | 1 | 1 | 2 |
| Turnkey | 0 | 1 | 1 |
| R.C. priest | 1 | 1 | 0 |
| Sweep | 1 | 1 | 0 |
| Police officers | 4 | 0 | 4 |
| Dissenting minister | 0 | 1 | 0 |

\* Dr Kennedy, D.D., of Shrewsbury School.

### The Shrewsbury election of 1857

The pollbook is in Manchester Reference Library, as political tract P. 2759. Mr John Kenyon of Toronto University kindly drew my attention to this item.

Result: Tomline, Liberal   706
Slaney, Liberal   695
Huddleston, Conservative   548
Phibbs, Conservative   484

Twenty-six freeholders and 100 householders did not vote. Twenty-two voters plumped for one candidate, and 75 gave a vote for one Whig and one Tory

*The Shrewsbury election of 1857 (cont.)*

candidate. The following analysis, however, includes only those who gave a straight party vote for two candidates. Unfortunately, about 200 of these, or about one-sixth of those voting, had no occupation stated. The following figures must therefore be treated with caution.

|  | Liberal | Conservative |
|---|---|---|
| I. Gentlemen | 31 | 37 |
| Clergy, teachers | 8 | 2 |
| Solicitors | 11 | 17 |
| Medical | 4 | 13 |
| Merchants | 21 | 8 |
| Masters | 8 | 9 |
| Professional, etc. | 1 | 9 |
| Clerks | 22 | 29 |
| Innkeepers | 53 | ·32 |
| Farmers | 4 | 0 |
| II. Butchers | 10 | 21 |
| Other shopkeepers | 106 | 51 |
| Bakers, confectioners | 20 | 2 |
| Grocers | 36 | 10 |
| Mercers, drapers | 17 | 7 |
| Hatters | 1 | 5 |
| Chemists | 5 | 5 |
| Cowkeepers | 7 | 6 |
| Ironmongers | 8 | 6 |
| Stationers | 2 | 2 |
| Fishmongers | 0 | 2 |
| Barbers | 6 | 4 |
| Wine merchants | 2 | 2 |
| Jewellers | 2 | 0 |
| Painters | 17 | 12 |
| III. Printing crafts | 12 | 13 |
| Smiths, metal workers | 20 | 23 |
| Luxury crafts | 8 | 12 |
| Building crafts | 42 | 30 |
| Tailors | 25 | 18 |
| Shoemakers | 40 | 19 |
| Furniture makers | 10 | 7 |
| Other trades | 21 | 14 |
| IV. Engine-drivers | 3 | 0 |
| Engineers | 18 | 0 |
| V. Unskilled | 23 | 21 |
| VI. Occupation unstated | 133 | 70 |

| Summary: | Liberal | Conservative |
|---|---|---|
| I. Commercial, professional, and property owning | 155 | 156 |
| II. Retailers | 116 | 72 |
| III. Craftsmen | 195 | 136 |
| IV. Engineers, engine-drivers | 21 | 0 |
| V. Unskilled | 23 | 21 |
| VI. Occupations unstated | 133 | 70 |

## The Shrewsbury election of 1868

The pollbook is in the Bodleian Library.

Result: Wm. J. Clement, Liberal     1,840
Jas. Figgins, Conservative     1,751
Robt. Crawford, Liberal     685

Figgins was a London typefounder, and sometime Sheriff of London and Middlesex. Clement was a practising surgeon, a former Mayor of Shrewsbury, a J.P. and Deputy Lieutenant of Merioneth, and the patron of a living.

| Selected categories | Clement | Crawford | Figgins |
|---|---|---|---|
| Turnkeys | 2 | 0 | 9 |
| Sweeps | 4 | 4 | 0 |
| Clergymen | 1 | 0 | 4 |
| Organist | 0 | 0 | 1 |
| Sexton | 0 | 0 | 1 |
| Vestry clerk | 1 | 0 | 1 |
| Postman and P.O. clerks* | 6 | 0 | 12 |
| Dissenting ministers | 8 | 6 | 0 |
| Bankers | 3 | 0 | 3 |
| Farmers | 6 | 1 | 7 |
| Gentlemen | 77 | 10 | 71 |
| Surgeons | 13 | 2 | 16 |
| Lawyers | 17 | 0 | 22 |
| Victuallers | 57 | 9 | 65 |
| Beersellers | 17 | 7 | 19 |
| Printers | 23 | 10 | 25 |
| Shoemakers | 101 | 50 | 92 |
| Tailors | 84 | 47 | 57 |
| Carpenters | 60 | 37 | 43 |
| Grocers | 23 | 6 | 18 |
| Butchers | 25 | 8 | 28 |
| Railwaymen | 73 | 38 | 58 |
| Labourers | 131 | 85 | 147 |

| Plumps | | Splits | |
|---|---|---|---|
| Figgins | 703 | Clement and Figgins | 1,047 |
| Clement | 147 | Clement and Crawford | 672 |
| Crawford | 30 | Crawford and Figgins | 2 |

\* The postmaster plumped for Figgins.

## The Shropshire election of 1831

An analysis of a Tory victory at the Reform general election of 1831 in the 'most Tory county in England'. The pollbook is in Manchester Reference Library.

Result: Sir Rowland Hill, Tory     1,824
J. C. Pelham, Esq., Tory     1,355
William Lloyd, Whig     835
John Mytton, Whig     395

### Voters A–G inclusive

| Selected categories | Hill | Pelham | Lloyd | Mytton |
|---|---|---|---|---|
| Gentlemen | 93 | 89 | 30 | 15 |
| Farmers | 230 | 175 | 84 | 46 |

The two Darbys of Coalbrookdale each split their votes between Lloyd and Mytton. Viscount Clive voted for Hill and Pelham.

### All voters except farmers and gentlemen

| | Hill | Pelham | Lloyd | Mytton |
|---|---|---|---|---|
| I. Clergymen | 99 | 89 | 15 | 2 |
| Parish clerks | 74 | 67 | 10 | 7 |
| Organist | 1 | 1 | 0 | 0 |
| Dissenting ministers* | 0 | 0 | 2 | 1 |
| II. Surgeons | 18 | 10 | 10 | 2 |
| Lawyers | 13 | 12 | 8 | 2 |
| Schoolmasters | 15 | 9 | 4 | 1 |
| Surveyor, auctioneer, bailiff, land agent | 22 | 15 | 12 | 4 |
| Vets., farriers | 5 | 2 | 2 | 0 |
| III. Bankers | 11 | 9 | 3 | 0 |
| Ironmasters | 4 | 2 | 6 | 1 |
| Builders | 12 | 8 | 6 | 4 |
| Innkeepers | 60 | 38 | 33 | 20 |
| Millers, maltsters | 62 | 51 | 36 | 11 |
| Brickmakers | 8 | 4 | 2 | 1 |
| Bargeowners | 9 | 9 | 4 | 1 |
| Merchants | 16 | 7 | 16 | 3 |
| IV. Butchers | 41 | 30 | 23 | 18 |
| Bakers | 10 | 9 | 11 | 3 |
| Chemists | 3 | 2 | 4 | 1 |
| Hairdressers | 4 | 3 | 3 | 2 |
| Ironmongers | 12 | 6 | 12 | 2 |
| Wine merchants | 8 | 4 | 5 | 1 |
| Booksellers | 1 | 0 | 3 | 2 |
| Drapers, glovers, hatters | 21 | 17 | 21 | 8 |
| Grocers and other shops | 42 | 23 | 49 | 18 |

* The votes of three Dissenting ministers who wished to vote for Lloyd and Mytton were disallowed.

*The Shropshire election of 1831 (cont.)*

|  | Hill | Pelham | Lloyd | Mytton |
|---|---|---|---|---|
| V. Labourers | 88 | 64 | 44 | 30 |
| Weavers | 4 | 3 | 2 | 2 |
| Miners, colliers | 11 | 7 | 10 | 2 |
| Servants, gardeners | 29 | 18 | 11 | 5 |
| Carters | 8 | 6 | 5 | 2 |
| Miscellaneous | 54 | 37 | 48 | 21 |
| VI. Shoemakers | 39 | 28 | 45 | 30 |
| Tailors | 22 | 15 | 22 | 14 |
| Printers | 4 | 1 | 2 | 0 |
| Coopers | 7 | 4 | 9 | 4 |
| Blacksmiths | 33 | 20 | 15 | 11 |
| Plumbers | 6 | 4 | 3 | 2 |
| Building crafts | 33 | 21 | 15 | 12 |
| Brazier, tinman, white-smith, watchmaker | 14 | 6 | 11 | 4 |
| Saddlers | 13 | 10 | 6 | 4 |
| Tanners, Skinners | 9 | 6 | 10 | 2 |
| Cabinetmakers, upholsterers | 12 | 6 | 6 | 5 |
| Curriers | 3 | 4 | 13 | 5 |
| Joiners, carpenters, sawyers | 33 | 30 | 22 | 17 |
| Painters, glaziers | 17 | 9 | 11 | 3 |
| Wheelwrights | 21 | 16 | 13 | 7 |

| Plumps | | Splits | |
|---|---|---|---|
| Hill | 275 | Hill and Pelham | 1,268 |
| Pelham | 46 | Lloyd and Mytton | 285 |
| Lloyd | 267 | Hill and Lloyd | 251 |
| Mytton | 71 | Hill and Mytton | 30 |
| | | Pelham and Lloyd | 32 |
| | | Pelham and Mytton | 9 |

### The Shropshire (North) election of 1832

The pollbook is in the Guildhall Library.

Result: Rowland Hill, Conservative 3,002
John Cotes, Liberal 2,104
Ormesby Gore, Conservative 2,032

Voters A–D inclusive:

| selected categories | Cotes | Hill | Gore |
|---|---|---|---|
| Clergymen | 8 | 18 | 16 |
| Dissenting minister | 0 | 1 | 0 |
| Ironmasters | 3 | 0 | 2 |
| Colliers | 10 | 0 | 0 |
| Parish clerks | 4 | 5 | 4 |
| Shoemakers | 22 | 16 | 6 |
| Gentlemen | 27 | 47 | 36 |
| Farmers | 192 | 307 | 192 |
| Labourers | 45 | 54 | 29 |

### The Southampton election of 1852

Result: B. M. Willcox, Liberal    1,058
Sir A. E. Cockburn, Liberal    1,012
A. B. Cochrane, Conservative    797
A. A. Vansittart, Conservative    770

| Selected categories | Willcox | Cockburn | Cochrane | Vansittart |
|---|---|---|---|---|
| Dissenting ministers | 4 | 4 | 0 | 0 |
| R.N., all ranks | 5 | 5 | 7 | 7 |
| Army, all ranks | 0 | 0 | 10 | 10 |
| Bankers | 2 | 2 | 0 | 0 |
| Railway, all grades | 16 | 15 | 5 | 4 |
| Boilermakers | 6 | 6 | 2 | 0 |
| Anglican clergy | 0 | 0 | 11 | 12 |
| Servants | 2 | 2 | 6 | 6 |
| Police, all grades | 5 | 5 | 0 | 1 |
| Saddlers | 4 | 4 | 2 | 2 |
| Pilots | 4 | 3 | 6 | 5 |
| Sexton | 0 | 0 | 1 | 1 |
| Surgeons | 10 | 9 | 9 | 10 |
| Master mariners | 4 | 3 | 4 | 3 |
| Mariners | 40 | 30 | 13 | 7 |
| Labourers | 27 | 27 | 11 | 11 |
| Merchants | 24 | 21 | 18 | 15 |
| Sailmakers | 2 | 2 | 4 | 4 |
| Shipwrights | 15 | 13 | 5 | 3 |

### The Staffordshire (West) election of 1868

The pollbook is in Cambridge University Library.

Result: Smith Child, Conservative    3,909
H. F. M. Ingram, Conservative    3,773
W. O. Foster, Liberal    3,295
H. W. H. Foley, Liberal    3,244

Clergymen:   for Ingram    60
for Child    60
for Foley    5
for Foster    6
Abstained    12 (mostly living at a distance)

### The Stockport election of 1847

Result: Cobden, Liberal    643
James Heald, Tory    570
James Kershaw, Liberal    537
John West, Radical    14

| All voters | Cobden | Kershaw | Heald |
|---|---|---|---|
| I. Gentlemen | 15 | 13 | 20 |
| Medical | 6 | 4 | 10 |
| Official | 6 | 5 | 2 |
| Other professions | 7 | 9 | 20 |
| Legal | 7 | 5 | 9 |
| | 41 | 36 | 61 |

*The Stockport election of 1847 (cont.)*

| All voters | Cobden | Kershaw | Heald |
|---|---|---|---|
| II. Textile workers | 16 | 38 | 20 |
| Cotton masters | 13 | 14 | 8 |
| Managers | 38 | 27 | 32 |
| | 67 | 79 | 60 |
| III. Butchers | 15 | 14 | 15 |
| Shopkeepers | 151 | 135 | 111 |
| | 166 | 149 | 126 |
| IV. Beersellers | 24 | 29 | 18 |
| Publicans | 42 | 30 | 52 |
| Brewers | 0 | 0 | 4 |
| | 66 | 59 | 74 |
| V. Building | 8 | 6 | 11 |
| Leather | 0 | 6 | 6 |
| Minor crafts | 7 | 4 | 13 |
| Metal | 14 | 15 | 21 |
| Wood | 8 | 8 | 16 |
| Tailors | 14 | 11 | 9 |
| Shoemakers | 11 | 6 | 11 |
| | 62 | 56 | 87 |
| VI. Dealers | 32 | 26 | 37 |
| Hat manufacturers | 9 | 5 | 1 |
| Minor manufacturers* | 29 | 25 | 19 |
| Builders | 2 | 5 | 6 |
| Farmers | 6 | 3 | 6 |
| | 78 | 64 | 69 |
| VII. Labourers | 0 | 1 | 1 |
| Servants, etc. | 3 | 5 | 4 |
| Clerks | 10 | 11 | 9 |
| Miscellaneous† | 14 | 21 | 54 |
| Carriers | 2 | 0 | 5 |
| | 29 | 38 | 73 |

| Summary | Cobden | Kershaw | Heald |
|---|---|---|---|
| I. Upper crust | 41 | 36 | 61 |
| II. Textile interest | 67 | 79 | 60 |
| III. Shopkeepers | 166 | 149 | 126 |
| IV. Drink | 66 | 59 | 74 |
| V. Craftsmen | 62 | 56 | 87 |
| VI. Small business | 78 | 64 | 69 |
| VII. Miscellaneous | 29 | 38 | 73 |

\* Mainly candlewick makers.            † Mainly outvoters.

No usable materials survive for the earlier elections, but there is a little further evidence that business was by no means always Liberal. Cobden, remarking that the millowners 'who neither changed their clothes nor closed their eyes for 36 hours' were working for him in 1841, stated 'these men were against me at the former election', i.e. they must have voted for an orthodox Tory candidate with strong local connections. See John Morley, *The Life of Richard Cobden* (1881), I, 176.

## The Suffolk election of August 1830

The pollbook is in the Guildhall Library. It does not state the occupations of voters.

Result: Sir H. E. Bunbury, Bt., Whig    1,097
        Chas. Tyrell, Whig    1,064
        Sir T. S. Gooch, Bt., Tory    627

Bunbury was a Whig, and Tyrell a Whiggish Tory. Gooch, who had been returned for 25 years unopposed, was a thick and thin supporter of ministers.

| | Bunbury | Tyrell | Gooch |
|---|---|---|---|
| Clergy | 26 | 23 | 72 |
| Dissenting ministers | 3 | 3 | 0 |

## The Suffolk West election of 1868

The pollbook is in the Guildhall Library.

Result: Major Windsor Parker, Conservative    2,500
        Lord Augustus Hervey, Conservative    2,389
        Charles Lamport, Liberal    1,704

Anglican clergy (distinguished by the prefix 'Rev.') voted as follows:

| Lamport | 3 |
|---|---|
| Hervey | 101 |
| Parker | 99 |

## The Tamworth election of 1837

The pollbook is in the Guildhall Library.

Result: Sir Robert Peel, Conservative    387
        Captain A'Court, R.N., Conservative    244
        Captain Townshend, R.N., Liberal    186

| Selected categories | Townshend | Peel | A'Court |
|---|---|---|---|
| Surgeons | 1 | 4 | 3 |
| Parish clerk | 0 | 1 | 1 |
| Butchers | 4 | 12 | 8 |
| Grocers | 3 | 7 | 4 |
| Shoemakers | 17 | 20 | 5 |
| Labourers | 28 | 46 | 27 |
| Innkeepers | 11 | 29 | 19 |
| Beersellers | 1 | 2 | 2 |
| Farmers | 11 | 32 | 26 |
| Town crier | 0 | 1 | 1 |
| R.C. priest | 1 | 1 | 0 |
| Woolstaplers | 1 | 1 | 1 |
| Miners | 3 | 2 | 0 |
| Coalmasters | 0 | 2 | 1 |

## The Tamworth election of 1841

The pollbook is in the Guildhall Library.

Result: Peel, Conservative    365
A'Court, Conservative    241
Townshend, Liberal    147

| Selected categories | Townshend | Peel | A'Court |
|---|---|---|---|
| Solicitors | 0 | 3 | 3 |
| Surgeons | 0 | 4 | 3 |
| Parish clerks | 0 | 1 | 1 |
| Butchers | 2 | 9 | 7 |
| Grocers | 1 | 11 | 7 |
| Shoemakers | 12 | 19 | 8 |
| Labourers | 27 | 47 | 23 |
| Innkeepers | 9 | 24 | 19 |
| Beersellers | 0 | 1 | 0 |
| Farmers | 9 | 32 | 28 |
| Relieving officer | 0 | 1 | 1 |
| Organist | 0 | 1 | 1 |
| Dissenting minister | 1 | 0 | 0 |
| Town crier | 0 | 1 | 1 |
| Paper manufacturer | 0 | 1 | 1 |
| Canal agent | 1 | 0 | 0 |
| Woolstapler | 1 | 0 | 0 |
| Cotton spinners | 0 | 2 | 2 |
| Bleacher | 0 | 1 | 1 |
| Coalmaster | 0 | 1 | 1 |
| Tape manufacturers | 1 | 2 | 2 |

## The Tewkesbury election of May 1831

The pollbook is in the Guildhall Library.

Result: John Martin, Whig    238
J. E. Dowdeswell, Tory    222
C. H. Tracy, Whig    170

Resident voters

| All voters | Martin | Tracy | Dowdeswell |
|---|---|---|---|
| Gentlemen | 10 | 6 | 7 |
| Stocking makers and weavers | 13 | 8 | 7 |
| Flax dresser | 1 | 1 | 0 |
| Wine merchants | 1 | 0 | 3 |
| Gardeners | 2 | 1 | 1 |
| Cabinet makers | 3 | 2 | 1 |
| Baker | 1 | 1 | 0 |
| Bookseller | 0 | 1 | 1 |
| Labourers, bargemen | 10 | 8 | 1 |
| Butchers | 3 | 3 | 5 |

*The Tewkesbury election of May 1831 (cont.)*

| All voters | Martin | Tracy | Dowdeswell |
|---|---|---|---|
| Grocers | 3 | 4 | 1 |
| Other shopkeepers | 9 | 9 | 4 |
| Lawyers | 2 | 2 | 1 |
| Innkeepers | 7 | 3 | 7 |
| Shoemakers | 5 | 3 | 6 |
| Farmers, yeomen | 8 | 6 | 4 |
| Gaoler | 0 | 1 | 1 |
| Dissenting ministers | 1 | 2 | 0 |
| Surgeon | 0 | 0 | 1 |
| Clergyman | 0 | 0 | 1 |
| Miscellaneous | 46 | 36 | 24 |

Non-resident voters

| All voters | Martin | Tracy | Dowdeswell |
|---|---|---|---|
| Innkeepers | 2 | 1 | 3 |
| Farmers, yeomen | 14 | 11 | 36 |
| Lawyers | 5 | 3 | 9 |
| Gentlemen | 37 | 20 | 42 |
| Butcher | 1 | 1 | 0 |
| Officers | 0 | 0 | 3 |
| Surgeons | 5 | 3 | 5 |
| Labourers | 3 | 1 | 3 |
| Shoemakers | 2 | 2 | 0 |
| Clergymen | 4 | 3 | 16 |
| Bankers | 3 | 2 | 2 |
| Merchant | 0 | 0 | 1 |
| Miscellaneous | 37 | 27 | 25 |

Splits and plumps

| | |
|---|---|
| Dowdeswell and Martin | 77 |
| Dowdeswell and Tracy | 15 |
| Martin and Tracy | 151 |
| Tracy alone | 4 |
| Martin alone | 10 |
| Dowdeswell alone | 130 |

## The Tewkesbury election of 1841

The pollbook is in the Guildhall Library.

| Result: Wm. Dowdeswell, Conservative | 193 |
|---|---|
| John Martin, Liberal | 189 |
| John Easthope, Liberal | 181 |

| All voters | Martin | Easthope | Dowdeswell |
|---|---|---|---|
| Craftsmen | 50 | 46 | 35 |
| Farmers, yeomen | 9 | 9 | 24 |
| Labourers | 2 | 2 | 3 |
| Gentlemen | 11 | 10 | 28 |

*The Tewkesbury election of 1841 (cont.)*

| All voters | Martin | Easthope | Dowdeswell |
|---|---|---|---|
| Stocking makers | 13 | 12 | 3 |
| Innkeepers | 6 | 6 | 16 |
| Shoemakers | 11 | 10 | 8 |
| Lawyers | 4 | 4 | 7 |
| Butchers | 2 | 1 | 4 |
| Grocers | 6 | 6 | 2 |
| Beersellers | 7 | 7 | 0 |
| Surgeons | 2 | 1 | 4 |
| Baptist ministers | 2 | 2 | 0 |
| Independent minister | 1 | 1 | 0 |
| Gaoler | 1 | 1 | 0 |

## The Wakefield election of 1837

The pollbook is in the Guildhall Library.

Result: Hon. W. S. Lascelles, Conservative    307
  D. Gaskell, Liberal    281

| Selected categories | Gaskell | Lascelles |
|---|---|---|
| Innkeepers | 23 | 29 |
| Gentlemen | 22 | 14 |
| Lawyers | 5 | 17 |
| Clothiers | 4 | 1 |
| Butchers | 9 | 9 |
| Watermen | 2 | 0 |
| Shoemakers | 12 | 7 |
| Corn merchants | 11 | 9 |
| Beersellers | 9 | 6 |
| Minister | 1 | 0 |
| Woolstaplers | 13 | 7 |
| Grocers | 9 | 8 |
| Surgeons | 5 | 11 |
| Dyers | 3 | 0 |
| Merchants | 2 | 2 |
| Boilermaker | 1 | 0 |
| Engineer | 1 | 0 |
| Manufacturers | 8 | 2 |
| Farmers | 1 | 2 |
| Clergymen | 3 | 6 |
| Wharfingers | 3 | 0 |
| Bankers | 1 | 1 |
| Worsted spinners | 2 | 6 |
| Ironfounders | 0 | 3 |
| Registrar | 0 | 1 |

## The Warrington election of 1847

Result: G. Greenall, Peelite 327
Wm. Allcard, Liberal 293

| All voters | Allcard | Greenall | | Allcard | Greenall |
|---|---|---|---|---|---|
| I. Gentlemen | 13 | 14 | Ironmasters | 18 | 8 |
| Farmers | 8 | 50 | Cottonmasters | 9 | 0 |
| II. Legal | 1 | 10 | Dealers and manufacturers | 4 | 2 |
| Medical | 3 | 7 | | | |
| Officials | 0 | 5 | VI. Labourers | 10 | 17 |
| Other professions | 15 | 12 | Textile workers | 10 | 0 |
| III. Publicans | 29 | 40 | Metal workers | 25 | 9 |
| IV. Clerks | 9 | 20 | VII. Butchers | 4 | 11 |
| V. Glass manufacturers | 0 | 6 | Drapers | 9 | 10 |
| | | | Other shopkeepers | 74 | 40 |
| Bankers | 0 | 3 | VIII. Tailor | 4 | 5 |
| Brewers | 4 | 7 | Shoemaker | 9 | 4 |
| Corn and flour | 12 | 9 | Wood | 9 | 14 |
| Coal | 0 | 2 | Leather | 6 | 5 |
| Builders | 2 | 0 | Others | 10 | 12 |
| | | | Painter | 0 | 3 |

| Summary: | Allcard | Greenall |
|---|---|---|
| I, II. Upper crust | 40 | 98 |
| III. Publicans | 29 | 40 |
| IV. Clerks | 9 | 20 |
| V. Business | 49 | 37 |
| VI. Labour | 45 | 26 |
| VII. Shopkeepers | 87 | 61 |
| VIII. Craftsmen | 38 | 43 |

## The Warwick Borough election of May 1831

The pollbook is in the Institute of Historical Research.

Result: John Tomes, Whig 698
Hon. Sir Chas. J. Greville, Tory 505
E. B. King, Whig 523

| Selected categories | Greville | Tomes | King |
|---|---|---|---|
| Gentlemen | 28 | 25 | 21 |
| Bankers | 3 | 1 | 1 |
| Surgeons | 6 | 6 | 4 |
| Lawyers | 5 | 7 | 7 |
| Clergymen | 3 | 1 | 0 |
| Dissenting ministers | 0 | 2 | 2 |
| Turnkey | 1 | 0 | 0 |
| Millers | 8 | 4 | 3 |

*The Warwick Borough election of May 1831 (cont.)*

| Selected categories | Greville | Tomes | King |
|---|---|---|---|
| Farmers | 34 | 11 | 4 |
| Publicans | 21 | 17 | 8 |
| Woolcombers | 1 | 15 | 15 |
| Woolsorters | 0 | 4 | 4 |
| Woolstaplers | 0 | 4 | 4 |
| Butchers | 18 | 16 | 13 |
| Grocers | 7 | 12 | 11 |
| Carpenters | 23 | 39 | 29 |
| Tailors | 23 | 35 | 28 |
| Shoemakers | 26 | 45 | 37 |
| Labourers | 47 | 73 | 64 |

| Greville: | splits | 203 | Tomes: | splits | 697 |
|---|---|---|---|---|---|
| | plumps | 302 | | plumps | 1 |

King: splits  518
plumps  5

## The Wigan election of 31 July 1830*

The pollbook is in the Guildhall Library.

| Result: | James Hardcastle, Radical | 116 |
|---|---|---|
| | Richard Potter, Radical | 112 |
| | J. A. Hodson, Tory | 54 |
| | Col. Jas. Lindsay, Tory | 45 |
| | J. H. Kearsley, Tory | 12 |

(No parties given.)

| All voters | Kearsley | Hodson | Lindsay | Potter | Hardcastle |
|---|---|---|---|---|---|
| Cotton spinners | 3 | 5 | 3 | 3 | 3 |
| Bankers | 0 | 2 | 2 | 0 | 0 |
| Gentlemen | 4 | 19 | 16 | 6 | 6 |
| Solicitors | 0 | 3 | 1 | 2 | 4 |
| Timber merchant | 0 | 1 | 1 | 0 | 0 |
| Yeomen | 0 | 1 | 1 | 1 | 1 |
| Cotton merchants | 0 | 0 | 0 | 3 | 3 |
| Farmers | 0 | 2 | 1 | 0 | 1 |
| Cordwainers | 1 | 1 | 0 | 4 | 4 |
| Iron merchants | 0 | 1 | 2 | 0 | 0 |
| Linen manufacturer | 0 | 1 | 1 | 0 | 0 |
| Linen merchant | 0 | 1 | 1 | 0 | 0 |
| Innkeepers | 1 | 1 | 1 | 17 | 18 |
| Butchers | 0 | 3 | 3 | 2 | 2 |
| Manufacturers | 1 | 1 | 2 | 6 | 6 |
| Surgeons | 0 | 0 | 0 | 4 | 4 |
| Tailors | 0 | 0 | 0 | 6 | 6 |
| Grocers | 0 | 0 | 0 | 6 | 6 |
| Divers other occupations | 2 | 13 | 11 | 52 | 52 |

* The returning officers refused the votes of many legally qualified voters, hence statistics given by Bean, etc., differ wildly from the above.

### The Yarmouth election of 1830

The pollbook is in King's Lynn Public Library.

Result: Hon. Col. G. Anson, Whig  946
C. E. Rumbold, Whig  945
T. E. Campbell, Tory  754
H. Preston, Tory  751

| Residence of voter | Anson | Rumbold | Campbell | Preston |
|---|---|---|---|---|
| Yarmouth and Southtown | 502 | 502 | 427 | 424 |
| Norfolk | 76 | 75 | 34 | 34 |
| Norwich | 51 | 51 | 44 | 44 |
| Suffolk and Essex | 67 | 67 | 67 | 67 |
| London, Middlesex, Surrey | 161 | 161 | 106 | 106 |
| Kent | 68 | 68 | 42 | 43 |
| Distant voters | 21 | 21 | 33 | 33 |
| | 946 | 945 | 753 | 751 |

Splits for Anson and Rumbold  942
Splits for Preston and Campbell  750

### In-voters

| Selected categories | Anson | Rumbold | Campbell | Preston |
|---|---|---|---|---|
| Parish clerk | 0 | 0 | 1 | 1 |
| Sexton | 0 | 0 | 1 | 1 |
| Publicans | 1 | 1 | 5 | 5 |
| Pilots | 2 | 2 | 1 | 1 |
| R.N. officers | 1 | 1 | 5 | 5 |
| Surgeons | 2 | 2 | 8 | 8 |
| Solicitors | 7 | 7 | 7 | 7 |
| Gentlemen | 21 | 21 | 32 | 32 |
| Merchants | 12 | 12 | 18 | 18 |
| Shipowners | 6 | 6 | 2 | 2 |
| Shipbuilders | 1 | 1 | 3 | 3 |
| Shipwrights | 56 | 56 | 60 | 60 |
| Mariners | 82 | 82 | 62 | 61 |
| Tailors | 10 | 10 | 6 | 6 |
| Cordwainers | 16 | 16 | 5 | 5 |

### Norfolk and Suffolk out-voters

| Selected categories | Anson | Rumbold | Campbell | Preston |
|---|---|---|---|---|
| R.N. officers | 0 | 0 | 3 | 3 |
| Pilots | 1 | 1 | 7 | 7 |
| Surgeons | 2 | 2 | 3 | 3 |
| Solicitors | 4 | 4 | 2 | 2 |
| Gentlemen | 21 | 21 | 20 | 20 |
| Farmers | 9 | 9 | 8 | 8 |
| Shipwrights | 11 | 11 | 12 | 12 |
| Mariners | 6 | 6 | 8 | 8 |
| Tailors | 7 | 7 | 1 | 1 |
| Cordwainers | 10 | 9 | 1 | 1 |

*The Yarmouth election of 1830 (cont.)*

### London, Kent and distant places

| Selected categories of out-voters | Anson | Rumbold | Campbell | Preston |
|---|---|---|---|---|
| R.N. officers | 0 | 0 | 6 | 7 |
| Pilot | 1 | 1 | 0 | 0 |
| Surgeons | 2 | 2 | 2 | 2 |
| Solicitors | 1 | 1 | 5 | 5 |
| Gentlemen | 12 | 13 | 16 | 16 |
| Shipwrights | 69 | 69 | 32 | 32 |
| Mariners | 28 | 29 | 12 | 12 |
| Tailors | 6 | 6 | 6 | 6 |
| Cordwainers | 10 | 10 | 2 | 2 |

## The Yarmouth election of December 1832

The pollbook is in the Institute of Historical Research.

Result: C. E. Rumbold, Liberal    837
Hon. Geo. Anson, Liberal    828
A. Colvile, Conservative    750

### Plumps

| Rumbold | 0 |
|---|---|
| Anson | 7 |
| Colvile | 688 |

| Selected categories | Anson | Rumbold | Colvile |
|---|---|---|---|
| Surgeons | 7 | 7 | 8 |
| Pilots | 6 | 6 | 11 |
| Parish clerk | 0 | 0 | 1 |

## The Yarmouth by-election of 1838

Result: Wm. Wilshere, Liberal    735
Thos. Baring, Conservative    702

| Selected categories | Wilshere | Baring |
|---|---|---|
| Officers | 4 | 0 |
| Surgeons | 5 | 15 |
| Pilots | 4 | 5 |
| Parish clerks | 0 | 2 |
| Organist | 1 | 0 |

## The Yarmouth election of 1841

The pollbook is in the Institute of Historical Research.

Result: Wm. Wilshere, Liberal    945
C. E. Rumbold, Liberal    943
Thos. Baring, Conservative    501
J. Somes, Conservative    494

### Freemen and householders together

| Selected categories | Wilshere | Rumbold | Baring | Somes |
|---|---|---|---|---|
| Officers | 6 | 6 | 0 | 0 |
| Mariners | 59 | 59 | 15 | 14 |
| Shipwrights | 82 | 84 | 65 | 62 |
| Sailmakers | 16 | 15 | 9 | 10 |
| Caulkers | 27 | 26 | 7 | 6 |
| Fishermen | 7 | 6 | 5 | 5 |
| Pilots | 2 | 2 | 8 | 8 |

### £10 householders only

| Selected categories | Wilshire | Rumbold | Baring | Somes |
|---|---|---|---|---|
| Surgeons | 3 | 3 | 5 | 5 |
| Grocers | 16 | 16 | 1 | 1 |
| Butchers | 7 | 6 | 2 | 2 |

## The Yarmouth election of 1847

The pollbook is in the Institute of Historical Research.

Result: Lord A. Lennox, Peelite    834
Octavious Coope, Peelite    813
C. E. Rumbold, Liberal    729
Francis Goldsmid, Liberal    698

| Freemen voters only: selected categories | Rumbold | Goldsmid | Lennox | Coope |
|---|---|---|---|---|
| Gentlemen | 25 | 25 | 27 | 25 |
| Surgeons | 4 | 2 | 4 | 5 |
| Solicitors | 11 | 11 | 8 | 8 |
| Cordwainers | 20 | 22 | 17 | 19 |
| Grocers | 5 | 5 | 6 | 6 |
| Tailors | 12 | 12 | 13 | 13 |
| Publicans | 5 | 5 | 9 | 8 |
| Mariners | 46 | 45 | 62 | 62 |
| Shipwrights | 34 | 39 | 62 | 59 |
| Pilots | 1 | 1 | 7 | 7 |

Freemen electors    918
£10 householders    644
Total poll    1,562

## The York City election of 1835

The pollbook is in the Guildhall Library.

Result: Lowther, Conservative    1,499
Dundas, Liberal    1,301
Barkley, Liberal    919

| Selected categories | Dundas | Barkley | Lowther |
|---|---|---|---|
| Watermen | 1 | 1 | 14 |
| Policemen | 3 | 2 | 0 |
| Chorister | 0 | 0 | 1 |
| Organist | 0 | 0 | 1 |
| Gentlemen | 99 | 55 | 100 |
| Surgeons | 14 | 7 | 19 |
| Farmers | 1 | 0 | 0 |
| Shoemakers | 127 | 104 | 124 |
| Weavers | 7 | 7 | 4 |
| Grocers | 1 | 0 | 1 |
| Butchers | 38 | 25 | 61 |
| Labourers | 23 | 8 | 49 |
| Dissenting ministers | 3 | 3 | 0 |

## The York City election of 1841

The pollbook is in the Bodleian Library.

Result: Lowther, Conservative    1,625
Yorke, Liberal    1,552
Atcherley, Conservative    1,456

Voters A–G inclusive only

| Selected categories | Yorke | Lowther | Atcherley |
|---|---|---|---|
| Stonemasons | 9 | 5 | 3 |
| Grocers | 7 | 9 | 8 |
| Butchers | 11 | 27 | 27 |
| Shoemakers | 57 | 42 | 37 |
| Farmers | 13 | 33 | 28 |
| Labourers | 13 | 14 | 11 |

Voters A–Z

| Selected categories | Yorke | Lowther | Atcherley |
|---|---|---|---|
| Surgeons | 16 | 20 | 20 |
| Merchants | 4 | 0 | 0 |
| Basketmakers | 3 | 6 | 5 |
| Saddlers | 15 | 18 | 13 |
| Comb makers | 52 | 33 | 31 |
| Clergy | 4 | 23 | 23 |
| Wesleyan ministers | 0 | 3 | 3 |
| Weavers | 17 | 8 | 6 |

*The York City election of 1841 (cont.)*

Voters A–Z (*cont.*)

| Selected categories | Yorke | Lowther | Atcherley |
|---|---|---|---|
| Railwaymen | 1 | 2 | 2 |
| Proctors | 1 | 4 | 4 |
| Choristers | 0 | 3 | 3 |
| Organbuilders | 2 | 4 | 3 |
| Organist | 0 | 1 | 1 |
| Vestry clerk | 0 | 1 | 1 |
| Policemen | 1 | 4 | 3 |
| Dissenting ministers | 2 | 0 | 0 |
| Sexton | 0 | 1 | 1 |
| Unitarian minister | 1 | 0 | 0 |

## The York City election of 1852

The pollbook is in the Institute of Historical Research.

Result: J. G. Smyth, Conservative 1,870
W. M. E. Milner, Liberal 1,831
Henry Vincent, Chartist 886

| Selected categories | Vincent | Milner | Smyth |
|---|---|---|---|
| Railway employees, all grades | 4 | 18 | 38 |
| Watermen | 2 | 7 | 14 |
| Policemen | 0 | 5 | 5 |
| Dissenting ministers | 0 | 3 | 0 |
| Clergymen | 0 | 1 | 3 |
| Vergers | 0 | 1 | 3 |
| Chorister | 0 | 0 | 1 |
| Organist | 0 | 0 | 1 |
| Bankers | 0 | 2 | 3 |
| Gentlemen | 24 | 99 | 141 |
| Lawyers | 2 | 25 | 34 |
| Surgeons | 0 | 12 | 24 |
| Farmers | 9 | 46 | 60 |
| Publicans | 12 | 56 | 52 |
| Shoemakers | 80 | 94 | 96 |
| Curriers | 9 | 25 | 30 |
| Tailors | 56 | 52 | 57 |
| Weavers | 5 | 10 | 7 |
| Grocers | 11 | 26 | 21 |
| Butchers | 19 | 70 | 72 |
| Labourers | 21 | 33 | 43 |

| Plumps | | Splits | |
|---|---|---|---|
| Smyth | 969 | Smyth and Milner | 881 |
| Milner | 563 | Smyth and Vincent | 20 |
| Vincent | 479 | Milner and Vincent | 387 |

# BIBLIOGRAPHY

## A. SOCIOLOGICAL THEORY AND SOCIAL STRUCTURE

Bellerby, J. R. 'Distribution of Manpower in Agriculture and Industry 1851–1951', *Farm Economist*, IX (1958).

Booth, Charles. 'Occupations of the People of the United Kingdom, 1801–1881', *Journal of the Statistical Society*, XLIX (June 1886), 314–44.

Clapham, J. H. *An Economic History of Modern Britain: Free Trade and Steel 1850–1886*. [There is a table of occupations drawn from the 1851 census on page 23.]

Dahrendorf, Ralf. *Class and Class Conflict in Industrial Society*. London, 1959.

Day, Clive. 'The Distribution of Industrial Occupations in England, 1841–1861', *Transactions of the Connecticut Academy* (1927).

Hirsch, G. P. 'The Size of Farm Holdings in England and Wales', *Farm Economist*, IX (1958), 87.

Report of Departmental Committee on Factory Statistics: *Parl. Papers* (1895), XIX, 583.

Return of all persons employed coming under all Factories and Workshops Acts. *Parl. Papers* (1871), LXII, 164.

Routh, G. G. C. *Occupation and Pay in Great Britain, 1906–60* (1965).

Tawney, A. J. and Tawney, R. H. 'An Occupational Census of the Seventeenth Century', *Economic History Review*, V (1934–5), 25.

## B. POLLBOOKS

British Museum. The Museum has a handlist, kept at the counter, of its holdings of pollbooks.

Camps, Anthony J. *Poll Books: a list of those in the Library of the Society of Genealogists*, 1961.

Cannon, John. 'Short Guides to Records: 2. Poll Books', *History* (June 1962).

History of Parliament Trust. *Draft Register of Pollbooks*. 21 Oct. 1953. [This is a list of some 1,750 pollbooks printed between 1694 and 1882, based on exhaustive enquiries in libraries all over the country.]

McCalmont, H. *Parliamentary Pollbook*. London, 1910.

Smith, Henry Stooks. *The Register of Parliamentary Contested Elections*. London, 1841.